100 Years

of

Illinois State Redbird

Basketball

By Bryan Bloodworth and Roger Cushman

Foreword by Doug Collins

ILLINOIS STATE
Redbirds ®

Dedicated to all Redbird fans, players and coaches
past, present and future

The authors are grateful for the steadfast support and everlasting encouragement
of their partners in life, Elaine Cushman and Lisa Bloodworth.

For information write:
Illinois State University
Department of Intercollegiate Athletics
Campus Box 2660
Normal, IL 61790-2660

Rick Greenspan, Director
Dr. Linda Herman, Associate Director
Leanna Bordner, Assistant Director
Larry Lyons, Assistant Director
Kenny Mossman, Assistant Director
Todd Reeser, Assistant Director
Nick Reggio, Assistant Director
Donna Taylor, Assistant Director

Photographs courtesy of Illinois State's Athletics Department, Dennis Banks,
Nelson Smith, Jerry Liebenstein, the Bloomington *Pantagraph*, the *Index* and
Einstein Photo. Editors: Kenny Mossman, Tom Lamonica and Jim Bowers.
Special thanks to Todd Kober, assistant athletics media relations director, and ISU Alumni Services.

Printed in U.S.A. by Multi-Ad Services, Peoria, IL
Prepublishing Services: Brandon Burwell, Cindy Hodel and Kim Simmons.

Bloodworth, Bryan, 1956–
    100 Years of Illinois State Redbird Basketball/by Bryan Bloodworth and Roger Cushman;
foreword by Doug Collins.
        p. cm.
    ISBN 1-56478-158-5
    1. Illinois State University—Basketball—History. 2. Illinois State Redbirds (Basketball team)—History. I. Cushman, Roger,
1933– . II. Title.
GV885.43.I52B56 1998
796.323'63'0977359—dc21   98-38461
                                                                                            CIP

FOREWORD

It is hard to believe that 25 years have passed since my final basketball game at Illinois State University because memories of that night are still so fresh in my mind. I shall never forget the tremendous outpouring of love and support from the fans who packed Horton Field House. It was one of the most emotional moments of my sports career.

Illinois State University is a very special place to me. Like so many incoming freshmen, I was a bit shy when I came to college from the Franklin County seat of Benton in southern Illinois. The Bloomington-Normal community opened its heart and became my second home. The knowledge and wisdom of my coaches, Dr. Jim Collie and Will Robinson, and the loyal support of my athletics director, Dr. Milt Weisbecker, helped me grow as an individual. They remain among my cherished lifetime friends.

I have been reminded of Illinois State's proud basketball legacy often throughout my 25 years as a player, coach and television commentator in the National Basketball Association. In fact, the chief of officials when I entered the NBA was a former Redbird basketball player, Darell Garretson, but that never helped me get any breaks on the calls!

Former ISU athletes Bubbles Hawkins and Jeff Wilkins joined other NBA teams when I was playing. When I became coach of the Chicago Bulls, I was associated with broadcaster Jim Durham, media relations director Tim Hallam and ticket sales director Keith Brown—all from Illinois State; also, the WGN television sports director, Dan Roan, had played freshman basketball during my junior season at ISU. When I coached the Detroit Pistons, I became reunited with my former college coach, Will Robinson, who has been in Detroit's scouting office since leaving ISU in 1975. One of my assistant coaches at Detroit was Brian James, another ISU graduate.

I mention these individuals to show that Illinois State's basketball influence extends far beyond the campus boundaries. The accomplishments of these people testify to the university's importance in their lives.

My academic and athletic experiences at ISU were very rewarding but not entirely unique. So many players in Illinois State's first century of basketball have enjoyed the thrill of competition and achievement. I am delighted that this book will bring renewed awareness of their accomplishments and I am proud to be part of this heritage.

After my last game at Horton Field House on that distant night in February 1973, I told the fans that if I could make my college decision all over again, I would come back to Illinois State.

The university continues to hold a warm place in my heart and I enjoy visiting the campus as often as possible. As the Redbirds enter their second century of intercollegiate basketball, let me say once again with pride: If I had it to do all over again, I would still enroll at Illinois State University.

—Doug Collins, '73

Table of Contents

1

Chapter 1

The Preeminent Game

(1899)

♦

5

Chapter 2

Establishing A Tradition

(1899–1908)

♦

11

Chapter 3

From Triumph To Despair

(1908–1910)

♦

15

Chapter 4

Restoring The Program

(1910–1917)

♦

19

Chapter 5

The World At War

(1917–1919)

♦

21

Chapter 6

Racial Diversity And

Russell's Last Years

(1919–1923)

♦

25

Chapter 7

Good-Bye To The

Old Castle Gym

(1923–1925)

♦

29

Chapter 8

A New Nest For Hatching

Don Karnes' "Red Birds"

(1925–1927)

♦

33

Chapter 9

Joe Cogdal's Reign Begins

(1927–1930)

37

Chapter 10

The Golden Thirties

(1930–1938)

43

Chapter 11

Years Of Glory And Grit

(1938–1949)

♦

49

Chapter 12

The Hometown Hero

As Coach

(1949)

♦

53

Chapter 13

The Pim Goff Years

(1949–1957)

♦

59

Chapter 14

Gentleman Jim Collie

(1957)

♦

63

Chapter 15

Illinois State's First

National Appearance

(1958–1965)

♦

69

Chapter 16

Arends To McGreal To Terry:

A Redbird Triple Play

(1965–1968)

♦

77

Chapter 17

One More Title For

Gentleman Jim

(1968–1970)

83

Chapter 18

Will Robinson, Trailblazer

(1970)

87

Chapter 19

Where There's A Will,
There's A Way

(1970–1972)

93

Chapter 20

Doug Collins, Olympic Hero

(1972–1973)

101

Chapter 21

Will Power

(1973–1975)

107

Chapter 22

MTXE: Gene Smithson's
Teams Win With Style

(1975–1978)

115

Chapter 23

New Style, Same Results:
Donewald Era Begins

(1978–1980)

119

Chapter 24

A Valley Full Of Fun:
Redbirds Join NCAA Elite

(1980–1985)

127

Chapter 25

The Last Years At Horton

(1985–1989)

131

Chapter 26

Bender Heals, Wins

(1989–1993)

141

Chapter 27

With Background A-Plenty,
Stallings Comes To Town

(1993–1995)

149

Chapter 28

The Gang's All Here

(1995–1997)

155

Chapter 29

Season No. 100 Is One
For The Ages

(1997–1998)

Chapter 1
THE PREEMINENT GAME
(1899)

With drums beating and banners flourishing, the Illinois State Normal University band and a cheering throng of students clad loyally in school colors escorted a delegation of 110 students and several faculty chaperones to the Illinois Central train station on Wednesday, May 3, 1899.

The delegation was headed for the Inter-State Oratorical Contest, a major event involving colleges from Illinois, Iowa, Kansas, Missouri and Wisconsin. In addition to the featured orator, the Illinois State party included champion tennis players, two glee clubs and members of the newly formed men's "basket ball" team.

When the group returned on Saturday, Illinois State had won the first intercollegiate basketball game in school history, a 12–4 victory over the "Bounding Elks" of Iowa State Normal School (now Missouri Valley Conference rival Northern Iowa). The event inspired a student reporter to describe the conquest poetically in the campus yearbook, closing the masterpiece with the exclamation, "Hurrah for the team of the I.S.N.U."

Illinois State basketball fans have been cheering their favorites through 100 seasons since. Players from a century ago would be astonished to see today's above-the-rim athleticism, but they would heartily approve of the record of excellence that includes all-American athletes, distinguished coaches, team championships and national tournament appearances. Illinois State went into its third season of basketball before tasting defeat. B.C. Edwards, a reading instructor who coached the first four seasons of men's basketball, had a 14-2

cumulative record with teams that competed successfully, though infrequently.

◆   ◆   ◆   ◆   ◆   ◆

That inaugural Illinois State game took place less than eight years after James Naismith, a physical education teacher at the Young Men's Christian Association (YMCA) Training College in Springfield, Mass., created the sport in 1891 to provide more interesting wintertime activities than calisthenics and other gymnastics exercises. Naismith drafted 13 rules, asked a janitor to nail two half-bushel peach baskets to the balcony of a cramped gymnasium measuring 50 feet by 30 feet, and introduced the new game to a physical education class on December 21, 1891.

The game's popularity soon spread from YMCAs to college campuses. In 1895, Hamline College of St. Paul, Minn., defeated the

Minnesota State School of Agriculture, 9–3, in the earliest recorded intercollegiate game. That game featured nine players per side, but the number was reduced to five a year later when the University of Chicago defeated Iowa, 15–12.

Rising interest in the new sport of "basket ball" (written as two words or hyphenated as "basket-ball" then) coincided with Illinois State Normal University's construction of the

A construction scene from Cook Hall, which opened in 1896. The castle-like exterior was cut from the stones in the foreground.

Gymnasium, a limestone fortress with towers and battlements suggestive of European castles. Campus President John W. Cook believed "aesthetic gymnastics" was an essential part of teacher education and persuaded the Illinois General Assembly to appropriate $40,000 in 1895 to construct the building. The campus yearbook, the *Index*, proclaimed that "Athletics now seem to have taken firm root in the school and by the aid of a new gymnasium building we hope in a few years to see Illinois State Normal University second to none in athletics and field sports."

Iowa Team Throws its only Goal.

The 1899 *Index* made fun of the referee from an Illinois State-Northern Iowa basketball game with a cartoon captioned "Iowa Team Throws its only Goal" and the tag "Iowa's Referee" on the back of the character.

The building, now known as Cook Hall, contained the campus library and science laboratories in addition to a gymnasium considered spacious for the times. The gymnasium proper was about 40 feet by 90 feet with a 28-foot ceiling. Nine feet above the floor, a 200-foot running track hung by iron brackets extended around the wall. A railing around the track provided a handy support for attaching basketball goals, which were present in the first photographs taken after the building opened in 1896.

Illinois State's enrollment was 826 students, dropping to 572 at the turn of the century. So the gym was large enough to accommodate students wishing to watch the games, plus interested townspeople. Seating was available in chairs placed along the walls at court level

and spectators could also stand in the gallery. Attendance at early games was seldom reported, but crowds of 300 to 500 were noted occasionally and a throng of 700 was estimated once during the gymnasium's second decade. The noise level could be so high in the brick-walled gymnasium that referees sometimes stopped the action to quiet the crowd.

Basketball goals were made of an iron rim and cord basket—much as they are today—but had no opening at the bottom because the first rules stated that the ball must stay in the basket in order to count as a score. The ball could be retrieved by ladder or by reaching over the balcony rail, but manufacturers also created a chain pulley to tip the basket and release the ball more conveniently. Not until the 1904–05 season did the seemingly

obvious solution of opening the bottom of the net arrive.

Basketball initially attracted Illinois State's women, who were eager to have an organized activity to parallel the men's interest in football and baseball. Soon after the gymnasium opened in 1896, an enterprising group known as the "Pioneer Team" became the first of 20 women's teams to form. Outside games were arranged with teams from Illinois Wesleyan University and Normal Community High School (NCHS) in October and November. Frank Dillon, a professional baseball player from Normal, was hired during his off-season for three hours a day at $25 a month to assist with gymnastic work and coach the women in basketball. Dillon eventually played five seasons in the major leagues, managed five Pacific Coast League pennant winners in Los Angeles, and established a lucrative apple pie business with his wife, the former Blanche Reitzel, who was one of his students at ISNU.

The ISNU women lost their first game to Wesleyan, 6–4, played a scoreless tie with NCHS, and defeated Wesleyan in a rematch, 2–0. "Normal had few games with other schools, as their aim was exercise and not glory," the 1897 *Index* reported.

B.C. Edwards, a graduate of Boston School of Oratory, came to Illinois State in 1897 as teacher of reading and gymnastics. Illinois State's men, dressed in trousers and turtle-necks, began organizing teams that year to represent the popular debating societies, the Philadelphians and Wrightonians. For years, the hotly contested rivalries of these two organizations would command greater interest than the varsity basketball teams. In at least one year, the entire squad from one of the societies represented the university against outside competition.

By the 1898–99 school year, basketball fever was sweeping the campus, resulting in games between faculty and students, between sections and classes, and between novelty teams such as the "Longs" (garbed in blue overalls) and the "Shorts." Not only was the game popular, but it provided valuable lessons for future teachers, according to the *Index*, which declared that "Basket ball is preeminently the game for the

Normal Schools." (The word "normal," part of Illinois State's original name, is defined as constituting an accepted standard, model or pattern, and was commonly used as a synonym for teachers colleges because their primary role was to set the standards—"norms"—for teaching in public schools.)

In March 1899, Professor Edwards assembled a squad from the class teams, perhaps to prepare for the trip to Iowa two months later. As part of the preparation, the team played the Bloomington YMCA on Saturday, March 18. "This is the first game the university boys have ever played with outside parties and it is expected to be a very interesting one," the Bloomington *Pantagraph* commented in an advance story the day of the game.

Edwards might have expected a good workout for his squad since YMCA teams had

This 1896 photo of Cook Hall's interior shows the basket mounted on the face of the balcony, gymnastics equipment on the main floor and exercise apparatus against the left wall.

many of the most skilled basketball players during the sport's early years. Naismith had developed the game in a YMCA and his disciples carried the torch around the country to similar institutions, which already had gymnasiums because of their interest in physical fitness. YMCA teams frequently defeated collegiate teams during the early years. However, the Bloomington team turned out to be too young and inexperienced to compete against the Illinois State squad.

Illinois State's student newspaper, the

In 1899, the first Illinois State basketball team took its first road trip with the debate team, departing from the Normal Illinois Central station with quite a send-off. The large advertisement for A. Livingston & Son, a Bloomington department store, is on the side of a building on Beaufort Street which houses Shanigans 100 years later.

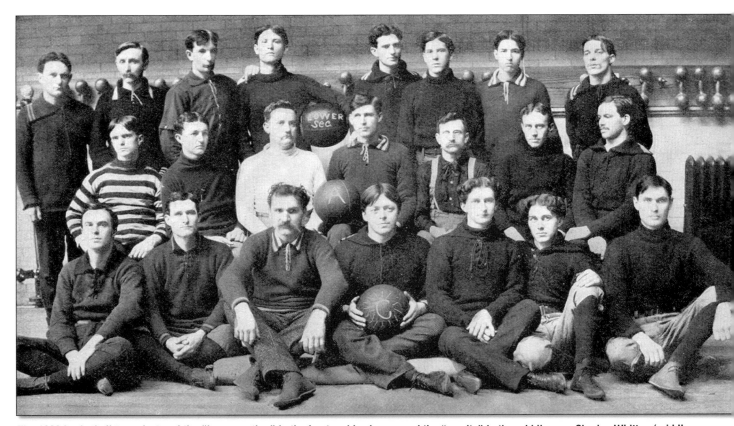

The 1899 basketball team featured the "lower section" in the front and back rows and the "varsity" in the middle row. Charles Whitten (middle row, second from right) later became the first executive director of what is now the Illinois High School Association.

Vidette, reported: "When the Bloomington team appeared in the 'arena,' the I.S.N.U. men were much chagrined to find that they were to play against boys. Several of the more experienced players wanted to withdraw from the game and substitute younger players, but Prof. Edwards had selected the team to play and would not allow any changes. The YMCA team, however, showed much skill for boys, but they did not understand the 'screen' throw, and consequently played at a disadvantage."

The teams played 15-minute halves. Illinois State, confusing its youthful foes by setting screens for open shots, led 13–0 at the half and coasted to a 21–4 victory. "The Bloomington team will have to practice some before they come to Normal again," the *Pantagraph* commented.

Nearly two months later, amid much hoopla, the university basketball players and 100 other students boarded three special chair-car coaches shortly before noon for the journey to Cedar Falls, Iowa. They paid $5.40 each for the round trip; their experience was a foreshadowing of modern-day Redbird fan junkets.

"It was the shortest long trip any of us ever took," the *Vidette* reported. "The day was spent in having a good social time. All formality was thrown off and all became acquainted as they had never been before. We gave vent to enthusiasm by singing school songs and by swarming out upon each station platform to astonish the inhabitants by that most fearful of all things, a school yell. With all the sights to be seen, and with cracker-jack and chewing gum as promoters of sociability, the delegation was kept fully occupied until dusk."

The group arrived in Cedar Falls at about 1:00 a.m. The students remained on the train until morning, "sleeping very little on account of a few irrepressibles," and took a streetcar two miles out of town to the Iowa Normal School campus. Baseball, tennis and rowing were among their social activities. Some students took an electric car to nearby Waterloo. Others watched Iowa girls teams play basketball on an outdoor field, with baskets attached to posts at either end of the field.

A poetic description of Illinois State's first intercollegiate game indicates that it was held

indoors, although the yearbook illustration shows a person apparently celebrating a basket on a grassy field. The caption reads, "Iowa Team Throws its only Goal." The grinning shooter wears a tag labeling him as "Iowa's Referee." Complaining about officiating is a traditional American pastime; even Naismith, the inventor of the game, once wrote about difficulties encountered with local officials.

The poem, which is the only description of the game available, gives an unflattering view of the hometown official. Apparently, the host team objected to setting screens, a practice Illinois State claimed permissible according to the A.G. Spalding sporting goods company rule book. After describing the controversy, the poem concludes:

A toss of the ball and a quick, cool run,
The first goal was made and the yelling begun;
So light o'er the ground the Normal boys played,
So light they threw goals, Hawkeyes were
  dismayed.
It is won! the gay Hawkeyes are beaten all thro',
Hurrah for the team of the I.S.N.U.

Chapter 2

ESTABLISHING A TRADITION (1899–1908)

The dawn of the 20th century came with a growth of basketball fever at Illinois State. President John W. Cook, a sports fan, left in 1899 to become president of the new Northern Illinois State Normal School in DeKalb. His successor, Arnold Tompkins, honored a student request by appointing B.C. Edwards, two other faculty members and five students, including Charles Whitten, to a permanent Athletic Association board.

With Edwards continuing as volunteer coach, the association arranged a game with the Decatur YMCA in January 1900 to test student interest in supporting an intercollegiate team. Illinois State, wearing baseball uniforms, vanquished the Decatur team, 44–3. Gate receipts easily exceeded expenses, and four more games were scheduled. Basketball officially became an intercollegiate sport at the university.

Despite the euphoria and a succession of strong teams, storm warnings developed early in Illinois State's first decade of basketball. Tompkins departed after only one year to become president at the Chicago Normal School. David Felmley, who lacked his two predecessors' interest in sports, began a 30-year reign as president in the fall of 1900 by presiding over the faculty's abolishment of football and baseball by the end of his first decade. That action caused several top athletes to leave school in 1910 and resulted in a temporary upheaval in the basketball program until the sports were restored.

But all seemed well in that 1900 basketball season when Illinois State romped through a five-game schedule with only one challenge, a

12–11 victory over Knox College in Illinois State's first home game against a collegiate opponent.

The whipping of the Decatur YMCA in the opener featured a 22-point outburst by David Wells, "enough to win several games" in an era when play stopped for a center jump after every score. Illinois State drubbed Eureka College, 43–1, and took back-to-back victories of 19–7 and 26–8 over Greer College of Hoopeston to conclude an undefeated campaign.

A key figure on that team and in the long-term future of Illinois State athletics was freshman guard Henry Harrison Russell. The Peotone native later would rescue the Illinois State sports program during its darkest hours at the end of the decade. Russell became athletics director and coach from 1910–23, restored athletics into the good graces of President Felmley and his faculty, and shepherded the program through desperate times during a world war and a national influenza outbreak.

But, as the 1900 season was becoming history, athletics enjoyed popular support, according to the campus newspaper. "The attendance at the recent games of basket-ball indicated that there is strong sentiment prevailing in the school in favor of athletics," one article read. "Never before was so much interest taken and spirit manifested in athletic contests as this year."

During the 1900–01 school year, the Athletic Association passed supervision of all intercollegiate sports over to a supportive five-member Board of Control. The two faculty members were Edwards, the reading instructor and basketball coach, and Whitten, a former

student-athlete then teaching science and mathematics at the university. Harrison Russell, a sophomore and the basketball team captain, Bessie Cardiff and C.L. Fink were the three student members. "Under their management the association has become one of the foremost organizations of the school," the campus yearbook proclaimed.

The opening basketball game on February 5, 1901, resulted in the first defeat and the first overtime game in school history. Illinois State and a Danville YMCA team played to a 14–14 tie in regulation time at the Normal gymnasium. The teams decided to play "extra time" and Danville won, 16–14.

Illinois State won its remaining four games, defeating sister institution Northern Illinois by 10–7 and 15–13 scores, the Danville YMCA, 27–17, in a rematch, and Eastern Illinois Normal, 32–11, with Russell scoring nine field goals for over half of his team's points.

Cook, in his second year as president at Northern Illinois, welcomed Professors Edwards and Whitten and the Illinois State players warmly when they arrived at DeKalb on February 9 for the first game between the state universities, feeding the group an oyster supper after the game.

◆   ◆   ◆   ◆   ◆   ◆

Attendance for intercollegiate basketball zoomed higher in three home games in 1902. In Edwards' final season as volunteer coach, the entire Wrightonian Society team represented the university. Brightly attired in red long-sleeved, collared baseball uniforms with ISNU in white lettering, the team responded with a 3-1 record. The closing game, a 24–20 victory over Northern Illinois, included attendance estimated at 400 or 500 persons.

A controversy arising from the game's ambiguous regulations at the time fueled Illinois State's only loss that season, a 22–18 decision to Northern Illinois at DeKalb. In a conflict reminiscent of Edwards' first team, which had to defend its practice of setting screens, Northern refused to allow Illinois State's 1902 team to carom shots off the backboard. In today's jargon, the bank was closed in DeKalb. "The boys were used to throwing goals by 'banking,' but there they were deprived of this means and had to resort to free goal throwing," the *Vidette* commented.

In an era fraught with rules disputes, it was not the first objection to Illinois State's practice of banking shots. The Decatur YMCA, still smarting from its 44–3 loss in 1900, was denied a place on the Illinois State schedule and responded with a sarcastic letter signed by L.D. White with the following postscript: "I understand that behind each of your goals a screen is placed and that from this screen most of the goals thrown in the game last year were deflected into the goal. In our gymnasium here we do not encourage throwing at the side of a barn and trusting to luck that the ball may enter the goal, but on the contrary we discourage this practice as much as possible, in most games even not counting as goals any that may touch anything besides the player's hands and the basket itself before entering the basket. In other words when a ball is 'banked' into the goal it does not count."

White suggested that Illinois State project the goals at least two feet from the screen to eliminate bank shots in future games. Obviously, Edwards ignored the advice.

As the Edwards coaching era came to a close, Illinois State began confronting the cold realities of athletics funding. Citing "financial embarrassments of the Athletic Association," the *Vidette* proposed in the fall of 1901 that students be assessed an athletics fee of 50 cents per term. That proposal languished and the university was unable to field a football team in the fall of 1902. The void was partially filled by basketball, with the university scheduling a December intercollegiate game for the first time.

◆ ◆ ◆ ◆ ◆ ◆

The 1902–03 basketball team featured the return of Harrison Russell, who had dropped out of school for a year to teach, and the beginning of Professor J.P. Stewart's four seasons as volunteer coach. The basketball team wore sleeveless tank tops above baseball knickers but posted a not-so-spiffy 3-3 record. Even so, the school yearbook, inspired to poetry once again, published 120 lines of verse, complete with cartoon caricatures of eight players and an illustration showing the team in front of a train station bearing the sign of "Podunkville." In 1903, the town of Normal had fewer than 4,000 residents and only two blocks of paved streets: Beaufort from Linden to the Illinois Central railroad tracks (now part of the Constitution Trail) and North Street from the tracks to Broadway. That fall, Illinois State's enrollment dropped to 386 students, the smallest number in 37 years.

◆ ◆ ◆ ◆ ◆ ◆

Despite the enrollment decline, Stewart assembled a basketball powerhouse that broke the point-a-minute barrier with an astonishing 42.1 average in January and February of 1904 on the way to a 7-1 record. Some histories credit Rhode Island State as the first to accomplish that feat by averaging 41 points in 1929, but Illinois State did it 25 years earlier. It must be added, however, that three of Illinois State's eight games were against non-collegiate opponents.

Illinois State nearly reached the 100-point mark in a 97–8 victory over the Bloomington YMCA, barely missing a plateau that would not be scaled for half a century. The front line of Perry Hellyer with 42 points, Wright Jackson with 24 and J.R. Steagall with 22 led the assault. The 89-point winning margin remains the greatest point spread in school history.

In an age before reliable automobile transportation was possible, the train was the primary means of traveling to away games. A convenient train schedule and the lure of a dance attracted the basketball team and approximately 25 followers to a game with Pontiac High School, 40 miles to the north, at the start of the 1904 campaign.

"Yes, we made the conductor laugh, and the brakeman laugh, and the porter laugh, and the passengers haw haw. But after about an hour's experience in getting married, in stealing peanuts, in getting divorced, and in smiling on

The 1900 team was the first to formulate and play a schedule. Seated are Harrison Russell (later ISNU coach), Wilson Perry, David Wells and Adam Hummel. Kneeling are Edward Flock, Coach B.C. Edwards, Lee Kinsey and Roscoe Steagall.

A 1904 *Index* illustration shows the "closed" net used on baskets of that era.

return from Decatur by hopping boxcars. The interurban improved transportation for sports teams to some extent but it was not until the 1920s that paved highways and automobiles would make travel more convenient to cities with limited rail service.

◆   ◆   ◆   ◆   ◆   ◆

The bottom, literally, fell out of the basket in 1905, ending the need to have someone retrieve the ball from the cylinder after each successful shot, and the team record also dropped to 4-4. The Bloomington YMCA, then known as the Banzais, strengthened its lineup with former Illinois star Fred Muhl and other good athletes after the previous year's embarrassment and scored two victories over Illinois State. However, the first meeting with Bradley was a 39–13 win and the season ended with a 22–21 thrilling inaugural against Western Illinois.

A *Vidette* article indicated that the most sensational plays of the game were one-hand goals scored by forwards Paul McWherter and Leo Stuckey—ahead of the times. The one-hander wasn't popularized until 1936 when Hank Luisetti of Stanford and his one-hander made a memorable and highly publicized appearance at Madison Square Garden in New York.

The 1906 team finished 6-2 despite limited practice time. It was Stewart's last season as coach and it took all of his persuasiveness to keep the team from walking out several times because of problems created by the gymnasium's popularity for social events. The varsity team disbanded at one time but reconsidered after student groups surrendered some time so home games could be arranged.

The *Vidette* blamed basketball's struggles on President Felmley: "The greatest trouble, however, with carrying on basketball, and athletics in general, is Mr. Felmley's firm belief that games should be between teams within the school, and not between teams representing this school and other schools." Felmley's opposition to any student missing a class to take part in athletic contests made it difficult to arrange games away from home as well, the *Vidette* reported.

one another, we reached Pontiac.

"There we had a hard game."

The college team edged Pontiac High School, 30–28, but perhaps the players had their minds on the dance.

The 1904 team's only defeat came at the end of a two-game road trip to DeKalb and Chicago at the close of the season. The team defeated Northern, 24–16, but absorbed a 39–12 shellacking from Lewis Institute (later the Illinois Institute of Technology). The student

newspaper blamed the loss on the romantic interludes fostered on the train trip and at subsequent social activities. "Many attributed this sad end to Captain [Abe] Newton's nocturnal habits and others to Hellyer's reflections on married life," a *Vidette* reporter wrote.

Train travel was not always so glamorous. In 1904, two years before an interurban electric railway line linked Bloomington and Decatur and three years before a second line was developed to Peoria, the football team had to

Eureka College's uniforms provided a comic moment during the 1906 season when the team showed up for a game at the Normal gymnasium with sleeveless jerseys and short pants. Illinois State players had worn red tank tops in some previous seasons but, perhaps prompted by complaints about immodest attire, the 1905 team modified the uniform by putting red T-shirts under the jerseys, eight decades before that style became fashionable. Legs were covered with baseball knickers and long stockings. When Eureka's team arrived on February 7, its players were shocked when Illinois State enforced a school policy against "skimpy" uniforms.

"An unfortunate feature of the game was the long delay about beginning," the *Vidette* reported. "Eureka had not been informed as to the requirements in the matter of dress, and when they were not allowed to play in their track suits, some of the players for a long time refused to play. The whole affair was unfortunate, but after all the matter of clothing is not so essential as the Eureka players seem to think, and the claim that the game was lost because they were compelled to wear heavier clothes than they were accustomed to, can hardly be given serious consideration."

Maybe, but the Eureka team avenged that 45–23 loss with a 38–17 victory on its cozy home floor at the end of the season. "Normal's defeat is due to two things—Eureka's small playing field, and the pushing, crowding, hugging game of their team," the *Vidette* alibied. "The playing field is very small—about 40 feet by 20 feet, about one-fourth the size of ours. The space is so small that team work is almost out of the question, and every man is both guard and forward."

Obviously, the home-court advantage has always been part of basketball. The *Vidette* suggested that a third game on neutral grounds would be needed to settle the dispute and proclaimed that Illinois State had "a good claim on the championship of the state outside of Chicago and vicinity, not including the University of Illinois." Illinois State had scored a 49–21 victory over Illinois' second team that

season. The only setbacks were to Eureka and to Wheaton which had "some Olympian medal winners in its lineup," the *Pantagraph* reported. The six victories included a 45–16 thrashing of Bradley when Francis Gray scored 24 points against the "boys of the still city," a reference to Peoria's thriving whiskey industry.

◆   ◆   ◆   ◆   ◆   ◆

For the next two years, Illinois State's athletics program continued to be led by student organizations and volunteer faculty coaches. William

A Suggestion as to How a Conversation may be carried on during a Basket Ball Game.

The basketball crowds of 1906 were forerunners of later eras. As evidenced by this *Index* illustration, loud crowds made it difficult to communicate during games.

Bawden, a manual training teacher originally from Buffalo, N.Y., continued the school's winning basketball tradition in 1907 and 1908.

The 1907 team, resplendent in new uniforms described as "the best that have been purchased by this institution," opened impressively when captain I.D. Frantz scored 28 points in a 46–12 conquest of Bradley. That was to be his final game, however. A doctor

diagnosed him as having yellow jaundice (hepatitis) and advised him to withdraw from school. The team elected Jay Crist to assume the captaincy and recovered to post a 5-3 season record marred by two losses to its new nemesis, Eureka College.

The Illinois State players thought Eureka had a difficult basketball environment, but they hadn't seen Lincoln College yet. "The room looked more like a bowling alley than a basketball field," one player told the *Vidette*, describing Lincoln's court as being 60 feet long and only 10 feet wide.

Illinois State won, 24–18, but was frustrated by the conditions. The *Pantagraph* reported, "It was the roughest [game] that any of the local men ever played in, due in a great measure to the room in which the game was played. Brick walls formed the boundary line for three sides of the field and the playing conditions were anything but satisfactory. Lincoln will play here later in the season an e result of this game will better tell the true merits of the two teams."

Illinois State won easily on its more spacious ourt, 47–9, and clipped Western Illinois, 3–10, in the season finale. The Macomb chool brought about 50 fans and a band to he game, which was scheduled at the time f the Inter-Normal Oratorical Contest late in March, boosting the crowd to a reported 400 500.

"The interest in basket ball seems to have een lagging for the past two seasons," the *idex* commented. "One reason only is given r this fact—the basket ball manager is not ected until late in the fall term, and as a onsequence the schedule is not what it should e or what it used to be."

The student manager for the 1908 team, Doc" Pulliam, attempted to arrange a more mbitious schedule but, according to the earbook, several opposing teams canceled.

Illinois State was left with only six games, three at home and three away. The team responded with a 5-1 record, losing only at Bradley, 41–23, a day or so after beginning practice. "The field was small and had six posts in it, which somewhat handicapped the Normal team," the *Vidette* commented. A second game between the schools was canceled because of the death of Bradley founder Lydia Moss Bradley.

Illinois State's 1908 roster contained some of the university's most highly regarded early players. The indomitable Harrison Russell, a member of Illinois State teams in 1900, 1901 and 1903, was back in school again after several years of teaching and eventually regained a starting position at forward. The other forwards were Clyde Hudelson, who was to achieve a distinguished career as Illinois State's agriculture department chair, and Earl Rosenberry. Grover Harrison, who stood about 6-foot-3, jumped center. The regular guards were captain Alfred Blackburn and Guy Ogle. Harrison's brother, Charles, was among a

talented group of replacements that sometimes beat the starters in practice.

After squeezing past Millikin, 23–22, at Decatur, Illinois State won three home games by lopsided margins over Shurtleff College of Alton, Monmouth College and the Pontiac YMCA. The season finale was a relatively easy victory at Macomb.

The Shurtleff coach, George Binnewies, must have been impressed with what he saw when Illinois State walloped his team, 40–20. By the time classes began in the fall of 1909, he had moved to Normal to become the university's first athletics director and full-time coach.

The era of faculty volunteer coaches and student-run intercollegiate programs was nearing an end. In its first 10 seasons, Illinois State Normal University had established a grand tradition with a 44-16 record. Binnewies would take ISNU basketball to greater heights in his first season and the athletics program to near-catastrophic depths during a turbulent second year.

Chapter 3

FROM TRIUMPH TO DESPAIR
(1908–1910)

The departure of John A. Keith, a distinguished faculty member who coached Illinois State's football team to an 8-2 record in 1907, aroused student sentiment for a full-time athletics director to lead Illinois State Normal University's intercollegiate sports program.

Keith was appointed president of Oshkosh Normal School in Wisconsin during October of that season, leaving his ISNU faculty position as director of teacher training. Illinois State students, encouraged by resident Board of Education member Charles L. Capen, almost unanimously petitioned to add a faculty position in athletics for the 1908–09 school year. The university's governing board granted the request.

President Felmley hired Wilfred George Binnewies, the popular coach at Shurtleff College in Alton. Shurtleff students collected $300 to induce Binnewies to remain, but President Felmley countered by increasing ISNU's offer by the same amount—a substantial sum of money at a time when monthly public school teaching salaries in Illinois averaged $82.13 for men and $60.70 for women. Binnewies, who taught German, joined the faculty in the fall of 1908.

Binnewies had been a prominent athlete at DePauw University, "a school famed for its athletic prowess," according to a yearbook article. Illinois State's athletics program prospered under his direction in 1908–09. "His work in Normal has proven most salutary," the *Index* assessed. "Mr. Binnewies is a conscientious hard-working and conservative man."

Indeed, Binnewies-coached teams produced records of 6-2 in football, 9-0 in basketball and 9-1 in baseball during the 1908–09 school year. The basketball team was crowned as the minor-college champion of the state after closing its unblemished campaign with a convincing triumph over DePaul. Illinois State was riding on top of the state's small-college sports. In the excitement of those heady achievements, few if any students suspected that the following year would bring conflict threatening to collapse their program.

Optimism reigned when Binnewies and team captain Guy Ogle assembled an impressive basketball squad in January 1909. The roster included:

◆ Leslie Hargitt, an imposing 6-foot-5 center. He had four years of experience on Normal High School and YMCA teams and was the football captain-elect at Illinois State.

◆ Grover Harrison, a rugged 6-foot-3 captain of the football team. A center on three previous teams, he moved to left forward with the arrival of Hargitt and gave the team dominating strength in the front line.

◆ Fred "Brick" Young, a 16-year-old freshman from Normal High School. A deadly accurate shooter, he moved into the starting right forward position and became an immediate sensation by scoring 34 points in his first college game. His nickname evolved from "Brig" after friends called him "little Brigham Young" because of his conservative manners. But in basketball, the yearbook described him as a "shark."

◆ Chuck Harrison, a brother of Grover and a veteran "stationary guard." The yearbook described him as a remarkable defensive player, "the largest number of goals being thrown by his opponent during any one game being two." He also played six years as a football end at Illinois State under that era's lenient eligibility regulations.

◆ Guy Ogle, the "running guard" and the "best all around athlete that the school has ever produced," according to a 1909 *Pantagraph* article. He was a star football halfback, baseball first baseman and recognized as the team's best basketball player.

◆ Previous starter Earl Rosenberry led a strong bench.

"Never in the history of the school have the conditions been more favorable for a winning team and never has the material been better," the *Pantagraph* assessed.

Illinois State overwhelmed Hedding College of Abingdon in the opener, 52–22, after leading by only seven points at halftime. The youthful Young was the team's designated free throw shooter, a common practice in basketball until the late 1920s, and celebrated his first college game with 12 baskets and 10 free throws.

Grover Harrison's 22-point outburst paced a 46–14 victory in the final meeting with the Bloomington YMCA, a game memorable for the *Pantagraph* giving Illinois State's basketball team a nickname. "Ogle, the captain of Normal, is one of the best basket ball men that has ever played for the teachers and his work always shows," read one sentence in the article. Illinois State teams soon became known as the Teachers (with a capital "T") and, as a variation, the Pedagogues or Pedagogs, until the current nickname of Redbirds was adopted during the 1920s.

Illinois State returned to its home court to

demolish four more opponents. Young scored 23 points in a 57–12 triumph over Bradley. Illinois State slipped past Binnewies' former Shurtleff team, 31–23, despite the absence of Hargitt. With the big center back in the lineup, the Teachers walloped Millikin, 70–19, as Young scored 30 points, Ogle 18 and Grover Harrison 16 in an awesome display of firepower. Undefeated Illinois College was expected to offer a stronger challenge, especially with Young home in bed with measles, but Illinois State rolled over the Jacksonville five, 68–12, to go 6-0 for the season.

With Young still out, the Teachers faced a difficult two-game western Illinois road trip against William and Vashti College in Aledo and Hedding College in Abingdon. Coach Binnewies might have shaken his head and exclaimed, "You can't get there from here," but he found a way to navigate an inconvenient transportation network.

The players left Sunday morning on the Illinois Traction System from Bloomington to Peoria, switched to the Iowa Central Railroad, and arrived at Keithsburg, along the Mississippi River, at about 8 o'clock that night. Monday at 5:30 a.m. they left for Aledo, taking two hours to travel about 15 miles. After chapel exercises, dinner and time to relax in a dormitory, they filed into a spacious gymnasium at 3:00 p.m. to face the largest crowd—and largest court—they had seen that season. "The gymnasium floor contained 4,000 square feet of playing space and had Normal not been used to a large floor the game would have been lost," the *Vidette* reported.

William and Vashti seized a 14–10 halftime lead but Grover Harrison and Hargitt each scored twice to open the second half and Illinois State held on for a 28–24 victory. Before leaving for Abingdon the next morning, the players were warned that "if they expected to win the game at Hedding College or have any chance of winning it, that they had better dispense with the services of umpire Kline of Hedding College, who has stuck with the home team thru thick and thin the last three years without a single defeat on their home court."

Illinois State had beaten Hedding by 47 points at the start of the season but the Abingdon school was advertising the game as being for the championship of Illinois. When the teams took the floor at 3:30, Hedding's lineup "was the same as it was in Normal, including Umpire Kline, who played forward, center and guard," the *Vidette* reported caustically. The first half ended with Hedding on top, 11–7.

Despite what was described later as something of a tug-of-war between Kline and Illinois State's traveling referee, a utility player named Harold Huxtable, Illinois State held Hedding to just three field goals in a 23–19 victory.

An undefeated season and state championship were on the line when Illinois State closed with a 44–23 home-court win against DePaul. Young's 17 points and a 29–8 halftime lead kept Normal in control.

The next day's *Pantagraph* carried a team photograph headlined NORMAL BASKET BALL CHAMPIONS OF ILLINOIS MINOR COLLEGES in all-capital letters, followed by a lengthy description of the players and season highlights. The article praised the impact of Binnewies on the program: "There is nothing like a good coach for a team and the Normal man has succeeded as is shown by the record of his men." Young, a freshman, averaged an extraordinary 22.7 points per game. He, Ogle and Hargitt would return in 1909–10, and Illinois State fans could hardly wait until next year.

◆   ◆   ◆   ◆   ◆   ◆

Next year was to become a bizarre disappointment. The 1909–10 team opened with five consecutive victories but was decimated by the

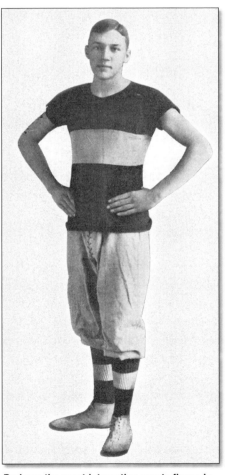

Perhaps the most interesting sports figure in central Illinois history, Fred Young was an outstanding athlete, a noted journalist and a well-known official and referee. He captained the 1910 basketball team at ISNU.

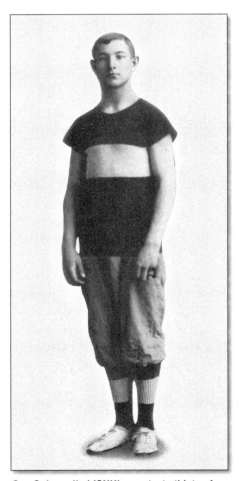

Guy Ogle, called ISNU's greatest athlete of his time, captained the 1909 unbeaten basketball team which won the state championship.

Coach George Binnewies holds the ball for the undefeated 1909 team, which featured Leslie Hargitt, Grover Harrison, Charles Harrison, Earl Rosenberry, Harold Huxtable, Guy Ogle and Fred Young.

ineligibility of four front-line players by mid-season. Sophomore "Brick" Young was elected captain to replace one of the departing starters and had to take Carrie Burtis and Frank "Dutch" Westhoff from the Academy (University High School) to finish the schedule. The team lost four of its last six games and finished with an 8-5 record. "Old Normal had the most unlucky season in the history of the school," the *Index* reported mournfully.

Illinois State had its squad intact for a season-opening triumph over Illinois Wesleyan, 43–31, in the Bloomington university's first collegiate game. It was a profitable venture for the schools. Gate receipts totaled $46.90, leaving Illinois State $22.20 after giving

Wesleyan $23.45 as its share and spending $1.25 for advertising.

A newcomer to the Illinois State lineup, scrappy forward Bob Roberts of La Place, scored 25 points in the opener, but academic problems held him out of all but one future game. In those years, faculty reviewed the academic progress of athletes frequently during the term. Students behind in their studies were "conditioned," a probationary status that left them ineligible to play.

Even without Roberts, the Teachers demolished Eureka College, 58–20, with Young playing his finest game at Illinois State. The star sophomore forward tossed in 17 field goals and 11 free throws for 43 points, a school scoring

record that stood for 45 years, converting several shots on inbounds passes.

Illinois State traveled to Peoria on Saturday, January 22, and defeated Bradley, 27–15, in a contest marred by rough play. The team was undefeated after three games but celebration was premature; five days later, Hargitt, the "giant" center, decided to leave school. The squad elected Fred Young to be captain for the remainder of the season.

Even without Hargitt, Illinois State scored an impressive 64–13 triumph over Shurtleff a couple of days later. Young, who might have stretched to six feet, moved into the center position and scored over half of his team's total with 11 baskets and 12 free throws for 34 points.

The Teachers defeated Lombard College, 37–25, in their next outing as Young again led the way with 17 points despite jumping center against a 6-foot-5 opponent. But they suffered their first loss of the season against Illinois College, 30–23, before 300 rabid fans at Jacksonville when Young again had to go up against a 6-5 center who was able to control the tips.

Illinois State was still thinking in terms of another state championship when it rebounded on its home court on February 11 for a 43–30 victory over a strong Monmouth team which had four starters over six feet tall. Young finished with 20 points. Glowing over the victory, the reporter concluded: "Hopes for the state championship are becoming all the stronger and with a victory over Knox on Friday afternoon we ought to add another nail on its hold."

Four days later, the hammer descended on Illinois State's athletics program. The faculty sent shock waves through the campus by voting to abolish baseball that spring. President Felmley explained the decision by saying baseball was a financial drain on the athletics treasury, that new uniforms would have to be purchased in order to continue the sport, and that the baseball team monopolized the field that other students should be able to use for their amusement and exercise.

The fallout was immediate. Ogle, a starting basketball guard, and Roberts, who had been trying to regain eligibility, left school the next day and enrolled at Illinois Wesleyan. "The loss to the basket ball team is a severe one, especially in the loss of Ogle, who is by far the best athlete the school ever had," the *Pantagraph* reported on February 17. "He is equally good in base ball. His popularity at the latter institution [Wesleyan] is attested in the fact that he was pledged a member of the Sigma Chi fraternity at a meeting held last night, this being one of the strongest in the country with chapters covering practically the entire United States."

Adding to the team's woes, L. Wyne Chamberlain, a basketball player who also was captain-elect of the football team, was "conditioned" by the faculty.

Young was left to pick up the pieces for the remaining six games of Illinois State's 1910 campaign. With Academy players Westhoff and Burtis moving into the lineup, Illinois State lost its first home game in two years, 44–33, to Knox, despite Young's 25 points.

Illinois State's only two victories in the remaining five games came against high school teams. State prep champion Bloomington fell, 46–18, and the Teachers downed Normal High School, 44–10. If the game's position on the schedule is correct as published in contemporary accounts, Young prevailed on former teammates Ogle and Roberts to rejoin him for what today would be considered an exhibition or scrimmage. Otherwise, the team limped to the finish line with decisive losses to Monmouth, Knox and Lombard. The record was published as 8-5 but without the high school opponents the team would have finished at 6-5. The state small-college championship of 1909 became a distant memory.

As a final irony, Young and Ogle both were chosen to a small-college all-state basketball team. Ogle had already transferred to Illinois Wesleyan and Young would join him there the following year and play four more seasons of basketball. The only lettermen who would be returning were captain-elect Claire Cox, a defensive mainstay at guard, and Jay Courtright, who showed promise as a "running" guard in his first season.

Just when it seemed that matters couldn't get worse, they did. Shortly before the end of the winter term in March, the faculty unloaded another bombshell by voting to drop football as well as baseball. A story in the March 30, 1910 *Vidette* gives several reasons for the action. "The leading ones were opposition to the game itself, the feeling that too few students participate in any form of athletics in the fall, and the undesirable conditions considered inseparable from inter-school athletics just at present."

President Felmley's role in the decision was not stated, but for several months he had been embroiled in a dispute with members of the football team over their athletics awards. The controversy began in November of 1909 when Felmley vetoed the athletics Board of Control decision to award sweaters to players by using a portion of the $300 in proceeds from the season's games.

The issue refused to die. In March, students attending general assembly at the school's new auditorium were treated to an unprecedented public debate between the university president and a student, Eugene Shaver of the football team, over what was being called "The Sweater Question." Shaver concluded his plea by asking for a standing vote by the student body and virtually every person in the auditorium rose to support him. Felmley remained adamant. "So long as the constitution is the way it is and so long as I am President of this Institution, sweaters will not be awarded to the foot ball team," he responded.

Later that month, football was abolished. George Binnewies, the school's first athletic director, left for the University of Chicago at the end of the academic year. With the program in shambles, Illinois State University needed a miracle worker to save intercollegiate athletics. It found one in Henry Harrison Russell.

Chapter 4
RESTORING THE PROGRAM (1910–1917)

President David Felmley responded to faculty concerns about the academic integrity of the athletics program in 1910 by summoning H. Harrison Russell to become director of athletics and coach of the few remaining men's teams in basketball, track and tennis.

Many faculty members knew Russell to be a young man of character and ability. In addition to being a prominent athlete as an undergraduate, he was a member of the 1908 debating team that won honors in the annual contest against Oshkosh Normal of Wisconsin.

Nearly a half-century later, Russell recalled for a *Pantagraph* sportswriter the circumstances that brought him back to his alma mater.

"President Felmley wrote me that athletics— these are not his words—are in sort of a mess and he wanted me to see if I could straighten it out," Russell explained.

Russell was finishing work in physical education at the Springfield (Mass.) YMCA training school, the place where basketball was born. He secured a loan, probably with Felmley's assistance, to study coaching at Harvard University in the summer of 1910. He returned to Illinois State that fall and began rebuilding an athletics program with no football, no baseball and limited facilities. About 200 men and 500 women competed for time on the single gymnasium floor, with intercollegiate athletics having a low priority.

Other obstacles were to surface during Russell's 13-year tenure: a world war that brought on a decline in male enrollment, a deadly flu epidemic that claimed more McLean County lives than the war, and the university's slender financial resources. His ability to keep the program alive and occasionally even to thrive was remarkable. The venerable Fred Young, an observer of the local sports scene for more than seven decades, often credited Russell with saving the university's athletics program.

One of Russell's first tasks was to form a competitive basketball team for the 1911 opener against Illinois Wesleyan. It was a formidable challenge. Two of Illinois State's best players from the previous season, Young and Guy Ogle, were on the Wesleyan team. Illinois State's most experienced players were L. Wyne "Single" Chamberlain, who had regained his eligibility, and three Academy recruits from the previous season: Carrie Burtis, Jay Courtright and Frank "Dutch" Westhoff. Russell chose Clare Dillon for the fifth starting position.

The *Pantagraph* gave Illinois State a slim chance for success. "Wesleyan is doped to win by a good score, but the Normal team is in the best possible condition, and are bound to give a good account of themselves," the newspaper reported. "There is no doubt but that it will be a game of fidget from the beginning until the last minute of play and should the 'hoodoo' which has been the feature of the last few games between these teams, make its appearance, the dopesheet is liable to be upset."

Illinois State scored the upset, 28–25, on its home court in a game marked by a dispute over one of the game officials during the second half. Wesleyan refused to continue playing until umpire Fred Telford, a former ISNU player, was removed. Illinois State relented and the game continued to its conclusion.

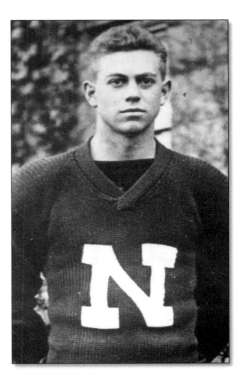

P.K. Benjamin.

"The game was a great surprise to every one, Wesleyan being supposed to have by far the better team, but the Normal boys have been putting in too much practice of late to let any team have a 'walk away' with them," the *Pantagraph* reported. Young had 19 of Wesleyan's points and Ogle had two of the remaining three field goals against their former teammates but Illinois State countered with 19 points by Chamberlain, including 13 free throws, and standout defensive guard play by Westhoff and Dillon.

The game was a financial as well as artistic success. Combined season ticket and single-game sales amounted to $118.62, a tidy sum considering that Illinois State had gross receipts of $17.50 and $28 in its next two

P.H. Miller, a center on the Teachers basketball team, eclipsed the national collegiate record for the javelin throw in a 1916 dual meet against Illinois Wesleyan.

home games. A single-game ticket cost 25 cents then.

It was a great start, but a 25–18 home-court loss to Bradley the following week showed how fickle sports acclaim can be. For reasons unreported, Russell elevated Roger Triplett from the Academy (University High School) team and started him at center. The student paper pilloried the move.

"Triplett gave the team the best he had which was not enough for the Bradley team," the *Vidette* reported, adding that "the Bradley game goes down as the biggest piece of 'bone-headedness' ever exhibited on the university floor."

By mid-February, the *Vidette* carried letters opposing the use of the high school players on university teams. The faculty apparently agreed and ended that practice the following year. But in 1911, skilled Academy players continued to work their way into the lineup on occasion.

Despite the promising start, Russell's first team slumped to a 6-7 record. It was Illinois State's first losing season in 13 campaigns.

◆　　◆　　◆　　◆　　◆　　◆

One significant development in 1911 was the establishment of the Illinois Intercollegiate Association basketball tournament at the Bloomington YMCA. The tournament, popular for the remainder of the decade, was a forerunner of the Little Nineteen Conference that contained all of the state's public and private "minor" colleges for several decades. Illinois State took fourth in the inaugural tourney, beating Eureka, 34–25, and Hedding, 35–14, and losing to Bradley, 43–18, and Wesleyan, 20–8.

In another exciting development, the faculty voted in January to lift the ban on baseball in 1911. When Russell sought in April to have football reinstated as well, the faculty voted 23 to 9 against. He was persistent, however, changing faculty minds in 1912 after the *Vidette* reported a study indicating that men competing on Illinois State's athletics squads achieved higher grades than non-athletes.

"I told President Felmley that I was going to work to get football reinstated," Russell said years later. "He said, 'Oh, the faculty doesn't want it.' But football had been out only two years, and I found that sentiment was strong that it should be reinstated.

"You can imagine there was quite a hulla-baloo. Some of the teachers said, 'This is too sudden,' but we insisted on a vote and the motion passed.

"President Felmley is always thought of as being autocratic," Russell added, "but Felmley said, 'My faculty has voted for football and football it is.' I call that real democracy."

Meanwhile, Russell's second basketball team endured a 2-8 season in the 1911–12 academic year. Student enthusiasm remained high, however, and the crowd at the annual home game with Wesleyan was so large that a number of spectators in the balcony were able to view the contest at only one end of the floor. Mindful of the previous year's arguments over officiating, Russell imported a referee from the

Chicago Basketball Association but the game was held up by controversy again when the official awarded Illinois State a free throw with the score tied 24-all in the closing seconds. After a little "rag chewing," the free throw was missed. Wesleyan won in overtime, 29–28.

The 1912 basketball budget was tight. The Athletic Board approved the purchase of two new basketballs, one for use by the high school team and one for the university team. The board also approved the purchase of "enough jerseys and pants...to make, with what we have, six complete suits." Contemporary photographs show players wearing unadorned sleeveless jerseys with short pants and baseball socks.

The school yearbook complained that the team was handicapped by two rule changes, one switching the team from AAU to Intercollegiate regulations and the other the rule against using Academy players, "this taking some of the best material in school." Indeed, the Academy lineup that year was dotted with names of players who had played for the university team a year earlier.

Center and captain Jay Courtright provided one of the few bright spots for 1912, receiving all-state honors. His play would be critical to Illinois State's resurgence during the next two seasons. Three of Jay's brothers also played for Russell during the decade, two serving as team captains. Opponents probably wondered when the Courtright dynasty would end but sportswriters reveled in reporting that "Courtright was 'right'" year after year in their game accounts.

◆　　◆　　◆　　◆　　◆　　◆

The 1913 and 1914 seasons showed Illinois State was "right." Those two seasons were among the best in the school's early basketball history.

The Teachers, as they were now called, posted a 12-4 record and finished third in the Illinois Intercollegiate Association Tournament in 1913 although star guard Ben Briggs was sidelined with mumps. Nearly 1,100 people jammed into the final session at Decatur to see Illinois State beat host Millikin in overtime for third place and Bradley score a one-point victory over Wesleyan for the championship.

Paul K. Benjamin, better known as P.K., captained the 1913 team. Courtright, John Kasbeer, Frank Westhoff and Sam Stout joined Briggs as other mainstays. An unheralded player named O.M. "Red" Smith was recruited from the senior class team to replace Briggs in the tournament and played a prominent role in the team's success.

In 1914, Illinois State finished 12-5 and took second place in the tourney by winning six post-season games before bowing to Wesleyan in the championship, 40–26. The teams had split two meetings during the regular season, which was Fred Young's sixth and final collegiate campaign. Normal had won, 38–15, a couple weeks before the tourney.

"That 1914 team was my best basketball team," Russell recalled nearly 50 years later. "I believe Jay Courtright was the best player I ever had."

Benjamin, Briggs, Courtright and Stout were joined by Oscar "Dutch" Schneider and Roy Diehl to form the 1914 squad.

Benjamin, an important sports figure at Illinois State, became the coach at University High, left the community for many years, and eventually returned during the 1950s to become the university's first full-time athletics trainer. He insisted that basketball was a rougher game when he was in college.

"There was more contact in the old days," he said in a 1957 interview. "We wore hip pads but our hips still got bruised. You could do almost anything as long as you had your hands on the ball. It was about like pass defense in football—you can almost kill a player as long as you went after the ball.

"We didn't have much money in those days," Benjamin added. "We had only two basketballs, one for practice and one for games, and we had to furnish our own shoes for all sports. But we had lots of fun. The old gym at Cook Hall was one of the best in the state at that time."

It was also one of the most crowded gyms when Illinois State and Wesleyan played. About 200 reserved seats went on sale several days before their late-season meeting in 1914. Two rows of chairs were set up around the court, and the balcony gallery was jammed with standing spectators. Illinois State outscored Wesleyan, 27–5, in the second half to bag a 38–15 triumph before what was described as a record crowd, although actual attendance figures were not published.

More than 1,050 saw Wesleyan turn the tables on the Teachers in the post-season tournament at Bloomington's YMCA. Although the tournament loss to their cross-town rivals must have been disappointing, the 1914 players joined their coach and president two days later at the Wesleyan celebration in the IWU chapel. Following Russell's example, they were as gracious in defeat as they had been in victory. Many of them spoke during the event to congratulate the winners.

After the great campaigns of 1913 and 1914, Illinois State's basketball teams struggled for many of the remaining years in the decade.

The 1915 slate began ominously when Russell Courtright, one of Jay's brothers, broke his leg in the season-opening loss to Wesleyan in January. Benjamin went down with torn ankle ligaments in the following game. High blood pressure sidelined C.D. Cox, and a severe attack of the grippe (influenza) took center Jean Petty from the lineup. The team limped to the finish line with a 3-10 record.

During the following summer, Courtright prepared with a threshing crew to harden his muscles for the football and basketball campaigns but he ended up missing half of the basketball season because of illness, and the 1916 team finished with a 6-10 record.

Coach Russell was absent during the Illinois Intercollegiate tourney in 1916 for reasons not explained in the press. University High coach Merton Lyon, who was called "the little wizard," coached the team in Russell's absence. Lyon adopted a liberal substitution policy that produced three victories and competitive showings in losses to Wesleyan and Bradley. "Lyon must have put the fear of the Lord into those fellows," Wesleyan star Norman Elliott remarked after IWU rallied from a halftime deficit to win the game.

The 1915–16 school year was memorable for many other reasons, not all involving sports. Europe was engulfed in war and former U.S. President William Howard Taft came to the campus in November to speak about America's national defense.

A week later, 30 members of the geography and geology classes ventured by automobile on a 25-mile field trip around the cities and as far away as Downs. It was a novel way to travel but the railroads remained the most reliable transportation for athletics teams. Former *Pantagraph* editor H. Clay Tate noted in his book on McLean County that 49 steam passenger trains and 62 electric interurban trains passed through the community every 24 hours at that time.

P.H. Miller, a member of Illinois State's basketball team, made headlines during the spring by eclipsing the national collegiate record in the javelin throw. He heaved "the seven and one-half foot missile" 180 feet, nine inches during a dual meet with Illinois Wesleyan and was invited to join the Chicago Athletic Club in the summer.

Illinois State's baseball team, which called itself the White Stockings a couple decades earlier when that Chicago professional team was the scourge of the National League, adopted the nickname of Braves for the 1916 campaign but the moniker did not stick as an official school name. Bradley Polytechnic had not become the Braves yet. Illinois State's student paper often referred to the teams from Peoria's hilltop as Cliff Dwellers, the boys from Whisky Town, or the Distillers during the latter part of the decade.

Illinois State's basketball team continued to be known as the Teachers during the 1917 season, the last campaign before the United States entered the world war. The Red and White crew rebounded for an 8-7 record and upset Bradley, 18–16, in the Illinois Intercollegiate Tournament opener. The resourceful Russell had scouted Bradley, a rarity in those years, and changed his lineup, replacing top scorer Fred Jones with Miller and stationing Miller under the Bradley basket to stymie the Peoria school's three-man offense.

However, the season was filled with sadness for Dudley Courtright and his teammates when his brother, Jay, died in February after a 15-month battle against tuberculosis. Jay Courtright, a former three-time all-state center, was principal and superintendent at Tonica High School when he contracted the disease and died at age 23.

"It is the consensus of opinion that he was the greatest player that ever donned a red and white uniform," the *Vidette* eulogized. "Tall, fair, and straight as a sapling, he was known, feared, and if we may use the word, loved by college students and players throughout the state."

The future would bring more difficult times. On April 6, 1917, the United States formally declared war on Germany.

The 1913 team placed third in the state intercollegiate tournament. In front, left to right, are O.M. Smith and Louis Moore. Seated are Arthur Farrel, captain P.K. Benjamin and John Kasbeer. In back are Talmage Petty, Ray Shotwell, coach Harrison Russell, Jay Courtright, Sam Stout and Frank Westhoff. The 1914 team, with many of the same players and the same coach, finished second in the state intercollegiate tournament.

Chapter 5

THE WORLD AT WAR
(1917–1919)

America's entry into the world war had an immediate impact on the Illinois State Normal University campus. From a pre-war total of 834 students including 185 men, the university enrollment plummeted to 605 students with 83 men in the fall of 1917 and to only 380 students with 57 men in the fall of 1918. One has to go back to the founding of the university in 1857 to find fewer men in attendance.

With President Woodrow Wilson urging the nation's colleges to continue their sports programs, Russell somehow assembled enough players to field a football team in 1917 and found a reasonable supply of talent for basketball season opening in January 1918.

Dudley Courtright returned to captain the team although he underwent surgery in December and missed the early part of the season. "Courtright is a shifty player with a good idea as to the location of the basket," the *Vidette* reported.

The team suffered another early squad loss when starting forward Byron Moore left after two games to join the Navy, but regrouped and won five of its last eight games for a 7-7 season record.

The turning point came when Illinois State upset Little Nineteen leader Eureka, 33–27. Courtright returned to action in this game and scored 18 points. "Little Nineteen" was a common nickname used for the Illinois Intercollegiate Athletic Conference (IIAC).

"Ain't it a grand and glorious feeling when your team that has not won a conference game suddenly comes to life and beats the team that is leading the Little Nineteen and has won every game so far?" the student paper crowed.

Illinois State's hot streak included surprising victories over Augustana, Bradley and Millikin in the Little Nineteen Tournament at Peoria before Eureka gained revenge in the championship game, 28–23. Courtright was chosen as a forward on the all-tournament team.

The team celebrated its tournament success with a banquet, the first in what has become an annual tradition. The menu featured such items as Double Dribble (soup), Umpire (pickles), Personal Foul (roast chicken), Free Throws (buttered peas) and Unnecessary Roughness (mashed potatoes). About 50 people attended the event at the Women's Exchange in Bloomington.

In April of 1918, the university displayed a military service flag containing 253 stars, two of them gold in memory of those killed in service. War news dominated the *Vidette*. A special Christmas issue, dated November 13 but probably prepared before the war ended on November 11, included this note from President Felmley (a staunch advocate of simplified spelling):

"We ar [sic] proud of you, proud of the fact that we ar [sic] almost unanimously a girl's school, that even before the last draft nearly all of our boys had enlisted. It grieved us sorely to lose you from the class rooms, from the athletic field, from the debating forum, from all the activities in which young men ar [sic] prominent. But with this great task before us we wanted you to go rather than stay even tho you must run the gauntlet of epidemics and machine guns."

The epidemics proved to be more dangerous than the machine guns. An outbreak of influenza killed an estimated 20 million worldwide, 548,000 in the United States. The Spanish flu claimed 242 McLean County lives during the last four months of 1918. The university closed for 15 days during the semester.

With that somber background, Illinois State prepared for the 1919 basketball season, bolstered by Dudley Courtright's return from several months in the Navy. "His record was nothing less than brilliant," the student yearbook proclaimed, but Illinois State managed only a 4-8 season record.

Courtright's talents helped the Teachers upset Bradley. Illinois State led 9–6 at the half but Bradley inched ahead at one point in the second half. Then Courtright "set the fans ablaze with 'pep' when he shot a basket over his head while facing opposite from the net, leaving the score 13 to 12 in Normal's favor," according to the *Pantagraph* account. Illinois State nursed a one-point lead into the final moments when Bradley misfired and Courtright scored again to make the final 19–16.

Captain Lyle "Farmer" Mohr was named to the Little Nineteen's all-tournament team after Illinois State won one of three games.

The quick end of the war had caught Illinois State officials by surprise. The university was in a weakened financial condition and funds were in short supply for a baseball team in the spring. Players volunteered to travel by car despite the primitive road conditions that still existed.

Through two lean war years, Harrison Russell had kept the program alive. He surely looked forward to more prosperous times in the post-war period.

Chapter 6

RACIAL DIVERSITY AND RUSSELL'S LAST YEARS (1919–1923)

Johnny came marching home again in 1919, boosting Illinois State Normal University's post-war male enrollment to 97 students that fall. The growth helped provide "an abundance of material of superior ability" in the words of the yearbook, and Harrison Russell produced the best basketball team in his final four years with an 11-5 record in 1920.

Most of all, the 1920 campaign should be remembered for the presence of Joe Ward, the university's first African-American basketball player.

Ward was one of 14 children born to Jesse and Mary Ward, both of whom were born into slavery. Jesse Ward entered a farming partnership in 1882 with C.W. Fairbanks, who became vice president of the United States under Theodore Roosevelt. Fairbanks owned farm property near Bellflower in southern McLean County, and Ward managed the acreage.

Before Joe Ward, two African-Americans had been involved in Illinois State athletics. George Green, a local barber, coached the baseball team during the 1896–97 school year, and Roy Williams was a starting lineman on the 1904 football team.

Still, Ward's appearance on the hardwood was a rare distinction. A dozen years would pass before another African-American athlete played basketball for the university. Ironically, UCLA standout Jackie Robinson—later the first modern-day African-American major league baseball player—would compete in a basketball game against Illinois State in 1940.

A standout athlete at Bellflower High School, Ward attended Illinois State for only one year but it was a memorable one. He and Jean

Harrison, a prominent local athlete, formed a stalwart backcourt combination that helped Illinois State win eight of 11 regular-season games and score upsets over potent Millikin and Augustana teams during the post-season tournament.

Ward often was credited with playing a strong game, especially on defense, in *Pantagraph* and *Vidette* accounts.

"The work of Joe Ward was a distinct feature," the *Pantagraph* reported after Illinois State edged Eureka, 26–24. "He put up a stellar defense."

A few days later, Ward scored four baskets as Illinois State captured its first victory over Wesleyan in six years, 25–22, before 900 fans at the Bloomington YMCA. He was scoreless, however, when Wesleyan won the return game, 25–17, before an estimated attendance of 700, the largest crowd ever reported at Normal's aging gymnasium in what is now Cook Hall. It is difficult to imagine that many spectators in such a small enclosure.

Illinois State's other two regular-season losses were to Millikin's powerful undefeated team, so ISNU was a distinct underdog when it drew Millikin as its first opponent in the ninth annual Little Nineteen Tournament at Rock Island. However, the Teachers snapped Millikin's 19-game winning streak, 24–23, on Harrison's late "ringer" under the goal.

The upstart Red and White five followed with victories over Illinois College and host Augustana (with Ward scoring three baskets) to enter the final round. The tournament had a double-elimination format, however, and ISNU placed fourth after losing rematches with champion Millikin and Augustana.

Ward and Harrison were on the all-tournament team "without dispute," the *Pantagraph* reported. "The showing of the Normal team was largely [due] to the stellar defense of the Normal guards, who also proved their worth as basket shots."

Ward returned to the farm after that season and never came back to college. He and his brothers formed an independent basketball team that played professional and semi-pro ball for 20 years. At one time, they had a record of 112 victories and only one loss.

Joe Ward also became a prominent high school sports official for 25 years before retiring to devote full time to farming 330 acres between Bellflower and Mansfield. He died in a fire at his home January 2, 1951, and was inducted posthumously into the Bloomington-Normal Officials Association Hall of Fame in 1978.

◆　　◆　　◆　　◆　　◆　　◆

Ward was not the only male student leaving school in 1920. Illinois State's male population dropped to 70 students that fall. It was a case of bad timing because coach Russell agreed to playing two hastily arranged games with Illinois during the 1920–21 season. Illinois State's female-dominated enrollment was only 439 while Illinois had about 7,000 students.

Harrison, also a starting quarterback in football, and Lyle "Farmer" Mohr were the only experienced players returning for the Red and White. The squad brushed up its techniques with an opening victory over Lincoln College before confronting the Illini in back-to-back games.

The games originally were scheduled by the

Bloomington Fans' Association independent team, a powerful squad with several former Big Ten Conference standouts and former Illinois State star P.K. Benjamin. Former Redbird star Fred Young, then the sports editor of Bloomington's afternoon newspaper, the *Bulletin*, was the coach and manager.

After University of Illinois faculty ruled against playing non-collegiate teams, local boosters invited Russell to match his Illinois State team against the Illini. He accepted the challenge. The first game was played December 20, 1920, at the new Bloomington High School gymnasium and, according to the *Vidette*, was attended by 400 "wild-eyed fans."

Excerpts from the *Vidette* article give a flavor of the historic meeting:

"An enthusiastic crowd was present to witness the contest and from the time the starting whistle blew until the final gun Normal yells and songs rang thru out the large gym. Fell Hall was out en masse and the local coeds lent their voices to the chorus of well-known Normal yells. On the other hand, a scattering of Illini grads and supporters were present so the big Orange and Blue team always got a welcome hand whenever it scored.

"In Gene [sic] Harrison the Illini basketeers met with a man of their own calibre. Time and again he broke up threatening plays and quickly returned the leather sphere to Normal's forwards. He forced the Illini clan to rush their shots causing the majority of tries to be made from long range.

"Not all the credit for a good game should go to Normal. Local fans saw a real Big Ten team in action. They saw a team formed from a student body of seven thousand persons, over twelve times that of Normal." The Illini won, 32–21.

The generous reporter praised the game officials, too. P.K. Benjamin was the referee and Jack McCord, a former Illini standout, was the umpire.

The Illini also won the second meeting, 42–18, before 4,500 spectators on the Illinois campus. It was the largest crowd that would see an Illinois State team play for many decades, probably until the 1950s when Illinois State played at Bradley's Robertson Fieldhouse.

The two games against the Fighting Illini

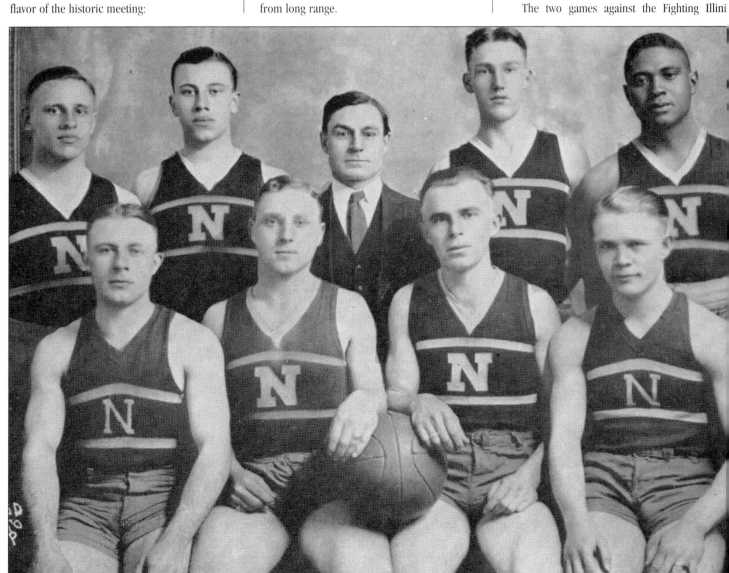

In 1920, Joe Ward (back row, right), whose parents were born into slavery, became Illinois State's first African-American basketball player. Jean Harrison (back row, left) was a stand-out guard and later a successful coach at Bloomington High School.

probably were the inspiration for the *Vidette* calling ISNU "the Fighting Teachers" later that season. That pugnacious appellation might have been an oxymoron in an era when teachers were expected to provide a model of decorum, but the expression gained favor for a few years.

The annual series with Wesleyan continued to have strong appeal. Six hundred "red hot fans and supporters of the two teams" jammed into Normal's cramped gymnasium for the first game and saw Wesleyan win, 25–24, on Glenn "Frenchy" Haussler's basket as time was expiring. Wesleyan also won a double-overtime struggle at the Bloomington YMCA, 36–31, which a breathless reporter called "the greatest basketball game in local history."

One of the Wesleyan players that season was William "Bunker" Young, brother of Fred. A few years later, he reversed the path his brother had taken by enrolling at Illinois State and playing for the Red and White.

Illinois State finished with a 5-11 record in the 1920–21 season and slumped to 2-11 for the 1921–22 campaign although male enrollment climbed to 157 to start an upward progression that solidified the base available for men's athletics in future years. However, the growth in male enrollment underscored the inadequacy of the 25-year-old gymnasium.

President Felmley appeared before the state legislature in March 1921 and requested $225,000 to build a gym that would contain basketball courts for both men and women.

"Pres. Felmley is a firm believer in athletics for every man the year 'round," the *Vidette* reported. "He said [that] during the winter months when we must stay indoors, the invigorating exercise of basketball should be enjoyed by not only the select ten or twelve men who make the team but by every able-bodied student."

Basketball players must have wondered who were the "select" men using the gym. The same *Vidette* story reported that during the winter "the Women's Athletic department had the gym from 8 a.m. to 3:40 p.m. and used it constantly while the men were crowded into it between

3:40 and 8 p.m.

"A new gym would do wonders to Old Normal and increase its male enrollment 100 per cent the first year," the *Vidette* concluded.

The *Pantagraph* reported the scheduling problems this way: "With over 300 woman students taking physical education work in their regular courses and others taking it as electives, the men are left practically without a gymnasium now. The present gymnasium was the finest in the state when it was erected many years ago but now it is a back number..."

The legislature did not grant Felmley's request then, but on June 25, 1923, state representatives awarded Illinois State and Southern Illinois $150,000 each to construct new gymnasiums on the Normal and Carbondale campuses. Illinois State would have a new gymnasium within two years but Harrison Russell would not enjoy using it. He decided to leave coaching after the 1922–23 season to pursue an academic career in geography.

Russell went out on a winning note with an 8-6 record. In 13 seasons, his teams won 86 and lost 97 games, a remarkable achievement given the scarcity of men on the campus and the frequent unavailability of the gymnasium for practice time, not to mention the perils of world war and a deadly flu epidemic.

Forty-five of the school's 157 men tried out for basketball that season. Russell dressed 16 players in uniforms featuring a white "N" between white bars on red jerseys. The color was probably cardinal red, but must have looked bright nonetheless.

The veteran Jean Harrison, absent in 1922, returned for his third season as a starter. Sophomore Stanley Changnon, a four-sport standout, was to achieve greater fame down the road as the coach of Mount Vernon High School's 1949 and 1950 state championship teams.

The big scoring star of the 1923 team, however, was Ernest Butzow, a transfer from Illinois Wesleyan who was in his second year as team captain. Butzow scored 154 points, nearly half of Illinois State's total for 14 games.

With better luck, Russell's last team might have enjoyed spectacular success. Bradley beat Illinois State twice by two points, once in

overtime. A loss by three points and two others by four left Illinois State mired with a 5-6 record and three home games remaining.

Illinois State won all three with a flourish. The most satisfying victory for Butzow and Paul Bolin, both Wesleyan transfers, came when the Teachers defeated Little Nineteen champion IWU, 29–26. Butzow scored 15 of Illinois State's points. Bolin added a pair of baskets and declared, "I attained the height of my ambition in basketball."

Two months later, Russell surprised the campus by announcing his resignation to take an assistant coaching position at Clark University in Worcester, Mass., and to study for a doctorate in geography under Professor Douglas C. Ridgley, a former ISNU colleague.

Russell completed his doctorate in 1926 and became a professor at Bloomsburg State Teachers College in Pennsylvania, rising to head the college's geography department. He returned to Normal after retiring in 1954, taught geography classes during the university's centennial year of 1956–57, and was a regular spectator at campus sports events. He died in 1968 at age 86.

President Felmley hired Russell to restore faculty confidence in the university's athletics program. Russell's success was illustrated by these comments from a *Vidette* editorial headlined "Finished a Clean Job," which was published April 18, 1923:

"It was Harry Russell who made Normal the cleanest school, athletically, in Illinois.

"Standing squarely upon a program of good sportsmanship, Mr. Russell has plodded along in his own unassuming way, turning out good teams, although no championship teams, for the past 12 [sic] years. He deplores unsportsmanlike athletics and never encouraged unclean athletics at Normal. In his own words he said, this week: 'I would not take a position at any school where unclean athletics are encouraged.'

"It is with regret and reverence to this man that we accept his decision to leave Normal, for he did put Old Normal on the map, not 'as a builder of champions, but as a builder of character.'"

Chapter 7

GOOD-BYE TO THE OLD CASTLE GYM (1923–1925)

I ronically, Illinois State endured its most unsuccessful basketball season during the brief coaching tenure of a congenial physical educator whose name would grace the university's basketball home four decades later: Clifford E. Horton, beloved by generations of admiring students as "Pop" and the man for whom Horton Field House was named during the 1960s.

When President David Felmley sought a successor for Harrison Russell in 1923, he took the advice of Douglas C. Ridgley, the former ISNU professor who influenced Russell's move to Clark University. Horton was coaching Clark's soccer, gymnastics and baseball teams while completing work on a master's degree. In effect, ISNU and Clark University traded coaches.

Horton won the position of athletics director and coach of men's sports over 46 other candidates. The *Vidette* introduced Horton to the campus with a story that included the following paragraph:

"Horton is not a large man, neither is [he] a man of words, but he has had some excellent training in physical education work and was recommended to Dr. Felmley very highly by Prof. Douglas C. Ridgley, a former member of the faculty at Normal who is now at Clarke [sic] University, Worcester, Mass., where Mr. Horton coached the past year."

Horton's undergraduate degree was from Springfield (Mass.) College, where he was regarded as one of the school's finest gymnasts. He captained the 1919 senior class swimming team and also played football, soccer, hockey and baseball on class teams.

He taught in the public schools of San Luis Obispo, Calif., and was an instructor at Ohio Wesleyan and Clark universities before coming to Normal. His background also included YMCA work in his home state at Spokane, Wash., and in Michigan City, Ind., and Mittineague, Mass.

Horton provided a lasting legacy at Illinois State with his wide-ranging sports interest, passionate love for gymnastics, and willingness to introduce new ideas. He initiated a model program of intramural activities for men soon after his arrival in Normal. He organized Gamma Phi, the honorary gymnastics fraternity, after his brief basketball coaching career ended and started the popular Gamma Phi Circus in 1932.

The summer before Horton's arrival in 1923, the Illinois General Assembly responded to President Felmley's numerous entreaties by appropriating $150,000 to build a new gymnasium at Illinois State. The amount was $100,000 less than Felmley's request but was welcome. By omitting a swimming pool and some other features, construction would begin the following spring for a new gymnasium with separate basketball facilities for men and women. Felmley secured an emergency appropriation of $25,000 to complete the women's gym, raising the building's cost to $175,000.

At the same time, the *Vidette* reported that Horton was preparing for his new duties by studying coaching methods under Walter Meanwell at the University of Wisconsin. "Dr. Meanwell…is one of the veterans in the basketball game and has developed a very successful short passing game which has been used by Wisconsin teams extensively. This type of playing has been used lately by Coach Russell

Clifford E. "Pop" Horton, for whom the field house was named, served as football coach, basketball coach, baseball coach and athletics director during his nearly four decades at Illinois State.

and has proven very successful with Normal teams.

"As a matter of duty," the *Vidette* continued, "every Normal student should help make Coach Horton's arrival the start of a new athletic period in ISNU—the most successful this school has ever enjoyed."

Horton confronted a daunting workload when he arrived at Illinois State in the fall of 1923. His assignment as athletics director

A construction photo of the new gymnasium from the 1925 *Index*. Growing fan counts and expanding programs made the gym in Cook Hall's Old Castle obsolete.

included head coaching responsibilities in football, basketball and baseball. He taught courses in anatomy, physiology, and growth and development. In addition, he organized the intramural program that provided an energetic outlet for a growing number of men on campus.

Great expectations for basketball success did not materialize. Horton's first squad posted a 6-8 record on the court, although that mark was reversed to 8-6 when two opponents forfeited games because they used ineligible players.

Horton had plenty of candidates for the 1923–24 season, but few experienced players were available to support captain Leonard Schneider and the redoubtable Stan Changnon, both four-year veterans. Bunker Young, a former Wesleyan athlete and Fred Young's brother, was on hand to provide some badly needed scoring punch but an injury ended his season after four games.

ISNU split its first four games with Young in the lineup, but struggled for most of the campaign. The team scored only nine points in a 17–9 loss to archrival Wesleyan, although the result was later overturned by forfeit.

The 1923–24 team photo shows that Horton had 17 men in uniform. He used 16 players in a 38–16 mid-season loss to Eastern Illinois State Teachers, which the *Vidette* described as "the poorest showing of the year" and "the most ineffective style witnessed this season."

Possibly stung by that criticism, the Fighting Teachers snapped a four-game losing streak with a 23–20 upset over Bradley in their next outing. They split their remaining four games. The 8-6 forfeit-aided final record was a winner, but not one met with enthusiasm.

Horton was responsible for more than basketball, of course, and he made a strong impact on the campus with his personal warmth, boundless enthusiasm and eagerness to serve the entire campus. He believed strongly in President Felmley's desire to provide physical education for all students. Fred Young, who had moved from the *Bulletin* to become sports editor of the Bloomington *Pantagraph*, noted in the summer of 1924 that Horton had four soccer teams, 13 basketball teams and 75 men playing baseball that year.

"Granted, the Teachers have not been hard to lick on the gridiron, basketball court, or diamond," Young wrote, "[but] the fact

remains that Horton is building up a stron athletic department and he is doing somethin that few physical directors in the conferenc are doing—he is providing stimulus for som form of athletic competition for every boy i his school.

"With the single exception of the Universi of Illinois, which has provided an elabora intramural system of athletics, which include over 6,000 students, no other school can sta in competition with Old Normal when it come to taking care of its students in this particula phase of college life."

◆   ◆   ◆   ◆   ◆   ◆

Basketball hopes were tempered by reali as the 1924–25 season approached. Captai Harold Gallaspie, a 5-foot-8 guard, an Bernhard Beck, a 6-foot center, were the mo experienced holdovers from the previou campaign. Beck, who was known as "Tiny was the tallest player on the team. Even by th standards of the 1920s, the squad was under sized; other players ranged from 5-5 to 5-10.

"The competition is unusually keen an although none of the boys have displaye

Originally, the gymnasium built in 1926 was named for then-President David Felmley. Shortly before Felmley's death three years later, he learned that a new science building would be christened Felmley Hall and the gymnasium renamed McCormick Gym for Henry McCormick, an early student at Illinois State who served the school as a faculty member for 43 years until his death in 1918.

anything superhuman or sensational, a survey of the squad indicates that ISNU will be represented by a strong and steady team when the Red and White clad warriors trot across the floor next Saturday night to match the five from Charleston Normal," the *Vidette* reported.

Illinois State absorbed a 33–14 loss in that game and the *Vidette* reporter expressed anxiety. "The Normal team did not play up to their standard of ability, and lacked the smooth teamwork that is so often evident in early season games. It is the earnest hope of the students that the team will find itself before long and put a few games on the win side of the column."

Anxiety turned to desperation as the losses began mounting. ISNU was winless in 13 games as it approached the last intercollegiate basketball game to be played in the Old Castle Gymnasium. The opponent was Illinois Wesleyan and the cross-town rivalry was enough to pack the gym, regardless of the team's record. An upset appeared possible when Illinois State surged into a 21–17 lead late in the game, but IWU scored the game's final four points and won a 22–21 decision.

"Every man was keyed up to the nth degree and they deserve loads of credit for the pluck and spirit they displayed, in the face of such a disastrous season," the *Vidette* opined. "They have done their best; they have always fought hard; they have fought clean. Give that team the time they need for practice, and they would have put a due number of games on the win side of the ledger."

Precious practice time would become available the following year with the opening of the new gymnasium. The *Vidette* took one last look at the small quarters that had been Illinois State's basketball home for nearly three decades:

"No longer will the warriors of Old Normal defend the school in the old castle gym. For 30 years it has been the scene of our inter-school hard court contests. If it could only talk it could indeed tell many interesting tales. How proudly it would boast of the old championship teams that the school used to produce! How it would acclaim to the world the suffering it has endured during the last six or eight years when large crowds swarmed its interior and made it groan under the strain. Yes, 'twould be a long

story, but now the basketball contests of the old gym are memories of by-gone days. It has served its purpose—we shall never forget how we packed ourselves into it during 1922–23–24–25 like sardines, to plead for our warriors to win."

There would be a new gymnasium for 1925–26 and a new coach as well. After two grinding years as head coach of all sports and director of the men's physical education program, Horton's load was eased with the hiring of a young University of Illinois athlete from Fairbury named Donald Karnes.

Horton continued as athletics director and head baseball coach for seven more seasons before the staff size was expanded again, enabling him to devote his full energies to physical education as the head of the department. In addition to starting the Gamma Phi Circus, he pioneered outdoor education by helping establish an eight-week summer session at East Bay Camp, Lake Bloomington, in 1938, and helped develop an annual summer camp for children with disabilities which continues six decades later.

His involvement with athletics continued for

many years as an official with the IIAC, the conference in which Illinois State teams competed prior to 1970. A member of the important eligibility committee since 1927, Horton was appointed IIAC commissioner when the group membership included only Illinois schools, and he retained that post after the formation of the "Interstate" Intercollegiate Athletic Conference in 1950.

Horton had an important role in the development of two athletics and physical education facilities at Illinois State. He was involved in the planning of Felmley Gymnasium (later renamed McCormick Gym) soon after his arrival in 1923 and of Horton Field House soon after his retirement in 1961. He was a revered community figure at the time of his death in 1981.

McCormick Hall was the home of Redbird basketball from 1925–63.

Chapter 8

A NEW NEST FOR HATCHING DON KARNES' "RED BIRDS" (1925–1927)

Two months after the close of the winless 1924–25 basketball season, Illinois State announced that Thomas Donald "Don" Karnes would become assistant athletics director and head coach of football, basketball and track. In this much-needed expansion of staff, Clifford E. "Pop" Horton would continue coaching baseball and directing the athletics and physical education programs.

The 22-year-old Karnes, a native of Fairbury, was prominent in basketball as a starting forward for two seasons under coach Craig Ruby at Illinois. The Illini tied for the Big Ten basketball championship in 1924 with Karnes in the lineup.

Karnes was a football end at Illinois under Bob Zuppke before injuring his right knee.

Harris Dean, later the president of the University of South Florida, was a 16-year-old freshman at ISNU in 1925. He recalls that students welcomed Karnes with enthusiasm.

"He was just out of the U of I and he was a great basketball player there," Dean said. "We were in awe of him for that reason."

The completion of a new gymnasium and adjoining sports fields also brightened the outlook in 1925. Karnes would have the distinction of coaching the first football and basketball games at new sports homes, which the Normal School Board named in honor of President Felmley because of his tireless efforts at securing funding. Felmley was surprised and somewhat uncomfortable with the honor and was pleased to learn before his death that his name would be used to identify a new science building instead. The athletics facilities were renamed McCormick Field and McCormick

Gymnasium in 1930 in honor of Dr. Henry McCormick, a faculty member for 43 years before his death in 1918.

A new coach, new facilities and even a new instructional program would boost Illinois State's athletics prospects.

"The moves made during the past year are destined to bring to Normal a new athletic regime," the *Vidette* commented in 1925. "With the new gymnasium, the finest in the state of Illinois, one of the finest football fields and cinder tracks, and a new two-year course for high school coaches with two competent instructors and coaches in charge, Normal enthusiasts see nothing but a great improvement in the general athletic record of the school."

◆   ◆   ◆   ◆   ◆   ◆   ◆

Students may have idolized Karnes but Dean remembers that some of Illinois State's veteran football players were "the orneriest bunch of fellows to work with" and took advantage of the new coach's relaxed discipline. An awkward incident near the end of the 1925 football season put the young coach under faculty scrutiny for the remainder of his two years at ISNU.

Following a football game at DeKalb, Karnes decided to take his team to Chicago for an evening in the big city before returning home. One player smuggled a gallon tin can of bootleg booze known as White Mule onto the bus and passed it around behind the coach's back. It was the "Roaring Twenties" and ISNU's prospective teachers were not cloistered from the outer world.

Some players were intoxicated by the time

the bus arrived in Chicago. The team was supposed to return to Normal at midnight but some players straggled in late by an hour or more. "It was rowdy and out of hand, no question about that," Dean recalled. Wisely, because of his youth, Dean had stayed close to the coach.

Rumors of the shenanigans circulated around campus and President Felmley appointed a faculty committee to investigate. The chairman, history professor William Andrew Lawrence Beyer, eventually questioned Dean.

"You were on the bus to DeKalb, weren't you?" Beyer asked.

"Yes," Dean replied.

"Where were you sitting?"

"I was sitting right behind the driver."

"Mr. Dean," the professor responded dryly. "Do you know you're the 18th man that's been sitting in that seat?"

President Felmley was not amused by the incident. He canceled the Thanksgiving Day football game at Illinois Wesleyan, a decision that cost each school at least $500 in gate receipts—big money in those days.

◆   ◆   ◆   ◆   ◆   ◆

With that background, Karnes greeted his first basketball squad in the new Felmley Gymnasium. The larger of the two gyms in the building could seat more than 2,000 fans compared to the 500 or so packed around and above the court at the Old Castle.

Illinois State counted 297 men among its 1,317 students in the fall of 1925, but that record enrollment offered slim pickings to Karnes after his years at Illinois. His best

Coach Don Karnes with the 1927 track team sports a light jacket with a Redbird insignia on the front—the earliest known photo of a Redbird logo.

available player, Bill "Bunker" Young, was older than Karnes and had started at Wesleyan four years earlier. Harris Dean, the precocious 16-year-old, was the biggest player in the lineup at six feet tall and 170 pounds. Between their age extremes were holdovers from a winless season and untested newcomers.

Problems associated with opening a new building also emerged. "The varsity squad in basketball has been laboring under great handicaps," the *Vidette* commented in December. "The new gym is not equipped with baskets so the only practice the boys get are on the fundamentals of dribbling, pivoting and passing."

Temporary goals brought over from Normal High School were erected for the opening game in December 1925 at Felmley Gym. The *Vidette* reported that "a large crowd" saw ISNU lose to the Chicago YMCA, 46–31. "Considering the fact that this was the opening game of the year for ISNU, Coach Karnes put a formidable team on the floor, and considering the fact that they average but 139 pounds, they put up a very creditable showing against their heavier rivals."

Young's scoring prowess helped Illinois State win two of its next four games against collegiate opponents but the undermanned Teachers managed only one more victory late in the season and finished with a 3-10 record. "The first year Bunker was all I had," Karnes said in a 1972 interview with the *Pantagraph.* "He was everything."

Besides Young's play, the highlight of the season was the welcome spaciousness of Felmley Gym. One sports column mentioned that the home game with Wesleyan had "all but two out of our thirteen hundred students present." The school yearbook added that "the modern gym surely did its part for basket ball at Normal."

❖   ❖   ❖   ❖   ❖   ❖

The 1926–27 school year brought renewed basketball hopes and a new team nickname, transforming the Fighting Teachers to the Cardinals for a brief period of time and then to the Red Birds. Students liked the new nickname and it quickly became official, usually expressed as two words for the next decade and eventually as one word: Redbirds.

A school-record enrollment of 1,424 (with 317 men) also meant more money for the athletics budget. The *Vidette* reported that men's athletics received $3,078 from the $12,140 available for student activities.

ISNU played three games in December tha[t] season and won them all by beating th[e] Chicago YMCA and Chicago Tech in the Wind City and scoring an impressive 48–19 victor[y] over Chicago Tech at Felmley Gym.

The *Vidette* unveiled the team's ne[w] nickname in the January 5 edition's headlin[e] reporting the home victory over Chicago Tech[.] The headline announced in capital letters:

CHICAGO TECH SNOWED UNDER
BY DON KARNES' CARDINALS

There was no reference to the "Cardinals" i[n] the story. Apparently the name was introduce[d] with little or no fanfare.

Reflecting on the change in the 1960[s] Horton said that he decided to call the team th[e] Cardinals because the school colors wer[e] cardinal and white. Karnes' role in th[e] selection, if any, is not known but a photograp[h] in the school yearbook shows him wearin[g] jacket adorned by the insignia of a cardina[l] perched on a limb.

The name of choice soon became Red Bird[s] (two words then) as the team winged to a five game winning streak by adding Wheaton an[d] Charleston Teachers to the list of victim[s.] "Don's Red Birds Take Another Step Towar[d] Conference Title," the *Vidette* bannered in th[e] January 19 issue.

The *Pantagraph* ignored the new nickname at first, although Horton credited sports editor Fred Young with suggesting the change from Cardinals to Red Birds to avoid headline confusion with the St. Louis Cardinals baseball team. The *Pantagraph* began switching between Teachers and Red Birds by mid-February.

"There was no trouble over dropping the name of Teachers," Horton recalled four decades later. "The fact of the matter is, I never heard a word about it. Everybody accepted the change. I thought it was right. In the long run, Redbirds has turned out to be a very desirable title."

◆   ◆   ◆   ◆   ◆   ◆

Meanwhile, basketball fever gripped the campus when the Redbirds polished off Charleston Teachers, 31–21, to run their record to 5-0 for the season. Harris Dean, now a sophomore, was the team captain and "the Don Karnes well coached machine" included such promising athletes as Henri Mohar, George Key, 6-foot-4 Everett Smith and Ralph Purcell Buckles.

The *Vidette* published eight stanzas of poetry that capitalized on the team's new nickname and early success. The first stanza provides a sample:

Four and one little Red Birds
Out there on the floor,
And when they scored a basket
*The crowd all yelled for **Mohar***

The *Vidette* continued having fun with the new nickname. One story opened with the image that "Don Karnes and his famous cage of Redbirds will journey to Eureka College…to do battle with the Eureka 'netsters.'"

Unfortunately, the 'Birds went south for the remainder of the season. After winning its first five, ISNU lost six games in a row, rose up to smite Carthage, 33–13, and then lost four more games to finish 6-10 for the season.

'Bird watchers kept flocking to Felmley Gym despite the losses. The *Pantagraph* reported that more than 2,500 attended the home game with Wesleyan: "A colorful crowd that jammed

A better look at the late 1920s Redbird on Harris Dean's jacket. Dean, captain of the 1928 Redbirds, later was acting president at the University of South Florida when the Redbirds played in their first Division I NCAA Tournament game on the school's Tampa campus.

every available inch of space in the new gymnasium witnessed the contest, over 500 persons standing the full forty minutes in order to see the contest."

The biggest basketball news was yet to come. Less than two weeks after the 1926–27 season closed, Karnes announced his resignation, effective at the end of the first summer term. The March 20 edition of the *Vidette* expressed

dismay that "one of the most popular coaches in the Little Nineteen" would be leaving.

"Karnes is very well liked by the student body and is held in very high esteem by all who know him," the *Vidette* commented. "It is a sad blow to lose our young mentor who has only been with us two short years."

In May, the *Vidette* announced in a page one story that Joseph T. Cogdal, a graduate of

Millikin University and the athletics director and coach at Assumption High School, would replace Karnes. But students were still grieving over Karnes' departure and the *Vidette* published numerous tributes to him over the summer.

A sports columnist named "Hap" Hazzard wrote the most poignant tribute, a sentimental ballad titled "Good by and Good Luck Donny Karnes." It reads as follows:

As I sit here alone this evening
I can't help but heave a sigh
The school year will soon be over
But that's not the reason why.

Oh, I'm just like the average fellow
I guess I'm glad to see it go
But with it goes a real old scout
Whom we all learned to know.

I suppose it is as some one has said,
"Even the best of friends must part"
But when our Thomas Donald leaves
There'll be many an aching heart.

For he's filled the job in this school
Filled it wisely, filled it well
And as to our Don's successor
Only time alone will tell.

This is our toast to you, Don,
This we would have you know,
May the best of luck be with you
Where ever you may go!

Karnes enjoyed a prosperous life after leaving Illinois State. He entered the insurance business while continuing for several years to coach track at Illinois Wesleyan and football at Bloomington's St. Mary's High School (later known as Trinity and now as Central Catholic). He also became a prominent area basketball official.

In 1933, Karnes joined the Illinois Department of Insurance as an examiner and moved up to chief state examiner before retiring in 1969. He also was controller for three insurance companies of the Illinois Agriculture Association for 10 years and vice president and director of Steel Insurance Co. of America.

Karnes maintained a strong interest in sports at Illinois State and in his hometown of Fairbury. He traveled with the Redbird basketball team to Hawaii in 1979 and frequently accompanied his old friend, *Pantagraph* sports editor emeritus Fred Young, to local and distant sports events. Karnes attended the Olympic Games on several occasions, including the Munich Olympics in 1972 to see Redbird basketball star Doug Collins gain international acclaim.

When Karnes died several months short of his 80th birthday in 1982, he left all but $50,000 of his $1.5 million estate to create a trust fund assisting college-bound graduates from Forrest-Strawn-Wing and Fairbury-Cropsey high schools (both of which became part of Prairie Central High School after a consolidation later in that decade).

And as for Karnes' successor at Illinois State in 1927, "Hap" Hazzard was prophetic in speculating that time would tell. Cogdal eventually achieved the longest tenure of any Illinois State coach, 22 seasons, and restored the Redbirds to their historic championship prestige in basketball.

Chapter 9
JOE COGDAL'S REIGN BEGINS (1927–1930)

Rugged, confident and handsome as the silver screen's leading men of his day, Joe Cogdal arrived at Illinois State in 1927 to open a 38-year term on the coaching staff, 22 as head basketball coach.

Cogdal was well cast for his role. During the early 1930s when actor Clark Gable was clean shaven, Cogdal was mistaken one day for the famous movie star while strolling down a Chicago street. Cogdal was surrounded in an instant and could not escape the celebrity seekers until he was able to convince them of his true identity.

Innovative and scholarly, he was much more than an icon at Illinois State. A brilliant basketball tactician, a champion of racial equality, a creative educator with diverse interests, Cogdal was well ahead of his time on many fronts.

His creative mind kept Illinois State at the pinnacle of state college basketball for most of his 22 seasons as head coach. He devised what he called a circulating offense, a system of pattern play foreshadowing today's popular motion offense. He also perfected the T-zone, a defense that baffled opponents for most of his coaching career.

"Jim Crow" racial practices of the era prevented Cogdal from showcasing Illinois State on the national scene. He turned down five invitations to the National Association of Intercollegiate Athletics (NAIA) Tournament at Kansas City because black athletes were not allowed to compete. Illinois State did not join the NAIA until December 1948 after it finally relaxed its long-time ban against African-Americans participating in the annual tournament to crown a national small-college champion. By then Cogdal was in the final year

of his illustrious basketball coaching career.

He continued coaching cross country and track until retiring in 1965 at age 68. At that time, he reminisced about his career with Dave Kindred, a talented *Pantagraph* sports reporter who became one of the nation's most respected sports columnists. Excerpts from the Kindred article provide interesting insights into the coach's background, beginning in 1908 when basketball came to Cogdal's hometown of Atwood, Ill.

◆　　◆　　◆　　◆　　◆　　◆

"The blacksmith pounded out some rings and they put up chicken wire for back boards and the basketball had big leather seams," Cogdal told Kindred. "I was in grade school then and we were derisive toward the high school guys playing basketball. At first we thought it was a pretty sissy type of game.

"We didn't have coaches or gymnasiums or athletic programs then. The boys had to get up the teams themselves. When I was in the grades, Thomas W. Samuels, a law student at the University of Illinois, encouraged them to have a track team.

"I was their slave, a mascot who did all the dirty work. And I was delighted to get to do it.

"I had more brass or guts or persistence so I became the leader my last two years in high school. Kenneth [Tug] Wilson, who went on to become the commissioner of the Big Ten, was the guiding light before me.

"So ever since I can remember I've been a coach.

"I graduated from Atwood in 1916 and went to Millikin for a year before going into the Navy.

At Millikin, I was on the track team with Joey Ray. I was a high jumper. Supposed to have been a pretty good one.

"I went to a submarine base at Norwich, Conn., and organized a track team there. I did the same at New London and then I served on the *U.S.S. Charles Whitamore*.

"The *Whitamore* was the last wooden battleship. It was a four-masted schooner whose purpose was luring U-boats within range so a sub with us could get them.

"My duties were organizing boxing, basketball, and calisthenics on board."

Cogdal returned to Millikin and graduated in 1921. He coached football and track at Winchester High School, went to Blue Mound in 1922, and to Findlay College in Ohio before returning to Illinois in 1925 at Assumption High School, where he organized the Meridian Conference, which still exists, and the Assumption basketball tournament.

Two years later, he began a legendary career at Illinois State. He coached football, basketball, cross country, track and tennis teams, and won 50 major championships and 45 second-place awards. Twenty-five times, Cogdal-coached teams won Illinois or Interstate Intercollegiate Athletic Conference championships.

His teams finished better than 10th in national competition on nine occasions, the best being a second place in the AAU's national cross country meet. He coached Jim Johnson, one of the world's six fastest humans in 1932, and Tidye Anne Pickett, who reached the semifinals of the women's hurdles in the 1936 Olympics.

His basketball teams won six IIAC championships from 1937–38 to 1943–44. His cross country teams duplicated that feat.

"When I came to Normal," Cogdal told Kindred, "eight of every 10 students were women and some of the men were older than I was."

Fortunately, that was about to change, and Cogdal was ready to make it work for Illinois State athletics fortunes.

◆ ◆ ◆ ◆ ◆ ◆

The Great Depression of the 1930s was a boon to male interest in the teaching profession.

The lure of stable jobs in education, coupled with Illinois State's introduction of specialized training for coaches, helped male enrollment more than double, surpassing 700 of some 1,850 total students in 1935.

Cogdal's leadership and creativity were the most important factors in the dramatic success of Illinois State basketball, however. His coaching innovations were described by the late Campbell "Stretch" Miller, a reserve center on the championship 1930–31 squad and later a member of the St. Louis Cardinals baseball broadcasting team.

"Joe was many years ahead of his time in strategy," Miller wrote in a collection of biographical anecdotes published in the book, *One Guy Called Me Stench.*

"When Loyola of Chicago won the NCAA cage crown in the early '60s, it was highly publicized that they put smaller rims inside their regular basketball rims for practice accuracy. Heck, Cogdal did that back in 1930.

"In the fifties there was an Eastern coach who got a lot of publicity because he put weights on the ankles of his players in practice to help their jumping. Cogdal had me playing in galoshes filled with sand for the same purpose—that was 20 years before.

"Zone defenses, at least the more complicated ones that are now used, were all in Cogdal's game plans. He had one, called a T zone [three men across the front, a man on the free throw line and the fifth man under the basket] that really baffled the opposition."

Cogdal was a stickler for discipline, fundamentals and physical conditioning. He drove his players hard. Each athlete was required to run three miles in a predetermined time based on the individual's weight, and Cogdal didn't make it easy.

Illinois State's greatest all-around athlete, James "Pim" Goff, played during the early 1930s and later noted how players felt about taskmaster Cogdal.

"Everyone thought they hated him," Goff told *Pantagraph* reporter Mark Wellwood after Cogdal's death in 1978. "But 10 years later I understood what a great guy he really was, and the things he taught us.

"He made you do things just right. You had to go over again and do it, do it, do it."

Goff, who eventually replaced Cogdal as head basketball coach, said Cogdal taught his players by example. "Part of his method of coaching was always playing with us in practice. He would play forward, center or guard. The only time the five starters played together at the same time was in games."

◆ ◆ ◆ ◆ ◆ ◆

Joe Cogdal's good looks complemented the creativity, dedication and diversity inside which served Redbird athletics for nearly four decades.

Harris Dean, a holdover from the Don Karnes era, saw other dimensions of

Cogdal's personality.

"He was hard-boiled and strict when he was coaching," Dean said in a 1997 interview, "but when it came to the evening he was not above associating with students. We were great friends."

Cogdal and his wife, Peg, were accomplished ballroom dancers. One night Dean and Gene Hill (another ISNU athlete who became a notable Redbird coach) were invited to bring their dates to accompany the Cogdals to a dance in Peoria. The evening's end showed another side of Cogdal. Dean, driving the coach's car, rolled through a stop sign in East Peoria and police pulled him over. Cogdal defended Dean so vigorously that he began scuffling with police, who promptly escorted the coach to the jailhouse. The group barely managed to come up with $12 to pay the fine and secure Cogdal's release.

"Joe was hot tempered," Dean said.

Dean and his coach remained friends through two seasons as Cogdal set out in 1927 to restore Illinois State's basketball fortunes following two decades of frustration. An indication of the difficulty of that task came when President Felmley gave some of the team's gym time away, then forced wholesale changes in the game schedule.

Aside from Dean, Cogdal's first team was inexperienced. Things got worse when Dean went down with the mumps late in the season. The Redbirds limped to a 2-13 record but Cogdal had made a clear statement that he was in command, including changing his starting lineup to reward players who gave up part of their Christmas vacation to return early for practice.

"It may not be his strongest combination, and probably isn't," the *Vidette* commented approvingly, "but at any rate, it proves that he intends to have discipline if nothing else."

◆   ◆   ◆   ◆   ◆   ◆

Cogdal set a similar tone when the Redbirds opened the 1928–29 season with a bus trip to Chicago. Some of his players sought entertainment in a shooting gallery but "Coach put a stop to that," the *Vidette* reported. The team

returned home with two victories.

Illinois State's lineup was more settled that season. Dean, voted the most popular student on campus, was back for his fourth year as a regular. Reed Needles, a transfer who had led Gridley College of Ohio in scoring for two seasons, and Ralph Kingery, a clever ballhandler, joined him in the backcourt. Bob Rowe, an experienced athlete, and Roland "Ike" Zook, a freshman, were paired at the forwards.

The key newcomer was Leslie "Mose" Moore, a lanky center who had spent a day or two at Michigan State before enrolling at Illinois State. Moore became the team's scoring, rebounding and defensive leader. The *Vidette* hailed the freshman center as "one of the best in the Little 19."

Illinois State entered the final two games of the regular season with a 9-5 record but dropped a 28–25 decision to archrival Wesleyan before 2,500 at Felmley Gym and lost at Eureka, 27–24. The loss of momentum was coupled with the loss of Dean, damaging the Redbirds' chances as they traveled to Macomb for the second annual Normal Schools Tournament.

Seventy-five Illinois State fans traveled the 120 miles to Macomb to see their team play five games in two days, a grueling assignment that proved the value of Cogdal's arduous conditioning drills.

The Redbirds opened with a 30–29 victory over Southern Illinois but had to play through the loser's bracket of the double-elimination tourney after bowing to Eastern Illinois, 36–27. They squeezed out another close decision over Southern Illinois, 28–27, and turned the tables on Charleston, 42–33, to enter the finals against the home team.

It was a wild scene, according to *Vidette* accounts: "…think of the team just before the final game marching through the streets of Macomb singing our school loyalty song, singing as they filed into the gymnasium, and running through Macomb's dressing-room to let them know that they still had some of the old fight."

One by one, Illinois State's regular players fell victim to the referee's whistle in the title match. With eight minutes to play, Moore was

the only ISNU starter on the floor and he had three personals with no one on the bench to replace him. But the Redbirds prevailed, 40–32, to capture their first basketball championship in 20 years.

Moore, who led the tournament in scoring with 46 points in five games, and teammate Zook were on the all-tournament team. Rowe was a second-team forward.

◆   ◆   ◆   ◆   ◆   ◆

As Illinois State began a new decade, the campus was saddened by the death of President Felmley. He lapsed into a coma shortly after Christmas of 1929 and died January 24, 1930.

At the time of Felmley's death, the basketball team was in the midst of an 11-7 season, including 6-0 at home. The school yearbook hailed it as "the most successful season in the last decade."

Cogdal opened the season with only two holdover starters—Moore at center and Rowe at forward—but continued a trend of attracting good athletes from a run of outstanding University High School teams. The newest campus-raised Redbirds were Dorrence "Red" Darling and Harry Caldwell, two well-rounded freshmen who moved into starting guard positions. Caldwell was Illinois State's second black basketball player, preceded only by Joe Ward's appearance 10 years earlier.

Team captain Bob Traughber filled a forward vacancy created when Zook took a teaching assignment.

It didn't take long for the newcomers to prove their mettle. In an early-season game described as "the wildest contest ever to be played on Felmley floor," the Redbirds scored a 28–26 double-overtime victory over Northern Illinois. Traughber's three-point play as time was running out forced the first overtime period.

"Then came the shot that drove the crowd mad," the *Vidette* reported, referring to the end of the first overtime. "Just as the scorer raised his gun to end the game, 'Red' Darling arched a shot from the middle of the floor and as the net quivered the gun sounded for the finish with the score still a tie."

Traughber's drive-in basket and a successful stall decided the game in the second overtime. "Those spectators who weren't in a state of collapse were in the nearby state of hysteria by the end of this hectic battle," a reporter commented.

Hysteria became commonplace, judging from the narrow margins in the following games. Illinois State lost successive one-point decisions at Wesleyan and at Charleston, then captured a typically tense 24–21 victory over archrival Wesleyan. Near the end of the regular season, Darling (whom the *Vidette* called the "the stolid little sorrel top") led his team to a 27–26 victory over Southern Illinois. Half of the team's regular-season games were decided by from one to three points.

Illinois State's defending champs split four games in the Normal Schools Tournament at DeKalb, losing twice to Southern Illinois. Traughber and Darling were voted to the all-tournament team. Moore and Caldwell were on the second team.

Dr. and Mrs. Ferd McCormick entertained the team with a post-season banquet in their beautiful home at 304 North Street to celebrate the basketball victory achieved against Wesleyan, which had dominated the series during the previous two decades. Ferd McCormick had been president of the campus athletics association as a student when the association was organized in 1897 and he continued to have a great interest in the university throughout his life.

Later in the spring of 1930, a faculty committee announced that Felmley Gymnasium would be renamed in honor of McCormick's father, Henry, the grand patriarch who had served 43 years on Illinois State's faculty before his death in 1918. The science building was named Felmley Hall, in honor of the late president.

The new president, H.A. Brown of Oshkosh, Wis., arrived in the summer of 1930 and described himself as an enthusiastic supporter of athletics. He tried to have students establish an athletics fee of one dollar for the fall term, increasing to two dollars by the spring term. The proposal passed by a six-vote margin in November but the turnout was so light that a

Led by freshman center Leslie "Mose" Moore, the 1928–29 Redbirds rode Joe Cogdal's innovative T-zone defense to the school's first championship in 20 years.

second ballot was distributed a week later and lost 595 to 581. Brown continued making waves, however, by abolishing the Athletic Board of Control in December 1930 and replacing it with a faculty committee on athletics which was dominated by the

coaches and their allies.

That was the setting as Cogdal prepared for his fourth, and perhaps his best, basketball campaign. Illinois State's "leading man" was about to lead Redbird basketball to new heights.

Chapter 10
THE GOLDEN THIRTIES
(1930–1938)

Campbell "Stretch" Miller began the 1930s as a reserve center for Joe Cogdal's Redbirds, finished the decade as a local sportscaster, and later called it the "Golden Thirties" of Illinois State athletics.

Miller's observations were based on an intimate knowledge of the program. Besides his playing experiences, he also wrote a sports column and was editor of the *Vidette* during those glorious years.

In 1930–31, the Redbirds racked up a 17-3 record, won their first state championship since 1909 with a 13-1 record in the Illinois Intercollegiate Athletic Conference (better known as the "Little Nineteen" although the unwieldy league had 22 members then), and tacked on their second Normal Schools Tournament title in four seasons.

The same lineup returned in 1931–32 and posted a 20-5 record, marking the first time that any Illinois State team reached the 20-victory pinnacle. Over those two seasons, Illinois State racked up a record 24-game winning streak, captured 30 of 31 games, and achieved 43 victories in 45 conference games. They were nearly invincible on their home court.

Colorful nicknames and talented left-handers abounded. The starters during those two seasons were:

◆ James "Pim" Goff, a freshman sensation in 1930–31, who emerged as the team's leading scorer with a 10-point average despite Cogdal's deliberate offense and a center jump after each basket. Goff lettered in football, basketball, baseball, track and tennis, earning recognition as the greatest all-around athlete in school history. Coaches arranged their spring schedules so that Goff could play tennis in the morning, pitch baseball in the afternoon, and throw the javelin between innings.

◆ Roland "Ike" Zook, who returned to school after a year of teaching to reclaim the other forward position with his former University High teammate.

◆ Dorrence "Red" Darling, a third former U-High athlete who was in his second season as a starting guard in 1930–31. Conference coaches voted the 5-foot-8, 148-pound Darling the Little Nineteen's most valuable player during the championship season.

◆ Harold "Sis" Swartzbaugh, who teamed with Darling to give the Redbirds a stalwart defensive guard combination.

◆ Leslie "Mose" Moore, the center who led the team in rebounding for four seasons and in scoring two years. He was an excellent defensive player as well and followed Darling as the league's most valuable player selection in the 1931–32 season.

Moore, Goff and Darling were left-handed. The other two starters were reputed to be ambidextrous.

The bench was solid, featuring three more ex-U-High stars: Ralph Kingery, Jimmie Tatman and Dick Peterson, who joined former starter Bob Rowe as key replacements. Alex Wade, Peter Miner and Howard Oetting were quality replacements at the guards. The 6-4 Miller provided size whenever Moore needed relief at center.

How good was this team? Cogdal was extravagant in his praise when, in the winter of his years, he reminisced about Moore's importance to the squad.

It was, Cogdal said, "a group of outstanding basketeers any one of which would have been welcomed by any team in the state. It took the play and leadership of Moore to make them one of the greatest if not the greatest basketball powerhouses in America. Moore's leadership made it so."

On the lighter side, Moore's talents meant that Miller usually occupied a seat on the bench. Miller did not question the coach's judgment but that didn't stop some friends in the stands from hollering for Cogdal to put him in with persistent chants of "We want Miller, we want Miller."

Cogdal finally motioned for Miller to get off the bench one night. Stretch stood in front of the coach, began removing his sweatshirt, and asked, "Who do you want me to go in for, Coach?"

"Who said anything about going in the game?" Cogdal said, pointing to Miller's boosters. "Go up and sit in the stands with those clowns. They're the ones who want you."

◆   ◆   ◆   ◆   ◆   ◆

The 1930–31 championship season began inauspiciously with a loss to the Chicago YMCA College when Cogdal experimented by playing all 15 of his men. Next came a loss to Indiana state champion Central Normal.

A few weeks later, the Redbirds were 4-3 after suffering their first conference loss, 15–11, in a rough game at St. Viator College of Bourbonnais. But they never lost again that year.

McCormick Gym was packed for the late-season rematch with St. Viator, and Goff rose to the occasion by scoring 10 points to spark the

Called the greatest all-around athlete in Illinois State history by many, James F. "Pim" Goff played as many as three sports in one day. He later returned to coach Redbird basketball from 1949 to 1957.

Redbirds to a 16–8 halftime lead en route to a 24–15 victory.

The enthusiastic Miller staked a claim to the mythical national championship in his sports column when Illinois State followed with an overtime victory over Northern Illinois to seize the Little Nineteen lead.

"If Northwestern is considered the outstanding team in the country then the following figures will make the Redbirds national champs," he asserted.

"Normal beat St. Viator.

"St. Viator beat Bradley.

"Bradley beat Iowa.

"Iowa beat Illinois.

"Illinois beat Northwestern.

"And there you are!"

Illinois State still had a difficult obstacle remaining at Illinois Wesleyan's Memorial Gym but the Redbirds won handily, 44–29, to claim their first state basketball title since 1909 and first ever in the IIAC, which began basketball competition in 1911.

They added the Normal Schools Tournament championship with four more victories at Carbondale, including a 33–28 triumph over Northern Illinois in the title game. Illinois State dominated the all-tourney team with three first-team selections (Zook, Moore and Darling) and one second-team choice (Goff).

To the victors came more spoils. The Associated Press chose Goff and Moore, and the *Pantagraph's* Fred Young selected Moore and Darling to their all-state teams.

Darling reaped the biggest individual honor of all when conference coaches voted him the league's most valuable player. He received 18 votes compared to 12 each for Goff and Wesleyan's Bill Meehan.

◆　◆　◆　◆　◆　◆

With the starting lineup intact for the 1931–32 season, hopes were high for another great season. The Redbirds knocked off four of the best small-college teams from Arkansas, Indiana, Ohio and Wisconsin during a strong non-conference schedule and ran their two-year winning streak to 24 games with league triumphs over Western Illinois, Illinois College,

Eastern Illinois and Eureka College.

The string snapped when Northern Illinois squeezed out a 16–14 victory at DeKalb. The Redbirds stayed in title contention by winning the next five games but dropped out of the race when they lost to Southern Illinois and Eastern Illinois on a disastrous road trip.

Illinois State had the home-court advantage for its title defense in the Teachers College Tournament (formerly called the Normal Schools Tournament). The Redbirds ran their season record to 20-3 by beating Western and Eastern but dropped a 33–30 decision to Northern and were eliminated by Western, a team they had beaten three times that year.

Although repeat championships proved elusive, more individual honors followed. League coaches named Moore the most valuable player in the conference and the Associated Press selected Moore and Pim Goff for its all-state team with Zook on the third team and Darling receiving honorable mention.

Even the coach got into the act. Illinois State students voted Cogdal the most popular faculty man on campus.

◆　　◆　　◆　　◆　　◆

Anticipation for the 1932–33 season was so strong that the Athletic Board voted to have all seats reserved for the conference schedule. McCormick Gymnasium was becoming too small just eight years after construction.

Goff, Darling and Swartzbaugh returned for yet another season together. Another U-High product, freshman Wilbur "Barney" Barton, an outstanding all-around athlete, became the third African-American to play basketball at Illinois State and eventually the first to captain the Redbirds in his senior season.

However, Goff and Darling both had knee injuries from football and the Redbirds sorely missed Moore, who graduated after dominating center play for four seasons. When Northern Illinois ended Illinois State's 21-game home-court winning streak by the shocking score of 49–18, it was apparent that this would not be a successful campaign.

Illinois State turned the tables on Northern at

DeKalb, 37–36, and beat Northern again in the last Teachers College Tournament to be played but finished with a 9-16 record.

◆　　◆　　◆　　◆　　◆

A continuing influx of talent from U-High helped Illinois State renew its golden touch under Cogdal for the rest of the decade and continuing through the World War II years,

Dressed in classic 1930s garb, Campbell "Stretch" Miller was a Redbird center during the Cogdal era and later the radio voice of the Redbirds and St. Louis Cardinals. Today, Redbird athletics' top service award bears his name.

culminating in an amazing run of six consecutive conference titles.

Goff led the Redbirds in scoring again with 120 points in the 1933–34 season and completed his career with 852 points, a school career record that stood for another decade.

Illinois State's season record was 13-8. Four losses by a total of eight points were the difference between sixth place and a championship,

which must have frustrated ISNU's No. 1 fan, first-year President Raymond W. Fairchild.

◆　　◆　　◆　　◆　　◆　　◆

Cogdal, whose self-confidence was unshakable, opened the 1934–35 season by using 15 players in a 31–30 victory over Arkansas State. The Redbirds rolled to a 12-5 record and placed third with a 9-1 record in the "Little Nineteen," which had dwindled to 14 members by then.

The coach continued refining his T-zone defense. He demonstrated his strategy at an assembly one day, using five of his players as props. His disdain for man-to-man defense was evident in the *Vidette* account, which paraphrased his comments as follows:

"The man-to-man defense…was one of the poor types, for to be successful the teams, man for man, must be about equal in height, weight and ability.

"The 'T' defense…does not require the men to be so well matched, and furthermore, covers well the area near the basket where the greater percentage of shots are made."

One of his demonstrators was Barton, now 84 and living in Indianapolis, Ind., after a career in coaching and school administration. Barton says the players weren't as enthusiastic about the T-zone, which stationed three players from the top of the circle down to the basket with two on each side of the free throw line extended.

"We hated it because it ran the hell out of us to cover the guys in the corners," Barton said. "Anybody who played under the basket had to run from one side to the other. It was something better done when we played in a gym with a track around it which meant you couldn't shoot from the corners."

Still, the push shot used in that era was not as accurate as today's jump shot so the T-zone and variations baffled many Illinois State opponents.

◆　　◆　　◆　　◆　　◆　　◆

Barton attended school on campus from first grade in Metcalf, the laboratory school,

Perhaps the best team in the first 50 years of Redbird basketball was the 1931 Little Nineteen champions with team mascot Rex Darling in front. Front row: Alex Wade, Roland Zook, Pim Goff, Leslie Moore, Harold Swartzbaugh, Captain Dorrence Darling and James Tatman. Back row: Manager Potsy Schwenn, Howard Oetting, Campbell Miller, Ralph Kingery, Coach Joe Cogdal, Peter Miner.

through graduation from ISNU in 1936. He captained the 1935–36 team, which achieved a 12-6 record, and was popular on campus. But when the Redbirds traveled, what seemed to matter most was the color of his skin.

"I was the only black on the team and we played in different places where they didn't want me to stay," he recalls. "Especially in Carbondale. I had to stay with a private family there. The team stayed at a hotel and came by in a bus to pick me up."

He said that Cogdal did what he could to soften the impact of racial discrimination.

"I admired Joe. We had a manager named Potsy Schwenn and Joe gave Potsy the job of going ahead of the team to see about eating. He said, 'If he doesn't eat, we don't eat.' That changed a lot of attitudes."

Barton wasn't allowed to play when Illinois State went to St. Louis during his freshman year

so Cogdal began scheduling away games in Wisconsin, Michigan and the Chicago area.

Ironically, discrimination surfacing in Chicago worked to Barton's advantage once.

When the team checked into a hotel near Lake Michigan, the hotel's management sought to avoid problems with older patrons by isolating Barton away from the team in a newly constructed wing. Other ISNU players were envious when they visited his luxurious accommodations.

"I had a suite of rooms overlooking the lake," he said. "They came in and said, hey, look at what he's got."

Barton, a tall player then at 6-foot-2, was the team's best rebounder. He usually had two or three other U-High graduates in the starting lineup with him during his four seasons as a regular. Herb and Don Adams, John White and Glenn "Wart" Jacquat were his teammates both in high school

and college. The emergence of Dick Kavanagh at center enabled Barton to play at his preferred forward position as a senior.

◆　　◆　　◆　　◆　　◆　　◆

Keeping up a personal tradition, Cogdal used 21 players in a 41–28 victory over Arkansas State. By the end of the season, he settled on a lineup with newcomer Marvin Hamilton of Atlanta at forward, joining veterans Don Adams at forward, Kavanagh at center, and Jacquat and Bill Balding at the guards.

It was a formidable cast with scoring balance with Jacquat leading the team with 168 points in 23 games. They broke from the gate with 12 straight victories and posted a 20-3 season record. But they missed out on a title because of two losses to Illinois Wesleyan (by three and four points) and a closing defeat to Western Illinois (by two points). ISNU managed to score

Wilbur "Barney" Barton was a four-year starter and, in 1936, became the first African-American to serve as a team captain at Illinois State.

saved. Fairchild was unmoved.

Wesleyan's president, Harry McPherson, responded by suspending relations in other sports as well, although that ban was lifted the following year when tensions eased. The schools did not meet again in basketball until wartime travel restrictions made the series desirable again in 1943–44.

The Little Nineteen Conference split almost in half after many of the private members adopted a freshman rule early in 1937. Eight of those private schools, including Wesleyan, departed by the end of that year. The IIAC, still known as the Little Nineteen, had but 11 members: Carthage, Elmhurst, Eureka, McKendree, Shurtleff, St. Viator and the five teachers colleges (Illinois State, Charleston, Carbondale, DeKalb and Macomb). More changes were on the horizon.

◆   ◆   ◆   ◆   ◆   ◆

During that transitional 1937–38 season, Cogdal was molding the ingredients for a remarkable championship run. Once again he sifted through his candidates by using 20 players in the season opener, a 38–24 victory over Arkansas State.

In an ever-changing lineup, Kavanagh was a tower of stability at center, with the steady guard Balding "specializing on killer-diller shots that mingle with the rafters but finally drop through and should count three points," according to a *Vidette* article.

Hamilton, under doctor's care early in the season, made a comeback at mid-January to provide offensive play which the *Vidette* called "the best seen on the McCormick floor since the days of Pim Goff." Hamilton's eligibility was in question for a time because of reports that he signed a professional baseball contract with the Philadelphia Athletics.

After ISNU's 15-4 season record, WJBC's Miller picked Kavanagh as the all-conference center with Balding and forward Byron Blakeman on the second team.

But the time Miller called the "Golden Thirties" had another year, and a good-sized "nugget" yet to be mined.

nly one field goal in the second half against estern but made 23 of 24 free throws, then a hool record.

The Wesleyan rivalry had become so bitter at President Fairchild, who graduated from

IWU and formerly taught there, announced after the season that the schools would no longer meet in basketball. Miller, then a broadcaster at radio station WJBC in Bloomington, pleaded for the series to be

Chapter 11

YEARS OF GLORY AND GRIT (1938–1949)

The arrival of John Scott and the start of six consecutive conference basketball championships initiated the best years of Joe Cogdal's coaching career.

Scott, an athletic 6-foot-2 with great leaping ability, came to Illinois State in the fall of 1938 from Centralia where he was well schooled in basketball fundamentals by legendary coach Arthur Trout. He also was an African-American more than two decades before that was acceptable on many of America's campuses.

While Scott may have stood out in a crowd, he quickly emerged from it even though he was one of 29 players Cogdal used in his annual pre-season tune-up against Wright Junior College of Chicago.

Scott joined veterans Marv Hamilton and Dick Kavanagh in the front line. George Matthews, John Baldini and Forrest Reid filled the guard posts.

After a season-opening 43–20 win over Illinois College, a *Vidette* article marveled at Scott's skills. "He was always close to that ball, intercepting passes, rebounding, passing, gaining jump balls with monotonous regularity," the student paper reported.

Illinois State was 4-4 after eight games, but had shown promise. The Redbirds held Eau Claire (Wisconsin) scoreless in the final nine minutes of one loss and turned in a respectable performance against the eventual national champion, Southwestern College of Winfield, Kan., before bowing, 44–33.

The Redbirds won eight of their next nine games, all against Illinois schools, to move into title contention in the Little Nineteen. Cogdal's mystifying T-zone held Western Illinois to three points, all free throws, in the first 25 minutes of

one game. When the Redbirds avenged their lone conference loss by whipping Northern Illinois, 45–29, they led the league with a 9-1 record.

The title clincher at Charleston came in a new $450,000 gymnasium. Normally, the rivalry would have drawn a boisterous crowd, but an influenza epidemic locked customers out. Illinois State won the silent battle, 44–30, before empty seats and clinched its first Little Nineteen title since 1931 with a 10-1 league record (17-6 overall).

Kavanagh, the rock-ribbed senior center, led the team in scoring and joined teammates Hamilton and Matthews on the all-IIAC team selected by WJBC's Stretch Miller, who also gave Scott a second-team berth, labeling him as "probably the best 'ballhawk' in the conference."

Miller praised Matthews as "the spark that brought the title to State Normal." Later generations know that name. Matthews' son, Denny, became prominent as the radio voice of the Kansas City Royals baseball team. In the 1990s, a grandson, Scott Matthews, was the starting catcher for Redbird baseball teams.

◆　◆　◆　◆　◆　◆

Scott was the only returning starter for the 1939–40 season. Cogdal constructed another championship lineup around him with sophomore Larry Kindred, who had followed Hamilton from Atlanta High School, and veteran Art O'Byrne at the forwards. Captain Charles Beck and Leroy Brandt were the guards.

Baldini was a valued guard off the bench and

later co-owner of his family's Bloomington restaurant, The Lucca. It was one of the most popular sports gathering places in the Twin Cities but, ironically, campus administrators frowned on Illinois State students hanging out there. President Raymond Fairchild believed that prospective teachers should abstain from alcoholic beverages, and he summarily dismissed more than one student caught drinking.

Fan enthusiasm for the 1939 season opener forced Athletics Director Howard Hancock to establish reserved-seat tickets to control the size of the crowd. WJBC was broadcasting the games regularly by now from a rakish-looking plywood booth mounted on the east wall above the main entrance to McCormick Gym. The booth was reachable by a removable ladder and held only one person.

The Redbirds won their first seven games. Cogdal was on top of the world. A photo of him in the student newspaper had the following caption: "Despite his more-than-casual resemblance to the male lead of 'Gone With the Wind,' Coach Joe Cogdal knows plenty of basketball." Who needed Clark Gable when you had Joe Cogdal?

Northern Illinois, a familiar nemesis, slowed the team's championship drive, 31–29, but the Redbirds rebounded to finish with a 10-1 league record and 20-5 overall.

Kindred turned in the grittiest performance of the season when he played half of the decisive victory over Southern Illinois with a broken ankle. Kindred was wearing a cast but Cogdal thought the 6-foot-2 sophomore could do the best job at his familiar defensive spot in the T-zone.

Talented John Scott scored as many points as the entire UCLA team (featuring Jackie Robinson) in a 1940 Redbird victory. The Redbird star led Illinois State to conference championships in all four of his seasons.

Scott and O'Byrne made Stretch Miller's all-conference team. Miller called Scott "the greatest performer in the state loop, sensational in every department—shooting, floor play, ball handling and defense."

◆   ◆   ◆   ◆   ◆   ◆

The school's 1931 championship cast helped preview the 1940–41 campaign with an exhibition against Cogdal's 23 varsity candidates. Nearly all of the 1,100 fans in McCormick Gym came to see the ex-champs, according to the *Pantagraph*. They were treated to Pim Goff making five of his famous hook shots, Red Darling and Ike Zook displaying their fancy dribbling, Leslie Moore rebounding with force and Harold Swartzbaugh sinking one of his long shots.

But the fans knew it would be a good season when the current varsity subdued the former stars, 45–31. Del Fagerburg moved into the starting front line with junior standouts Scott and Kindred. Captain Leroy Brandt and Baldini were the starting guards. When illness felled Baldini, Dane Walker and Jim McBride proved to be productive replacements.

The basketball world found out how good the Redbirds were when UCLA and its great athlete, Jackie Robinson, came to McCormick Gym December 21, 1940.

Seven years before Robinson broke the major league baseball color barrier with the Brooklyn Dodgers, he was a collegiate star in football, basketball and track at UCLA. The *Pantagraph* called him "the kingpin of all Pacific Coast athletes" in the caption of a posed action photo that appeared three days before the Illinois State game.

Kindred remembers Robinson well. They collided and Kindred had to leave the game for x-rays early in the second half, but he totaled eight points while Robinson managed just two baskets.

Scott matched the UCLA point total as Illinois State scored a prestige-building 37–21 victory. Illinois State catapulted to a 15–2 start and commanded a 22–6 lead at halftime. UCLA narrowed the gap to 27–18 before the Redbirds put on a closing rush to preserve the victory that had Cogdal beaming with pride.

The 1938–39 seniors who began a string of six straight Illinois Intercollegiate Athletic Conference titles for the Redbirds: (L to R) Jerome Ignerski, Forrest Reid, Dick Kavanagh, Howard Lester and George Matthews, who was the first of three generations of Redbird athletes. His son, Mike, played baseball at ISU in the 1970s and a grandson, Scott, was a Redbird catcher in the 1990s.

"You should have seen him walking around campus after the UCLA game," Kindred said. "You'd have thought that we were national champions. But it didn't surprise him that we won."

Cogdal's team posted a 15-4 record that season, with just two losses in the conference (each by two points). The Redbirds won their final five conference games to bag a third straight title in the Little Nineteen, which had dwindled to eight schools.

United Press placed Scott and Brandt on the Little Nineteen all-star team. Scott led the team in scoring with 241 points in 20 games.

◆   ◆   ◆   ◆   ◆   ◆

Hopes for a fourth straight league title in 1941–42 rested on veterans Scott, Kindred, McBride, Fagerburg and Walker. They did not disappoint, but Japan's December 7 attack on Pearl Harbor played a key role in the team's composition.

Fagerburg and team manager Everett Osborn left school for active service in the Navy at the end of January with the Redbirds enjoying a 9-3 record (all three losses to Indiana non-conference opponents). Sophomore Gerald Frieburg took Fagerburg's place in the lineup and the team kept up the pace with three more victories to run their winning streak to eight games.

Cogdal's juggernaut overwhelmed Western Illinois, 74–40, in the final home game for Scott, Kindred and McBride. Kindred and Scott both tied a McCormick Gym record with 23 points.

Scoring totals could have soared higher but Cogdal kept a tight rein on his talented squad.

"We wanted to fast break," Kindred said. "Jim McBride, my roommate, did run a couple of times. Joe would tell me, 'Now Larry, I don't want you to fast break; I want you to slow it down and run our plays.'

"He had an unusual knack about him. He got you prepared the day before the game and also before the game started. At halftime he wouldn't let you talk. Nobody said anything. You just stretched out and rested.

"The refs would knock on the door with two minutes to go. Then he would say, 'O.K., here's what you do.'"

Cogdal still scrimmaged against his players in those years. "We'd wink at each other and try to knock him on his butt," Kindred said. "But he was pretty tough.

"We used to call him Smokey Joe, but not to his face. He was a great guy. I learned a lot from him."

Scholarly Joe Cogdal enjoyed his interactions with student-athletes. Cogdal here is surrounded, left to right, by Bob Lockhart (capt.), Dick Baldrini, Jake Schoof, John Jorstad and Louid Baker.

The Redbirds finished with a 17-5 record, going 9-1 in the conference for their fourth consecutive title. Scott, who worked his way through school as a Normal dairy employee and a carpenter's assistant, broke Pim Goff's career scoring record with 912 points and received an offer to play for the New York Renaissance professional basketball team. He played a couple of seasons with the Harlem Globetrotters and settled in Chicago as a chiropodist.

Kindred signed a professional baseball contract with the New York Yankees but after one season went to the U.S. Marine Corps for combat in the South Pacific. McBride joined the Naval Air Corps.

◆   ◆   ◆   ◆   ◆   ◆

The war brought an increasing military presence and a declining civilian enrollment to Illinois State. Army pilots arrived in the summer of '42, replaced by Navy V-5 flyers that fall who were succeeded by a Navy V-12 unit of 300 men the next summer.

The apprentice sailors helped keep the university afloat because civilian enrollment dropped from 1,820 in 1940 to 779 by 1943. Only 56 civilian men were in college during the second semester of 1943.

Cogdal had few experienced players beyond captain Walker for the 1942–43 season, but he put the pieces together for a fifth straight IIAC championship. The old Little Nineteen now went by its formal name (Illinois Intercollegiate Athletic Conference) because only the five state teachers colleges remained as members.

Center Joe Swank emerged as the team's scoring leader, and freshman Bob Lockhart took over a key ballhandling role.

Illinois State entered February with three conference losses but closed with victories over Eastern Illinois and Southern Illinois to bag the championship in a year of parity. The final standings showed Illinois State alone at the top with a 5-3 record, followed by Southern Northern and Eastern at 4-4, and Western at 3-5.

Lockhart and center Jake Schoof were the only members of the squad still in school by the end of the semester. Lockhart would soon be gone for the duration of the war.

◆   ◆   ◆   ◆   ◆   ◆

The arrival of 300 apprentice sailors for the V-12 program in 1943 provided Cogdal with the material for a sixth straight IIAC championship, which turned out to be the final basketball title in the coach's illustrious career.

Schoof, now in the Navy V-12 program, was the tallest player at 6-foot-4 inches and the only carryover from the previous campaign.

All but one of the other 1943–44 players also came from the V-12 program. They included experienced college athletes Frank Olivieri (Northern Illinois), Bob "Tab" Talkin (Monmouth) and Warren Collier (Eureka).

Wartime travel restrictions helped bring ISNU and Wesleyan back together on the basketball court again, and the Redbirds won both contests, 51–34 and 62–32.

Olivieri led the league in scoring after having placed second as an NIU freshman. He set a home-court scoring record for ISNU with 28 against Western Illinois.

The team rolled through the IIAC with a 7-1 record—the only loss a four-pointer at Northern Illinois. ISNU was 16-7 as Olivieri and Talkin were honorable mention on the Converse Yearbook All-America team.

Cogdal was at the pinnacle of his career. He coached the basketball team five more seasons but there would be no more championships.

Illinois State's basketball fortunes declined during Cogdal's final five seasons. Starting with 1944–45, his teams were 7-15, 7-14, 7-13, 7-15 and 9-11 in 1948–49. One of Cogdal's best athletes, captain Lockhart, missed nearly a month of the 1948–49 season with a heart ailment and was able to play only half-time after his return. He made the most of his minutes, scoring 23 points during 20 minutes of action in his last home game. He was the team's most valuable player for the second straight year.

Incidentally, the team wore uniforms with "Illinois State" printed on the jerseys that season for the first time, even though Illinois State Normal University would remain the school's official name until 1964.

Improved baseline shooting had caught up with Cogdal's famed T-zone during his final five years. Recruiting was also a problem, according to Pim Goff, the former playing star who returned as Cogdal's assistant coach

Larry Kindred was a key player in the 1940 victory over UCLA.

Don Prince, the 1945 team MVP, was one of the V-12 apprentice sailors who bolstered the Redbird sports programs during WWII.

in 1947.

"Joe really wasn't a recruiter," Goff said. "He never recruited outside the county. His thing was to play the guys who showed up, and to teach them."

Fans began grumbling about the reversal of Cogdal's basketball fortunes but the coach continued doing it his way. An unpopular player move resulted in a thrilling Illinois State victory once, and student journalist Tom Gumbrell memorialized the event in an amusing poem for the campus yearbook under the title, "The Vindication of Bloody Joe."

The ninth stanza describes the critical moment after the team's star fouled out and Cogdal sent the player (given the fictitious name of Horsehead) into the game.

Not Horsehead, please! the crowd did wheeze
In one convulsive roar,
But Joe, concrete, cried from his seat,
"There's one coach here, no more!"

The substitute made the winning basket, amazing the fans but not the coach, and the 12-stanza poem concludes:

While his reward men do accord
In sport's heroic lore,
Joe rubs his shin and strokes his chin,
And calmly eyes the floor.

Cogdal resigned, no doubt grudgingly, after the 1948–49 season to focus on cross country and track, where he won eight cross country titles and two track championships before retiring in 1965. Ironically, he was inducted into the National Association of Intercollegiate Athletics Hall of Fame—honored by a group Cogdal had resisted joining until his final year as basketball coach because of its racial policies.

Goff, the school's greatest all-around athlete, was elevated to head basketball coach in 1949. He served eight years.

"I didn't really want the job," Goff told a *Pantagraph* reporter after Cogdal died in 1978. "But I felt Joe would have wanted one of his own boys in there instead of an outsider."

Chapter 12
THE HOMETOWN HERO
AS COACH
(1949)

If anyone was destined to become the head basketball coach at Illinois State, it was James "Pim" Goff. His multi-sport athletic exploits contained legendary performances. He was a knowledgeable teacher of sports technique, a good recruiter and a close friend of President Raymond Fairchild.

Goff, the scoring leader for Illinois State's 1930–31 championship team as a freshman, is the only five-sport letter winner in school history. He won letters in football, basketball, baseball, tennis and track during his junior year and totaled 13 letters in his collegiate career despite limiting his play to basketball and baseball as a senior. He won the same number at University High School.

It is almost an understatement to say that athletics were the major interest in Goff's life. Some claim he seemed to consciously block out nearly everything else.

Duffy Bass, the winningest baseball coach in Illinois State history, caught for the Redbirds when Goff was assistant baseball coach. Bass, ISU's baseball coach for 26 years, penned a tribute to Goff's dedication to sport in a profile.

"His walk through life in the Midwest was focused on what he did best," Bass wrote. "Pim Goff was, in the view of many, the greatest athlete of all-time in Central Illinois. He was casual, lanky, bordering on frail. With rounded shoulders and weathered face, Pim never gave an impression of Mr. Athlete.

He communicated verbally with merely enough language to convey a thought or an attitude.

"For all of his active days, Pim was serving, putting, pitching and hitting, shooting and dribbling—season after season. He knew all of the strategies, the shots and techniques, and neither cared for, nor spent much time on, many of the ordinary chores to which most of us must tend. His devoted wife, Katherine, shared her marriage to Pim with his football, basketball, baseball, tennis and track world."

◆   ◆   ◆   ◆   ◆   ◆

A left-hander, Goff was so good in all five sports that he couldn't decide upon which to concentrate:

◆ He was an all-conference halfback in football, punted up to 70 yards and quick-kicked 50 yards before a knee injury during his junior season ended his gridiron exploits. Even so, he was a strong candidate for the 1934 College All-Star football game in Chicago before deciding on a pro baseball career instead.

◆ He set a career scoring record in basketball with 852 points, a flashy number during a low-scoring era when the ball was put in play with a center jump after each basket and the clock ran during jump ball situations. He was all-conference four years and most valuable in the conference his senior year.

◆ He struck out 126 batters in 101 innings for a school baseball record in 1934 and missed the conference batting championship by one hit. He was inducted into the National Association of Intercollegiate Athletics Baseball Hall of Fame in 1961.

President Raymond Fairchild's hand-picked choice to succeed Joe Cogdal was Redbird legend James "Pim" Goff, shown here plotting strategy with assistant coach Warren Crews.

◆ He won javelin and discus events in his street clothes one day when coach Joe Cogdal responded to Goff's horseplay as a spectator by entering him in both events. Goff became a consistent point scorer in the javelin during his junior year.

◆ He won conference tennis championships in both singles and doubles (teamed with Charlie Sweet). He also teamed with Professor Richard Browne, who later became the first executive director of the Illinois Board of Higher Education, to win amateur events throughout the Midwest over many years.

◆   ◆   ◆   ◆   ◆   ◆

On two documented occasions, Goff participated in baseball, track and tennis on the same day. Once when Western Illinois teams came to Normal, he won singles and doubles tennis matches early in the afternoon, pitched a baseball shutout victory later in the day, and dashed to the track between innings to take first place in the javelin throw.

On another day against Illinois College in Jacksonville, he scored victories in tennis and track and arrived at the baseball diamond just in time to hit a pinch-hit home run to send the game into extra innings and went to the mound to pitch those extra frames.

Goff wrote this description of his busy day in Jacksonville:

"We got started late in tennis but we won the doubles and I won my singles, and then I hustled out and threw the javelin. When I got over to the ball game, we were in the ninth inning and one run behind.

"Their ball diamond was rather short, especially in right field, which was where the college president's house was located. When I got to the game [coach Howard] Hancock was excited and said, 'Hurry up. I want you to pinch hit.'

"Well I did, knocking the ball clear over the president's house, and tying the score. Unfortunately the ending was sad but my only warm-up pitches were on the mound and they got a run to beat us."

Goff signed with the St. Louis Browns after his senior season, played professional baseball for 10 years, and also played pro basketball four years. He won seven games in 14 days including both games of a doubleheader in the Kitty League one season. While pitching in the rain in 1936, he injured his arm. But he continued playing baseball into 1944 with Kansas City of the Triple-A American Association.

Pim Goff enjoyed playing sports his entire life. In fact, he even put on shooting exhibitions at halftime of high school games he refereed.

He also played semi-pro baseball for several seasons and once pitched two no-hitters in five days with a two-hit shutout in between. Two of those gems came in the state semi-pro tournament at Elgin.

Goff launched his coaching career at Bloomington's Trinity High School in 1937 and also coached at Donovan High School, Millikin University and Eastern Illinois University before returning to Illinois State as an assistant coach of football, basketball and baseball in 1947.

He took command of Illinois State's basketball program in 1949 with his president's enthusiastic support. President Fairchild came to Illinois State in 1933 when Goff was at the peak of his collegiate sports fame and developed a friendship with the personable young athlete. Fairchild had been a high jumper in his undergraduate years at Illinois Wesleyan and he enjoyed a close association with coaches and athletes throughout his presidency.

"Pim was the guy he wanted to coach," said J. Russell Steele, who was Illinois State's first sports information director in 1946, serving in that capacity for two decades.

And Fairchild offered extraordinary help and support to Goff's coaching. Accustomed to managing every detail of campus decisions, the president sought to influence Goff's coaching decisions.

"Fairchild would keep a box score and notes to talk to Pim about the next day or two," Steele recalled. "I don't think it bothered Pim a whole lot. I don't remember it changing his way of coaching."

If the president knew anything about defense, his advice might have helped. Goff's teams became characterized by a hair-trigger offense and casual defense that invited derision one night when the Redbirds scored 109 points—and lost. Northern Illinois won, 111–109.

"The contest had its serious and humorous aspects," Jim Barnhart of the *Pantagraph* wrote. "The comedy occurred when the players on both teams would shout to each other, 'Defense!'"

During eight seasons as head coach, Goff managed a total record just one game over the .500 mark despite churning out a steady progression of shooting stars. Glen Honsbruch, Bill Sarver, Al Meyer and Fred Marberry took turns elevating scoring records to ever-greater heights.

Goff was the first Illinois State basketball coach to devote a great deal of attention to recruiting, despite his busy campus schedule with a full teaching load and assistant coaching positions in football and basketball. In addition, he officiated football and basketball games at area high schools. He usually stayed on the floor at halftime and entertained the fans by shooting baskets from the center circle at halftime. He made plenty of them, too.

"Pim was a 'hail fellow' all his life and had friends everywhere," Steele said. "He worked his field contacts the way the modern coaches do. People like Stretch Miller tended to help him recruit people so he had a network."

Goff never forgot a good athlete. He recruited Dave Schertz from the small central Illinois community of Hopedale in 1950, but Schertz didn't stay long and eventually went into the U.S. Army. After his discharge in 1955, Schertz planned to attend Eureka College, but came to Normal first to visit with relatives.

"I was walking down the street across from the theater and someone in a car hollered at me," Schertz said. "Lo and behold, it was Pim. He got me in the car, asked where I had been, and before I got out of the car, he said, 'I'll take care of all the paperwork and you show up in the fall.' Pim had a great personality and did a lot for young people."

Schertz proved a bargain. Forty years later, Schertz still ranks among the Redbirds' career scoring and rebounding leaders.

At times the flow of capable athletes was so abundant that a player might perform well in a B team game one night, start for the varsity the next night, then rejoin the B team again. That happened frequently, sometimes several times during a season.

Gene Jontry, a fine shooting guard who followed Sarver to Illinois State from Chenoa, was caught in that revolving door for most of three seasons.

"The movement of players between the B team and the varsity was characteristic of how Pim took a look at recruited talent," Jontry said. "If Les Hellemann, as an example, would have a hot shooting night in the B team game Pim would use him as a spot shooter for about four or five minutes and when Les went in there he was expected to put it up."

High-scoring Glen Honsbruch developed as a shooting star during Pim Goff's early days as head coach.

The Redbirds might not know who would start on any given night but they sure knew how to score. The Goff era produced the first 100-point games in school history. His teams reached the century mark 18 times with a high mark of 120–99 over Central Michigan near the end of the 1954–55 campaign.

On the other hand, opponents scored 100 or more points 16 times. The worst defensive disaster came during the 1955–56 season when Western Illinois romped to a 126–92 victory. Illinois State surpassed 100 points five times that season but opponents did it six times.

"I don't think Pim spent much time teaching defense," Steele said. "His idea was to get the shots flying with people like Fred Marberry and Bill Sarver. He tried to get shots for the guys who had the high percentage. That was probably his strong point.

"That works and it doesn't work, you know. On the night when you're not hitting you're going to lose if you can't play the rest of the game."

Jontry verified that Goff put his emphasis on a productive offense.

"He thought the best defense was a good offense," Jontry said.

"He wanted the ball moved up the floor and once you were within range it was a good shot without the defense hanging all over you. I shot a lot of shots from 25 feet down to 18 feet for Pim because he thought that was my range.

"He would yell from the bench, 'Fire!' You could hear him from the sidelines. It wasn't in a negative nature, just assertive. He would never yell at you for shooting too much. You couldn't shoot too much in his philosophy."

Chapter 13
THE PIM GOFF YEARS (1949–1957)

A handful of veteran players, led by guards Leon Heinle and Dick Baldrini, greeted Pim Goff and his new assistant, Warren Crews, for Goff's first season as head coach in 1949.

Glen Honsbruch, a sophomore on his way to a school career scoring record, moved from center to forward because of three promising centers: 6-foot-7 Marvin Block, 6-foot-5 Don Richard and 6-foot-4 Bob Brenneman.

In a season-opening 70–61 loss to Millikin, Goff's free-wheeling offense outshot the Big Blue, 86–57, in attempts. Trouble was, ISNU made just 21 of its tries.

Muscular Frank Chiodo, later a legendary football coach at U-High, and Dean Burridge, only 5-foot-9 but a fine athlete in football, basketball and baseball, quickly joined the starting group as Goff showed he was willing to make changes on short notice. He did that often in a 9-15 campaign.

An unexpected change came with the loss of Burridge not long after he scored 23 points in a 70–57 upset over traditional rival Illinois Wesleyan late in the first semester.

The IIAC eligibility committee, headed by Pop Horton, ruled that Burridge, a junior, had only one more semester of eligibility remaining because of previous enrollment at Northwestern and Clinton (Iowa) Junior College.

Co-captain-elect of the 1950 football team, Burridge decided to drop out of school for a semester so he could play football in the fall. His accurate place kicking led the football Redbirds to an unbeaten season and a bid to the Corn Bowl. He was named the conference MVP, bringing that honor to Illinois State for the third straight season (following

John Dal Santo and Dick Baldrini).

Goff's spirited team inspired fan support far surpassing its won-loss record. More than 700 fans had to be refused admission for one game, leading President Fairchild to declare that the university greatly needed a new field house for athletics and intramural sports.

The major off-court story that season was the announcement that the Illinois Intercollegiate Athletic Conference would expand to seven members by adding Central Michigan University and Michigan Normal (now known as Eastern Michigan University). Anticipating that Ball State and Indiana State would also join, the league planned to call itself the Tri-State Conference, but when those schools did not come in, the traditional designation of IIAC was preserved as the Interstate Intercollegiate Athletic Conference.

◆　◆　◆　◆　◆　◆

Goff's 1950–51 team produced the school's first winning season in seven years: 14-12 with a potent lineup that introduced freshman set-shot artist Bill Sarver.

Sarver, a 5-11 guard, teamed with Stan Albeck, of later fame as head coach of the Chicago Bulls and at Bradley, on one of the best prep teams (Chenoa) in McLean County history.

Honsbruch, a junior, led Illinois State in scoring for the second straight year and fell just five points short of the career scoring record. Center Bob Brenneman scored 35 points against Eureka College, erroneously pronounced a school record by younger fans unaware of Fred Young's 43-point splash against the same school in 1910.

◆　◆　◆　◆　◆　◆

Goff's third season was his most successful: a 17-7 record, second place in the IIAC with a 9-3 mark, and the school's first post-season tournament appearance in the National Association of Intercollegiate Athletics district playoffs.

Honsbruch, the team captain who shattered the career scoring record in his first game that season, finished with 1,254 points. Sarver set a McCormick Gym scoring record with 30 points in an 86–68 victory over Illinois Wesleyan.

Brenneman was drafted into military service but Don Richard emerged as a potent offensive weapon at center with his stiff-armed hook shot.

Two Murray State transfers, Tom Molloy and Al Austin, rounded out the top five. Both quality athletes, Austin became the Redbirds' most valuable player in basketball and Molloy won MVP honors in baseball that year.

The only barrier to a conference title was Eastern Illinois, a small-college power which thrashed the 'Birds, 103–84, in its 41st straight home victory. Five all-conference players saw action in that game: Honsbruch, Sarver and three of the EIU starters.

Millikin defeated both Illinois State and Eastern Illinois in the district playoffs to win the state's berth in the national tournament at Kansas City.

As a sidelight, results of Illinois State's earlier commitment to educating high school coaches showed well as its alumni hauled down the top three places in the Illinois High School Association tourney. Hebron became the only district (now Class A) champion to win a state title under the guidance of Russ Ahearn, one of Goff's former baseball teammates.

Fred Marberry, Essic Robinson, Rich Bennett, Dave Schertz and Art Buesking model the special blue uniforms designed by coach Pim Goff worn by the Redbirds during the Illinois State Normal University Centennial year of 1956–57.

Quincy was second under George Latham and Mt. Vernon was third under Stan Changnon, whose Rams had won back-to-back state titles in 1949 and 1950.

❖　❖　❖　❖　❖　❖

Goff armed the Redbirds with an arsenal of explosive weapons during the next five seasons, but only twice did they finish as high as one game above the .500 mark.

During the 1952–53 season, junior guard Bill Sarver broke Honsbruch's four-year record with 1,282 points, set a single-season standard of 568 and fell two points short of Young's ancient single-game record with 41 points against Eastern Illinois. The redheaded sharpshooter was named the most valuable player in the IIAC and led Illinois State to its first triple-digit game, a 101–87 victory over Southern Illinois, but Illinois State finished 12-12.

The Redbirds were entertaining, even in

defeat. Webster Kirksey (46 points) of Michigan Normal and Sarver (30 points) staged a memorable duel when the Hurons outgunned ISNU, 102–99, before more than 2,000 fans squeezed into McCormick Gym.

A few games later, Redbird guard LeRoy Eicken brought another capacity home crowd to its feet by sinking a 65-foot desperation shot at the buzzer to force overtime against Wesleyan. WJBC broadcaster Gus Grebe was so excited he nearly fell from his cramped perch in the booth mounted high on the wall. It seemed anticlimactic when Wesleyan won the game, 77–72.

❖　❖　❖　❖　❖　❖

Even though Sarver set a record with every point he scored and future sensation Fred Marberry made his Illinois State debut, the 1953–54 season was a 9-15 disappointment.

Bureaucracy and geography landed

Marberry in Normal. Illinois had recruited Marberry with a track and field scholarship after he placed in two events at the 1953 state meet in his only year of track competition at Peoria Manual High School.

"By this time I really wanted to play basketball, too, but Illinois had only one black ballplayer before," Marberry said. "I was in this [registration] line about two blocks long and by the time I got up to the window, I had talked myself out of going."

So Marberry headed back toward Peoria, stopped off in Normal, and registered at Illinois State instead. He came unannounced, but was in the starting lineup when the Redbirds opened against Bradley. He was awed when he took the Robertson Fieldhouse floor against Bradley players he had admired as a high schooler.

Marberry proved their equal with 18 points and 14 rebounds. Bradley won the game but Marberry quickly became a fan favorite at ISNU with his 33-inch standing vertical jump and

Soaring Fred Marberry, a leaper for all basketball eras, snags a rebound in front of teammates Al Meyer (4) and Bob Riggenbach (21).

accurate fade-away jump shot.

"My heart fluttered on some of those shots," Goff once said. "He fell so far back, I was afraid he would hit his head on the floor."

Marberry, who also set the school high jump record during track season, enjoyed playing basketball for Goff. "Pim had a beautiful personality," Marberry said. "He treated me equally as a man, and this was in the 1950s. Things weren't that way then."

Despite the losing record, Sarver continued to reap individual honors. IIAC coaches named him the league's most valuable player for the second year in a row.

◆   ◆   ◆   ◆   ◆   ◆

Bill Sarver personified the Pim Goff philosophy. An all-around athlete, he played football, captained the baseball team and played two summers with the State Farm Insurance Companies' fast-pitch softball team which placed third in the World Tournament in

Clearwater, Fla.

"He was a great athlete and competitive, but you never would guess it talking to him," said Warren Crews, the Redbirds' assistant coach for more than two decades. "He was just a regular guy and had a lot of friends on the team."

Crews still marvels at Sarver's shooting range. He recalls one game when the Redbirds were nursing a slim lead against Eastern Illinois. About a minute and a half before halftime, Goff told his team to hold the ball for the last shot.

Sarver cradled the ball on his hip nearly 40 feet from the basket and slightly to one side of the court against a motionless Eastern Illinois defense as the clock ticked away. The rules did not require action then, so no one moved.

With three seconds left, Sarver raised the ball and pumped in a one-handed set shot over the stationary Eastern defense.

After graduating, Sarver played two years at Fort Chafee in Arkansas on an all-Army championship team. He and two teammates,

future Boston Celtic Sam Jones and future Philadelphia 76er Al Bianchi, were invited to the 1956 Olympic trials at Louisville, Ky.

After military duty, he played a half-dozen seasons for Allen-Bradley of Milwaukee, in the fast-paced National Industrial Basketball League and later when it became a power in the Amateur Athletic Union.

Sarver still ranked fifth on Illinois State's career scoring list with 1,798 points as late as 1998.

"He definitely was an offensive-minded coach," Sarver said of Goff. "That's why I ended up scoring so much. His philosophy was if he had someone who could put the ball in the hole, get the ball to him and let him do it." Bill Sarver could do it.

◆   ◆   ◆   ◆   ◆   ◆

Even after Sarver's graduation, the Redbirds under Pim Goff remained "offensive." Marberry, a sophomore, continued scoring

Bill Sarver (5) drives around a Gonzaga opponent in a 1953 win at McCormick Gym.

points in bunches, and quick-shooting guard Al Meyer took over Sarver's backcourt role for the 1954–55 season.

Add Jim Jones—a 6-foot-3 player with an 85-inch wingspan, destined to become a legendary sports official in central Illinois—plus Herman Shaw and Bob Riggenbach to the lineup, and the Redbirds were off and running for a 103–74 conquest of Quincy College in the opening game of the 1954–55 season.

When Riggenbach went down with a serious ankle injury, Art Buesking and Adrian Winters stepped in to keep the offense humming.

With two freshmen, two sophomores and one junior in the starting lineup, the Redbirds faltered early. They salvaged a winning record by averaging 104 points to win their final three games.

An 88–86 victory at Northern Illinois was the sweetest, avenging an earlier 111–109 loss. The Redbirds trailed by two points with 1:40 remaining but Buesking stole the ball twice, scoring once himself, then passing to Marberry

under the basket for the winning shot with six seconds left.

Marberry averaged 19.6 points a game that season and was voted the most valuable player in the Interstate Conference.

◆　◆　◆　◆　◆　◆

Goff had to start almost from scratch for the 1955–56 season when mainstays Buesking, Jones, Shaw and Winters went ineligible or left school.

Still, the Redbirds kept on firing. With Marberry, Meyer and Riggenbach back in the lineup, they sprinted to a 116–100 opening victory over McKendree, including a school-record 51 points by Meyer, officially breaking Fred Young's 47-year-old record.

Ironically, McKendree's head coach was Jim Collie, who would succeed Goff at Illinois State two years later. Collie's team was in the midst of a five-year reign as champions of the Prairie Conference. The Bearcats' captain, Rich

Herrin, would become better known to ISU fans as the prep coach of future Redbird all-American Doug Collins and a respected coaching rival at Southern Illinois University.

The Redbirds rang up five games with more than 100 points in 1955–56, but their opponents turned the trick six times. The most dismal night came when they scored 92 points but lost by 34 to Western Illinois (126–92). Essic Robinson's ineligibility weakened the Redbirds at the semester break and they finished with a 10-14 record.

Marberry was sensational again, however. The spring-legged junior broke Sarver's single-season scoring record with 645 points (a 26.9 average) and led the Redbirds in rebounding with a 13.8 average. He also broke Sarver's IIAC scoring record and, like Sarver, was voted the league's most valuable player for a second year in a row.

President Emeritus Raymond W. Fairchild died June 12, 1956—six months short of the university's centennial year and less than two months after his successor, Robert G. Bone, became Illinois State's ninth president.

◆　◆　◆　◆　◆　◆

Innovative footwear, unusual uniforms and a wealth of height decorated Goff's strongest roster for the 1956–57 season. He decked them out in bright blue uniforms with red and white trim in honor of the university's centennial year.

"We're not trying to change the school colors," Goff said of the uniforms. "I think they're good looking, but our colors are still red and white."

The team also forsook traditional tight-binding high-tops for low-cut basketball shoes created by Goff and Converse representative Grady Lewis.

The Redbirds were a "small college" team with "tall college" size. Two talented freshmen, 6-foot-8 center Tony Cadle and 6-foot-4 forward John Zuzevich, joined the explosive Fred Marberry in the starting front line. Six-foot-eight sophomore Rich Bennett, muscular 6-foot-4 forward Robinson and husky 6-foot-5 University of Arizona transfer

Charley Brannan rotated with them. Art Buesking and co-captains Dave Schertz and Parker Lawlis worked at the guards. Lawlis was the only senior.

One of the interesting early-season games was against McKendree College in Lebanon. Jim Collie, the future Redbird coach, had a plan for his Bearcats to prevail after losing the high-scoring affair the previous year.

"I told my players that if we could hold Fred Marberry under 35 points we could win," Collie said. "He scored 34 and we won [87–86]. He was a great player."

ISNU went 9-4 the first semester as Marberry put up hefty scoring numbers: 43 points against Tennessee A&I, 41 against Lewis, 39 against Platteville and 37 against Southern Illinois. His 29.5 average led the nation in scoring.

"Then came heartbreak city," *Pantagraph* sports editor Jim Barnhart reported in one of his columns. Marberry became ineligible for the second semester.

Students had to maintain a C average after their sophomore year to stay eligible at that time. Marberry went into his senior year even-up (a 2.0), Barnhart reported, but he received three C's, one B and one D. The B was in a two-hour course and the D in a three-hour course. That left him one honor point short and he was out of school.

Ironically, if he had received a B, instead of a D, in football coaching he would have been eligible. The D in a social studies course licensed Goff.

"He got shafted and I raised hell about it," Goff bristled two decades later in a conversation with Barnhart. "It was the worst situation ever and I'm still bitter about it.

"I went to that instructor and raised Cain. He told me that if he had known it would cause that much trouble, he would have given him a C. I told him he should have given him a C anyway."

For years to come, Marberry was more disturbed about the football coaching grade. Other students in the class had obtained an advance copy of the only exam given and one of them shared the information with him. Although Marberry's involvement was limited, he became the only person penalized by having his grade lowered and subsequently

Al Austin (9) wins a jump ball from an Illinois Wesleyan opponent in McCormick Gym in the early 1950s. Note the narrow lane, called a "keyhole."

A layup by Bob Riggenbach (21) is the center of action, but note the cramped conditions in McCormick Gym in the mid-1950s: fans jammed in the seats, the media row packed into the left corner (with the WJBC banner), and coats slung over the guy wires (upper right). The referees wore numbers and Illinois State's uniforms said "Red Birds" on the front.

losing his eligibility.

"That really broke my heart," said Marberry, who subsequently played for a nationally ranked AAU team in Joliet and two seasons for the Harlem Globetrotters.

Marberry's ineligibility broke the hearts of Illinois State fans, too, but it didn't break the Redbirds' spirit.

The spark came from 6-0 guard Gene Jontry, a three-year B-team member, who scored 31 points in an 82–77 win over previously undefeated IIAC opponent Western Illinois.

Illinois State also put up a good battle against major college opponent DePaul before losing, 87–77. Once a familiar member of the century club, the Redbirds cracked the 100 mark only once after Marberry's departure. They laced Eastern Michigan, 104–92, with Jontry scoring 24 points, Cadle and Zuzevich with 22 each, and Buesking with 18.

Illinois State finished the regular season with a 14-12 record and earned a spot in the new NCAA small-college tournament. They lost a first-round game to Evansville, 108–96. They also lost their coach.

Goff surprised the community by accepting a five-year contract for more than $9,000 a year—significantly higher than his Illinois State salary—from Quincy College, effective June 1, 1957.

Goff had second thoughts after resigning his tenured faculty position at Illinois State but it was too late. He took three of Illinois State's tallest and most promising young players (Cadle, Bennett and Zuzevich) with him to Quincy and led the Hawks to an NAIA Tournament berth in Kansas City his first year, but was terminated two years later after losing records.

Goff entered private business, then was a school counselor at Athens High School and Bloomington's Trinity (now Central Catholic) High School. Illinois State's greatest all-around athlete died in his sleep on February 27, 1980 while vacationing in Tucson, Ariz.

Chapter 14

GENTLEMAN JIM COLLIE (1957)

Dr. James Collie brought impeccable academic and coaching credentials to Illinois State in an era when coaches held faculty rank, taught a full schedule of classes, and could secure academic tenure. He had a doctoral degree, which was important for advancement on the salary schedule, and he had produced a series of championship basketball teams at McKendree College in Lebanon, Ill.

Collie was announced as the new Redbird coach in May 1957. His name invited puns, of course, and the campus newspaper couldn't resist the opportunity. It didn't take long before someone at the *Vidette* referred to him as the new "watchdog" of the Redbirds.

The university's popular president, Robert G. Bone, joined in the fun. It was not unusual for a collie to fetch a bone, the president declared at a pep rally, but this was the first time on record that a Bone had fetched a Collie.

Collie appreciated the humor of the situation. Although he approached basketball with an analytical mind, he was never stuffy about it.

"Jim Collie was a gentleman and a scholar type of guy," former sports information director J. Russell Steele said. "He was studious and organized. He taught the total game in a satisfactory way. He was the type of person you would often find in some other profession than coaching. But he wanted to coach and he did it rather well."

Collie, in fact, never intended to become a coach. He studied physical education at Murray State in his hometown of Murray, Ky., and at Indiana University with the goal of establishing an academic career.

"Throughout my undergraduate and graduate training I did not plan to coach because I didn't appreciate the abuse that coaches sometimes get from the public and school boards," he said.

"I was ready to start my last semester of graduate work at Indiana with that philosophy."

At that point, Collie was recommended for a coaching vacancy at Friends University in Wichita, Kan. He accepted the position after being assured that the school's only emphasis would be on educational values.

"They did not misrepresent the case at all," Collie said with humor. "The record indicates as much."

Collie's teams were 19-41 in three seasons but he discovered that he enjoyed coaching immensely.

"Somewhere along the line, I got the bug," he said.

So after receiving his doctorate from Indiana in 1952, Collie became athletics director, head basketball and head baseball coach at McKendree.

Success was instant and continuing. Collie's basketball teams won Prairie Conference titles in each of his five seasons as coach and posted a glossy 101-42 record. His baseball teams captured four conference titles in a row.

Collie's teams split a pair of basketball games with Illinois State in the two years before he became coach of the Redbirds, leading him to joke later that he was auditioning for the position.

He coached 13 seasons at Illinois State. There was nothing unlucky about the number. His teams won four Interstate Conference championships, received invitations to seven post-season NAIA and NCAA tournaments, and posted a record of 209-139.

His 1966–67 squad finished fourth in the NCAA College Division Tournament at Evansville. His 1967–68 team ranked third in the United Press International coaches poll and fourth in the Associated Press sportswriters poll for college division teams.

In 21 years of coaching at three schools, Collie had a 329-222 record.

Although Collie brought a greater emphasis on defense to the Redbirds, he enjoyed coaching a fast-breaking offense that reached its peak when the 1967–68 team averaged better than 90 points a game and strung together an 18-game winning streak en route to a school-record 25-3 campaign.

"This is spectator basketball," he said as he prepared the Runnin' Redbirds for the following campaign during a time when dunking was banned from the college game.

"The pros know what the spectators want to see and I think it's too bad that the colleges have been dragging their feet. One example is taking the dunk shot out of college basketball. That was a mistake. The fans like the dunk. It adds excitement."

The collegiate basketball world eventually returned to Collie's way of thinking by restoring the dunk to the game in the mid-1970s.

Although Collie most enjoyed the fast-breaking brand of basketball, he did not ignore the team's defense. Gene Jontry, the sharp-shooting guard who played for both Goff and Collie, said that Collie taught the total game.

"He stressed fundamentals," Jontry said. "He worked on basics such as screening out for rebounding, using your body properly, footwork on defense and proper shooting techniques. He took some people who were

Gentleman Jim Collie earned it all during his 13-year head coaching career at Illinois State. Here, he's honored with the "key to the cities." In front of the podium is the Redbirds' NCAA hardware.

weak in the fundamentals of shooting and made very good offensive players of them."

Collie, a deeply religious man in private life, approached his players with an even-tempered enthusiasm.

"He was calm and emotionally controlled at all times," Jontry said. "But you knew he was sincere and had a deep desire for you to win and do well."

Dave Schertz, the most valuable player under both Goff and Collie, saw the same qualities in Collie.

"He was quite a gentleman," Schertz said. "Most of us felt that we wanted to win so he would be happy. That was a paradox because he was not ever noticeably unhappy if we lost. He brought out the best in everybody."

Steve Arends, a standout on two championship teams a decade later, also took note of Collie's kindness and integrity.

"It was a wonderful experience playing for Coach Collie," Arends said. "I would want my son to play for a coach like Coach Collie because he has good, solid morals. He wanted to win as bad as anybody, but when he didn't it wasn't the end of the world. I can't remember him ever raising his voice. He treated us like young men and with respect."

Collie was the last basketball coach at Illinois State to hold academic rank as a professor of physical education. He believed so strongly in the educational value of athletics that he once took his team across the border into Mexico for a tour on the day of the third-place contest in a holiday basketball tournament in southern Texas. After touring the Reynosa market during the day, the Redbirds lost that night.

"We probably would have won the game by staying at the motel," Collie said, "but some of our players might never have another chance to see Mexico. It was an important experience for them."

Collie once explained his philosophy of coaching in this way: "I believe that coaching provides the opportunity for the highest type of teaching. Anyone who can teach can coach if he is motivated to do so.

"We in coaching have the opportunity to put our efforts on display before 5,000 people. We find out how effective our teaching has been.

Coaching provides a much sounder testing program than what any teacher could institute in the classroom. The teacher of English, say, who teaches composition for a semester and never sees the student again will not know if he has taught him or not.

"Athletics are certainly just a part of the educational picture, however. The basic job is to make good citizens. If the young man becomes a better individual and better citizen, this is important.

"I take a lot of pride in the fact that our athletes are students. Very few lettermen here fail to graduate. I know of only two in my years here. We are interested in the man who wants to be a college graduate.

"We try to be fair with every individual. The poorest player is just as important as the strongest one."

Collie's former players are a testament to his approach. Many of them went on to significant positions in education and other professional fields. Two prominent alumni were Kenneth "Buzz" Shaw, a chancellor and president of Syracuse University, and Steve Fisher, who coached the University of Michigan to a national championship in basketball. Two others, Stan Ommen and Bob Rush, became bank presidents in Bloomington. Shaw was the only player in that group to win a regular position on the basketball team but all of them received Collie's full attention.

◆   ◆   ◆   ◆   ◆   ◆

When Collie came to Illinois State in 1957, he inherited a squad diminished by the transfer of three tall and talented underclassmen who followed their former coach to Quincy College.

The only returning starters were forward Dave Schertz, the Army veteran who was voted most valuable player as a sophomore, and Gene Jontry, the refugee from the B team who became the scoring leader for the second semester of the previous campaign.

Collie teamed them with Buzz Shaw, Jerry Odell, a sophomore from the previous year's B team, and Charles Brannan, a senior center who had seen limited action.

It was no surprise when the team lost by 50

points at Bradley in the opening game but when the Redbirds were still struggling against Greenville College in the fourth game of the season, they seemed confused. "We had been ding-batting away the first half against a team that couldn't punch their way out of a paper sack," Schertz recalls.

The players filed down the back stairs to the McCormick Gymnasium locker room, took their seats on the hard benches, and waited for instructions from their new coach.

Finally, Collie entered the room. He gazed at his squad in silence. Then he spoke.

"Well, you guys figure it out," he said, and walked out of the room.

"We sat there feeling abused for awhile," Schertz said. But the players came together in a self-evaluation and began the second half with a purpose. They stormed back from an 18-point deficit in the final 18 minutes to win, 76–64.

Schertz gathered 20 rebounds in one game that season, the highest ISNU total on record at the time, and the Redbirds were practically unbeatable on their home court. They won their first nine games before undefeated Western Illinois snapped the string, 97–93, before an overflow crowd at McCormick Gym.

Jontry set two free throw records that still stand by making 35 in a row during one span and meshing 47 of 50 attempts during the season for 94 percent.

The Redbirds finished their schedule with a 13-13 record, tied for second place in the IIAC, and gained a post-season tournament bid for the second straight year.

They ran into their former coach for the third time that season in the opening game of the NAIA District 20 playoffs at Quincy College. Curiously, all three games were at Quincy: one in a holiday tournament, one on the regular schedule and one in the post-season playoffs. Quincy won them all but Illinois State nearly scored an upset in the playoffs before bowing, 63–62, after Jontry's desperation shot from near the half-court line grazed the ring with time running out.

"It was difficult losing to them," Jontry said. "We really wanted to prove to Dr. Collie that we could defeat that team in spite of the abilities they had. We played them tough."

Chapter 15

ILLINOIS STATE'S FIRST NATIONAL APPEARANCE (1958–1965)

Illinois State basketball fans saw red during Jim Collie's second year when his team had a storybook season with a 24-5 record, the school's first conference championship in 15 years, and the first-ever trip to a national basketball tournament.

President Robert Bone, the team's No. 1 fan, set the tone by wearing a red vest to the basketball games. When Illinois State defeated four-time defending champion Western Illinois, 94–85, in the conference showdown game late in February, the stands were ablaze with school colors of red and white.

"The most colorful crowd in Normal's half century of basketball saw the 'Birdies [a common reference of the day] avenge their defeat at Macomb last month," the *Pantagraph* reported. "Two-thirds of the overflow crowd were dressed in red sweaters or red shirts, and a committee from the student body even presented Coach Jim Collie with a red blazer so he could be in style, too."

It was one of the most memorable basketball campaigns in school history and a season with a dual personality.

Collie's starting lineup for the first half of the season had senior Dave Schertz and sophomore Jerry Odell at the forwards, sophomore Buzz Shaw and senior Rex Parker, a transfer from Beloit College, at the guards, and 6-foot-4 senior Ed Koch at center.

Waiting in the wings was Ron English, a 6-foot-7 transfer from Central Michigan. When he became eligible for the second semester, Koch moved to forward and Odell became a key sixth man.

"Jerry is still a very good ball player and of tremendous value to the team," Collie said after his team won the NAIA District 20 playoffs for a berth in the 32-team national tournament at Kansas City.

"Remember—admitting that English has been a big help—we weren't a bad team when Jerry was playing regularly. We were 5-1 for the first half of the conference season and finished the second half at 5-1 with English."

The emergence of Koch as a strong player was one of the heart-warming stories of that

The 1958–59 team won its first two games in the NAIA Tournament in Kansas City. Kneeling are coach Jim Collie and assistant coach Warren Crews. Standing are Buzz Shaw, Jim Hill, Rex Parker, Lindell Huisinga, Tom Tucker, Ron English, Ed Koch, Dave Schertz, Jerry Odell and Carl Franklin.

Dave Schertz (23) was the Redbirds' MVP in 1957, 1958 and 1959 and captained the 1959 IIAC Champions and NAIA District 20 Champions. Jerry Odell (4) trails the play as Schertz scores against Lewis.

Both had solid Illinois high school state tournament backgrounds: Shaw for 1956 runner-up Edwardsville and Parker for 1955 state champion Rockford West.

Schertz, the glue that held the team together, was in his third season as most valuable player and co-captain. "His value could not be measured," Collie said, because Schertz brought so many intangible qualities of leadership to the court.

With that lineup, Illinois State opened the season with a nine-game winning streak before suffering a three-point loss at Western Illinois, the conference champion for the previous four years. As the second semester began, the Redbirds were 12-3.

Enter English, who brought much-needed size into the pivot for the stretch drive. The Redbirds scored 100 or more points in four of the first five games after English entered the lineup and won 12 of their last 14 games, including four victories in post-season play.

"He's played in only 11 games but has given us a tremendous boost, particularly in rebounding," Collie assessed before the national tourney. "He helps in taking the pressure off Koch because Koch had to guard the other team's big man."

The Redbirds polished off Lewis College and North Central in the District 20 playoffs at McCormick Gym to go undefeated in 15 home games. English had 36 points and 12 rebounds in the title game, Schertz chipped in with 21 points and 11 rebounds, and Koch added 16 points (on 8-for-10 shooting) and nine rebounds.

With 200 scarlet-clad fans following them to Kansas City, the Redbirds drubbed Troy State of Alabama in the opening round, 98–50. Fairleigh-Dickinson fell in the second round, 68–64, after Schertz broke a 57–57 tie on a basket with 3:29 left, English scored from the floor, and Parker added a layup and five free throws in the final two minutes.

That brought the Redbirds face-to-face with Tennessee A&I (now Tennessee State), the nation's top-ranked small-college team. The Tigers lived up to their reputation. Future NBA guards John Barnhill and Dick Barnett popped in 25-foot jump shots with unerring accuracy.

season and a testament to Collie's coaching patience and work on fundamentals.

Koch had played for Collie as a freshman at McKendree College. After transferring to Illinois State, Koch was cut from the basketball team and lettered in swimming during his sophomore year. When Collie came to Illinois State, Koch tried out for basketball again and became a reserve player as a junior.

Koch refined his moves, perfected a deadly hook shot, and set a school record as a senior

by making 136 of 248 field goal attempts for a .548 percentage.

"I've known Ed since he was in high school and I don't know of a basketball player anywhere that has improved as much as Koch," Collie said. "He has tremendous desire."

Shaw, a deadly long-range shooter, made a run at Jontry's free throw record by making 85.4 percent of his attempts (76 of 89). Parker was an outstanding defensive player who usually guarded the opponent's best scorer.

Kenneth "Buzz" Shaw not only was a Redbird scoring leader, but became an educational leader as chancellor at Syracuse University and the first chair of the NCAA Division I Board of Directors.

Gene Jontry still holds the Redbird single-season free throw record, 47-50, .940 in 1956–57. He sank 35 in a row that season, which is No. 1 in Redbird history.

The Tigers shot 70 percent as a team and blitzed the Redbirds, 131–74. It was a tough finish to the winningest season in the first 60 years of Illinois State basketball.

◆ ◆ ◆ ◆ ◆ ◆

It would be hard to top that year for excitement but the Redbirds made a strong run during the next two seasons with records of 18-8 in 1959–60 and 19-7 in 1960-61.

Schertz and Koch were gone, but Shaw, English and Odell were joined in the starting lineup by forward John Hornacek and guard Dale Haywood.

Hornacek is best known today as the father of Utah Jazz star Jeff Hornacek. While at Iowa State, Jeff helped Johnny Orr's Cyclones upend the Redbirds in 1985 with a backcourt steal in the final seconds. John was the player who stepped up in 1959 to help Illinois State vault to an 8-2 record including the championship of the Ottawa (Kan.) Holiday Tournament.

The season crashed with three road losses in January, the ineligibility of English at the end of the first semester and a career-ending injury to Odell.

English, the leading center in the conference, was declared ineligible for failing to carry a required number of class hours. "I've made my bed and I've got to sleep in it," he told the *Pantagraph's* Jim Barnhart.

Illinois State recovered from that loss because John Swart, an outstanding 6-foot-5 athlete from Hartsburg, Ill., came in from Lincoln College for the second semester. Swart checked in with 28 points when the Redbirds avenged an earlier loss to Northern Illinois but Odell went down in that game with a broken cheek bone. Abe Booker, the Huskies' massive center, cracked Odell with an elbow while clearing a rebound. Odell was the team's second-leading scorer and rebounder at the time.

"We missed him more than I thought we would," Collie said. "That kind of serious injury is also a tremendous psychological blow to the rest of the boys."

The Redbirds were still dangerous, though. Swart had 28 points and a school-record 24 rebounds in a 98–83 loss to Eastern Illinois. Shaw gave Illinois State a two-point lead over Western Illinois with five seconds left but the Leathernecks managed to tie the score and win in overtime, 75–74, for a first-place tie with Southern Illinois.

Illinois State still had a role in determining the league champion. The Redbirds ambushed high-flying Southern Illinois, 95–84, at McCormick Gym and forced the Salukis to share the IIAC title with Western. "Over their heads, way over their heads," moaned SIU coach Harry Gallatin, shaking his head in disgust. But his talented team couldn't counter the Redbird balance of Shaw and Haywood with 21 points each and Swart's 20.

The 1960–61 Redbirds had hopes for another title bid with sophomore Jim Ringel, brawny Tom Tucker and agile Wardell Vaughn moving into the forward positions alongside returning center John Swart.

Illinois State opened with an 11-2 mark and successfully defended its Ottawa (Kan.) Holiday Tournament championship by beating Pittsburg (Kan.) State in overtime, 83–80.

But when Southern Illinois' powerful squad, led by high-scoring Charlie Vaughn and Tom McGreal, avenged the previous year's upset by 40 points, Collie knew his title hopes were slim.

"We would still like to place second," he said. "No one is going to stop Southern. I'm not sure that any team in the state, with the exception of Bradley, could beat them on their own floor."

The Redbirds did finish second. Ringel's two free throws with one second left beat Northern Illinois, 74–73, and ignited the club again. Illinois State won nine of the last 11 regular-season games and received a bid to the NAIA District 20 playoffs. Lewis College stopped the Redbirds in the first round, 74–69.

Shaw capped his four seasons as a starter by gaining all-conference and all-NAIA District 20 honors. He ranked third in career scoring behind Fred Marberry and Bill Sarver with 1,396 points and set a record for career free throw accuracy by making 83.1 percent of his attempts. He still holds school freshman and sophomore free throw records.

An unorthodox shooter, Shaw wrapped his left hand around the front of the ball, put his right hand behind the ball with its thumb pointing down, and brought his knees together as he rose for the jump shot.

"Opposing coaches used to wonder when they saw Buzz why we didn't change his technique," Collie said. "Then they knew why. He made a fantastic percentage for shots back then. He was a great shooter for his time."

Shaw received an NCAA Silver Anniversary Award for career achievements by former student athletes in 1986. The Syracuse University president contiues to have an active involvement in athletics as the first chairman of the NCAA Board of Directors.

◆ ◆ ◆ ◆ ◆ ◆

The 1961–62 season produced a 16-11 record, another second-place finish in the Interstate Conference, and a trip to the NCAA Great Lakes Regional Tournament at Valparaiso, Ind.—the Redbirds' fourth tournament bid in Collie's first five seasons as coach.

Only the absence of standout center Swart

Wardell Vaughn (42) shares the Redbird single-game rebounding record with 24 against Eastern Illinois, January 5, 1963. His long high school coaching career produced many stars, including future Redbirds Billy Lewis and Dwayne Tyus.

The Redbirds said good-bye to aging McCormick Gymnasium in the 1962–63 season. The 37-year-old facility could no longer accommodate the growing legions of people excited about Redbird basketball, driven in part by a growing student population.

Long lines of fans waited outside of the building on game nights for public tickets to go on sale a half hour before game time. Few were available because students usually filled the gym before then.

Those who squeezed into the 2,000-seat gym saw a scrappy Redbird team rally from a 1-6 start to post a winning 15-11 record. The Redbirds won 13 in a row at one stretch but faltered again near the end to tie for second place in the five-team IIAC with a 4-4 record. Still, they won their final game at McCormick Gym, 63–59, over Central Michigan.

Ringel, the team captain, was the only senior in the starting lineup. Junior Bob Sorrell emerged as the team's top scorer, junior Wardell Vaughn led in rebounding, and sophomores Preston Jordan at center and John Cruser at guard gave Redbird fans hopes for a brighter tomorrow in the new field house that was going up on the west side of campus.

◆ ◆ ◆ ◆ ◆ ◆

After 107 years as Illinois State Normal University, the school became Illinois State University on January 1, 1964.

This came less than a month after the Redbirds opened their new basketball home. On December 4, 1963, a crowd estimated at 3,000 fans saw junior guard John Cruser score the first basket after 29 seconds of action, but Indiana State spoiled the Horton Field House premiere, 58–55.

The next game produced the first of many Horton victories as the Redbirds beat Eastern Illinois, 86–82. The crowd was estimated at 2,400 for this game, well above the capacity of old McCormick Gym, but less than half of Horton's listed capacity of 5,645.

However, university enrollment more than doubled in Collie's first six years to 6,600

from the final eight games prevented the Redbirds from finishing with an even better mark and possibly advancing to the NCAA's elite eight in the national finals at Evansville.

Swart, a mid-season transfer from Lincoln College in 1960, ran out of eligibility at the close of the first semester. He was the team's top scorer with an 18.5 average and was the IIAC's top marksman in both field goal (.539) and free throw (.823) percentage.

The Redbirds had a 14-5 record while Swart was playing but lost four of their last six regular-season games and both of the NCAA regional contests, one in double overtime.

Still, they had a fine season with balanced scoring from the other season-long starters: Jim Ringel, Keith Rieger, Vaughn and Haywood.

The Interstate Conference dwindled to five teams after this season when league champion Southern Illinois withdrew to move into the major college ranks and Eastern Michigan pulled out to de-emphasize its program.

An era ended in Redbird athletics as physical education director Clifford Horton, who came to the university as head coach in 1923, and Athletics Director Howard Hancock, who came as football coach in 1931, both retired.

students and the onslaught of baby boomers reaching college age would double it again in the next five years, so it was just a matter of time before the field house was packed.

Illinois State had a 15-10 season record but slumped to 2-6 in the conference in their new surroundings. The Redbirds were weakened midway through the season when forward Vaughn lost his eligibility.

Cruser was the team's most consistent performer, averaging 18.6 points and securing all-conference honors.

He put together another MVP season in the 1964–65 campaign, averaging 19.5 points, but the Redbirds suffered through hard times. Starting center Jordan left school for military service and, just when the Redbirds needed an influx of new talent, the NCAA passed a rule barring freshmen from varsity play.

The 1964–65 team managed only a 6-18 record. One of the few highlights was forward Mike Akin tying Swart's school record by hauling down 24 rebounds in a 109–88 victory over Sioux Falls.

It was time to rebuild the Redbirds.

John Swart (55) came in as a transfer from Lincoln College and scored 28 points and 24 rebounds against Eastern Illinois February 6, 1960, just two weeks into his Illinois State career.

Chapter 16

ARENDS TO McGREAL TO TERRY: A REDBIRD TRIPLE PLAY (1965–1968)

The tireless trio of Steve Arends, Jerry McGreal and George Terry brought fans to Horton Field House in record numbers, keyed a resurgence of Redbird basketball success and paved the road to Division I basketball at Illinois State during their three varsity campaigns for coach Jim Collie.

Arends, a broad-shouldered, 6-foot-4 forward from Gibson City, Ill., was a mail-order athlete for the Redbirds.

"Coach Collie sent me a [recruiting] letter and I followed up with him," Arends explained. "I really liked him as a person. No promises were made, but he said he would give me a chance to play, and that was fair enough."

So, for the cost of a postage stamp, the Redbirds gained a player who battled for every rebound as though the ball was his last possession. He wound up with school rebound records for a season and three-year career, and became an all-conference choice and team co-captain in his final two years.

McGreal, a slender 6-foot-2 athlete from Rantoul, Ill., came to Illinois State to play for Milt Weisbecker's golf team after being overlooked his senior year because of an injury.

The left-handed McGreal got his break when the freshman basketball team's starting guards lost their eligibility at the end of the first semester. He moved from forward to guard, where his quickness and shooting skills became a valuable combination.

McGreal became an all-American, the second-highest scorer in Redbird history with 1,542 career points in three years and was drafted by the Indiana Pacers of the

American Basketball Association.

Terry, a husky 6-foot guard from Alton, Ill., braved financial and physical problems to become a prime-time shooter for the Redbirds. Terry earned his room and board by working as a recreation counselor at the Illinois Soldiers' and Sailors' Children's Home for four years.

Afflicted with arthritic gout, Terry often played basketball with painfully swollen legs and inflamed joints. He also had a broken foot bone at tournament time in his junior year. He caught an elbow hard in the mouth once at Central Michigan but didn't miss a game when equipment manager John Farris constructed a special mask to protect the injury.

Through it all, Terry became noted for winning games with last-second shots, like a 20-foot jumper with five seconds left for a 78–77 win over Pittsburg State.

"I used to have a game-ending play," Collie recalled, but during Terry's career the coach devised a more basic strategy: "Give the ball to George and get George a shot."

A pair of juniors rounded out the all-underclass starting lineup. Don "Buzzy" Feek, a former Bloomington High School star who transferred from Bradley University, was a 6-foot-3 forward possessing a deadly hook shot and the speed to run with the frisky sophomores. Duane Bruninga, a 6-7 center, was in his second year as a starter and provided strength in the middle.

The Redbirds improved after a 1-6 start, posted a 12-14 season record and tied for second in the IIAC. All five starters averaged in double figures, with Terry high at 16.7. "Coach Jim Collie seems to have a crowd-pleasing and

winning team for next season," the campus yearbook accurately forecast.

◆　　◆　　◆　　◆　　◆　　◆

Everyone associated with Illinois State's basketball program anticipated a great season in 1966–67. Collie had all five starters returning. His coaching staff was bolstered by the return of trusted assistant Warren Crews after three years of other assigned duties.

In the final year of Robert Bone's presidency, a new athletics partnership of Arley Gillett, head of men's physical education, health and athletics, and Milt Weisbecker, athletics director, brought in a new mobile bleacher section to the northern end of the field house, raising seating capacity to an estimated 8,500. They also initiated the Varsity Club, forerunner to the Redbird Education and Scholarship Funds (RESF).

Everything was in place except a favorable early-season schedule. After its home opener with Wayne State, the Redbirds played 10 straight on the road.

During that span the team traveled by air for the first time in school history. They played at Missoula, Mont., Spokane, Wash., and Alamosa, Colo.—where the temperature fell to minus-31 degrees—coming home with a 5-6 record.

But the Redbirds showed depth and resiliency. When Terry's gout flared up, Lexington's Ed Brucker, a 5-foot-10 transfer from Joliet Junior College, moved into the lineup and scored 22 points against Wisconsin-Milwaukee. McGreal had 33 in a lopsided victory at Platteville State, and all five of the

Tom Taulbee (54) scored between Southwest Missouri State stars Lou Shepherd (left) and Curtis Perry (right) in the 1967 NCAA College Division National Tournament semifinal game against Southwest Missouri State at Evansville, Ind. Redbirds Don Feek (far left) and George Terry (right) are ready to crash the boards.

starters were averaging in double figures.

Tom Taulbee, a sophomore center from University High, keyed the emergence of the team's running game. Collie inserted Taulbee into the starting lineup as a surprise move just after the holiday break and the Redbirds scored a 77–75 overtime victory over Washington University.

Although just 6-foot-5, Taulbee's ability to jump and run the floor enabled him to out-rebound many taller opponents and trigger the fast break. The team became known as the Runnin' Redbirds and won nine of its first 11 games after the winter break.

"Tom had the most explosive vertical jump of anyone I coached," Collie said. "You've heard of the movie, 'White Men Can't Jump.' Well, Tom could and he was a good rebounder for the size people we played back then."

One of Taulbee's most vivid memories came in a victory at Illinois Wesleyan, a traditional rivalry that took on family significance when his brother Kent later played basketball for the Titans.

"I remember that I was way out of position at the top of the key when Buzzy Feek intercepted a pass," Tom recalled. "I headed down the court, yelled for the ball, and dunked the ball two-handed. When I was running back a bunch of fraternity guys in the stands began to razz me and I looked up and winked at them. It was always a high for me to play Wesleyan."

Illinois State shared the IIAC championship with Central Michigan and, thanks to a vigorous lobbying effort by Weisbecker, secured the home court for the NCAA Midwest Regional. It wasn't supposed to make a difference, though. The University of North Dakota, coached by Bill

Fitch, was heavily favored with 6-foot-8 Little All-America forward Phil Jackson in its lineup.

Jackson, best known as Chicago Bulls coach three decades later, set a Horton Field House record with 51 points but it didn't matter because those points came in a consolation game. Jackson had fouled out early in the second half of the opening game and the Fighting Sioux were upset by a towering Louisiana Tech squad coached by Scotty Robertson, who, like Fitch, later had an NBA coaching career.

Illinois State nudged Parsons College in its opening game, then got its running game in high gear for an 89–66 upset of Louisiana Tech. Terry, playing despite a painful bone chip in one foot, scored 31 points and McGreal had 28.

Illinois State students were so excited by the school's drive into the Elite Eight that about

Celebrating the 1966–67 NCAA College Division Regional Championship. **Front: Don Feek, Steve Arends, Jerry McGreal, Ed Brucker, Gerry Sytar. Standing: Tom Taulbee, Blaine Royer, George Terry, Mike Green, Martin Bailey, Duane Bruninga, Bob Brewe.**

1,500 of them marched to President Bone's house demanding that classes be dismissed to allow them to attend the NCAA College Division National Tournament in Evansville, Ind.

Those who went to Evansville released a red-tinted pigeon named Ralph inside of Roberts Municipal Stadium before Illinois State's game against San Diego State, the nation's third-ranked college division team. With Ralph looking on from a safe perch, the Redbirds rallied from a 13-point halftime deficit to send the game to overtime.

The teams battled through three overtime periods before a pair of free throws by Feek and two more by Arends gave Illinois State a stunning 77–76 upset.

The Redbirds lost their next two games to Southwest Missouri State and 1966 champion Kentucky Wesleyan, and had to watch from the stands as the fabulous Earl "The Pearl"

Monroe—later Phil Jackson's teammate on New York Knick championship teams—led Winston-Salem to the title against the SMS Bears.

Still, the fourth-place finish was a signal honor.

A parade and pep rally, including mayors Charles Spear of Normal and Robert McGraw of Bloomington, were held to honor the basketball and wrestling teams, which both finished fourth in the NCAA that year. Even the immaculately tailored former British prime minister, Sir Anthony Eden, in town for a Stevenson Lecture, joined the players on stage during one of the most rousing celebrations in Illinois State basketball history.

❖   ❖   ❖   ❖   ❖   ❖

Basketball fans could hardly wait to see what the Redbirds would do for an encore in 1967–68. *Basketball News* ranked Illinois

State ninth in its pre-season college division poll. Four starters were back from the national tourney squad and all of them had made somebody's all-conference, all-tourney or all-opponents team.

Tom Cirks of Beecher, a 6-foot-4 transfer from Olney Community College, earned the fifth starting spot and immediately established a reputation as a quick-reacting defensive player, a solid rebounder and a bashful shooter. He didn't even attempt a shot in the opening game, a 110–85 conquest of Wisconsin-Whitewater.

"I was pretty nervous," Cirks said. "I just didn't have much confidence in my shot, so I didn't take any."

But he elevated his teammates as the Redbirds won their first seven games.

Terry scored 40 points in a 93–76 victory over Montana and 39 points in a 90–88 decision over Western Michigan as the

The left-handed Jerry McGreal (5) attacks the basket in Horton Field House. When he graduated in 1968, he was the Redbirds' No. 2 all-time scorer behind Fred Marberry and was named to the Associated Press Little All-America team.

George Terry (43) lays in two of his 40 points in a victory over Montana December 2, 1962, in Horton Field House. Tom Cirks (44) is on the left.

A ferocious competitor at just 6-4, Steve Arends, the No. 4 career rebounder in Redbird history, averaged 10.4 for his career.

Steve Fisher wasn't a prime-time player with the late 1960s Redbirds, but he later gained fame by coaching Michigan to the 1989 NCAA Championship.

Redbirds beat their only two major college opponents.

The seventh victory came by one point over Lamar University in the Pan American Tournament at Edinburg, Texas. Collie had kept a promise to seek a warmer climate. It was 70 degrees in southern Texas, more than 100 degrees warmer than Alamosa the previous year.

Host Pan American stopped the streak in the semifinals and, after the Redbirds spent an afternoon in the market across the Mexican border, Central Oklahoma thumped them in the third-place game, too.

They won their next 18 games, the school's longest winning streak in the same season and second only to the 24 games in succession that extended over two seasons in the early 1930s.

Meanwhile, Terry continued his scoring rampage. He scored between 32 and 40 points in six of the team's first 11 games and held a 28.2 scoring average. Arends and McGreal were joining in the parade. By early January, all three of them were over 1,000 career points.

The team had superb bench strength, too. Mike Green, a scrappy 5-foot-11 junior from Forest Park, Ill., cast a flinty glare at the person who referred to the replacements as subs. "Don't call us the subs," he growled. "Call us the Bandits."

It was not an empty boast. Green and the other members of ISU's second unit combined for 37 points in 10 minutes of play against nationally ranked Pan American College. That blistering pace would have been 148 points over 40 minutes.

The other Bandits were 5-foot-10 Ed Brucker of Lexington, 6-foot-1 Blaine Royer of Elgin, 6-foot-6 Bob Rath of Flossmoor, and 6-foot-7 Bob Brewe of Marseilles, Ill. Brewe and Brucker, the two seniors, started when illness or injury afflicted the regular cast. Wisconsin transfer Dave Handy, a 6-foot-3 forward from Watseka, Ill., joined them for the second semester.

The depth came in handy during an unusual conference schedule created to compensate for the withdrawal of Northern Illinois University in 1966, which left the league with only four members. The remaining schools agreed to play each other four times during the 1967–68 season, with back-to-back games on each court.

The extra games intensified emotions. The situation turned ugly one night when an Eastern Illinois player slugged Arends from behind as he rushed to assist McGreal, who had been pushed on a fast-break layup. Arends fell to the oor, unconscious, while players and fans milled round. The offending player had to retreat to enter court to stay out of the reach of angry spectators crowding behind Eastern's bench.

Game officials restored order and the second game was played the next day without incident. ISU wound up with a 12-0 conference record. Arends, McGreal and Terry never lost to Eastern or Western in three seasons.

Illinois State's 77–76 victory over Southwest Missouri was a memorable battle between nationally ranked teams that brought more than 8,000 fans into Horton Field House.

In a reprise of the previous year's national tournament, someone released a red-dyed pigeon (Ralph II) and the bird made one pass around the court before perching high on a wooden cutout of the school seal, seemingly to watch the game. When public address announcer Richard Godfrey said, "And starting for the Redbirds…," it took four minutes before he could continue introducing the team to the frenzied fans.

"The player who can't be fired up out of his mind with that support has already died and been embalmed without knowing it," wrote Dave West, a reporter for the *Canton Ledger.*

The game lived up to its billing. Tension ratcheted until, with about 15 seconds left, Southwest Missouri missed the front end of a bonus free throw opportunity while leading by one point.

The rebound skittered to the sideline near the corner. Illinois State's Taulbee sprinted to the spot and leaped over the line to retrieve the ball before it could fall out of bounds. With an acrobatic mid-air twist, he passed to teammate Bob Rath, who tossed the ball upcourt to the breaking McGreal.

With SMS all-American Lou Shepherd in his path, McGreal pulled up at the free throw line and rose for a jump shot that nestled in the net to give the Redbirds a 77–76 lead with nine seconds left. SMS missed a long-range try at the buzzer and fans swarmed onto the floor for a wild victory celebration.

Illinois State was host again for an NCAA regional and survived an upset bid in the first round when Terry swished a 20-footer with three seconds left for an 83–81 victory over DePauw. It was the Redbirds' 18th consecutive victory and ran their season record to 25-2.

The magic ended the next night. Fred Hardman, a muscular forward who had played high school basketball 15 miles up the road at Lexington, had a big game, and Indiana State ended the dream of a return to the national tourney, 98–93. The Sycamores went on to finish second in the NCAA Tournament.

But it had been a great season. The Associated Press tabbed McGreal for its Little All-America team and awarded Terry honorable mention. McGreal was the team's MVP for the third straight year and won the same honor in the IIAC for the second year.

Terry scored 609 points, the second-best season in school history then, and averaged 22.6 points while McGreal averaged 20.5. Arends set a school rebounding record with 11.2 per game and joined McGreal and Terry on the all-conference team.

They were three of a kind—all aces.

Chapter 17
ONE MORE TITLE FOR GENTLEMAN JIM (1968–1970)

F ew fans expected another great season from the Redbirds in 1968–69 after the talented trio of prime-time players had graduated, but the cupboard was not bare.

Center Tom Taulbee and forward Tom Cirks, the lone returning starters, were joined by four of the previous year's scrappy reserves who called themselves the Bandits: guards Blaine Royer and Mike Green, and forwards Bob Rath

and Dave Handy.

Added to the mix was Jerry Crabtree, a 6-foot-3 transfer from Miami (Fla.) University who could play either forward or guard.

They broke from the starting gate fast. Cirks, the reluctant shooter, led the team in scoring with 21 points in the opener, and Handy dialed 21 with 12 rebounds in a 116–83 drubbing of Whitewater State.

The Redbirds carried a 3-0 record into the IIAC Tournament (created so that the schools could return to a more traditional league schedule) and captured impressive victories of 77–65 over Central Michigan and 101–84 over host Eastern Illinois.

The left-handed Royer emerged as the most outstanding player in the tournament with 22 points against Central Michigan and 30 against

Coach Jim Collie (front) leads the celebration in front of the bench as the Redbirds won the 1969 NCAA Regional Championship at Valparaiso, continuing on to the NCAA College Division finals at Evansville.

Photographer Nelson Smith (center) was a fixture with Redbird teams for more than 53 years. Besides photographing and filming games, Smith chaperoned the Redbird cheerleaders. This group included Sherry Moore, Carolyn Lauing, Rose Warner, Nelson Smith, Linda Bitner, Karol Oltmanns, Janis Finch and Joan Love. The general services building was renamed for Smith, who died July 21, 1998, as this book was being completed.

Eastern Illinois, and backcourt partner Green joined him on the all-tournament squad.

"I know this is hard to believe," said Central Michigan coach Ted Kjolhede, "but these guards are faster and they shoot as well as last year's team."

The Redbirds lost to a pair of major college opponents in the Southern Invitational at Hattiesburg, Miss., but won their next five games for a glittering 10-2 start.

"These players don't want to be embarrassed," Collie said. "They know people are going to compare them to last year's team and they don't want to fall on their faces."

But the Redbirds lost their best rebounder and the nation's seventh-ranked field goal shooter when Cirks tore ankle ligaments scrimmaging with the Beecher (Ill.) High School team while home on vacation. He missed the rest of Illinois State's scheduled games.

Handy stepped up during the Hatter Tournament at DeLand, Fla., and scored 32 points in a 92–91 upset of Stetson University at the school's claustrophobic Armory. Handy was voted the most outstanding player in the tourney.

But with Cirks out of the lineup, the Redbirds lost five of their next six games. Still, they had enough left to tie Eastern Illinois for the IIAC championship and secure their third straight NCAA regional bid.

"What a great accomplishment for this team," Collie said. "This is the most successful team I have ever had. They have done more with the ability they have than any team I have ever coached. Who would have foreseen the possibility of our being co-champion in the conference and a national tournament team with only two regulars back this year, and one of those for only 10 games?"

The Redbirds weren't through yet. They won a nail-biter over North Park in the opening Great Lakes Regional game and rallied behind Cirks' courageous comeback to shock the host team, Valparaiso, and its coach, Gene Bartow.

Despite his painful ankle injury, Cirks played in the championship game and hauled down 12 rebounds. He wasn't the Redbirds' only hero.

Royer was voted the tournament's most outstanding player after scoring 34 points in the title game. Crabtree won all-tourney honors, too, with 28 points. Green, shut out in the first half, hit 13 in the second to help upend Valpo.

It was one of the career highlights for Taulbee, the starting center on three NCAA teams and a rebounding standout during the tourney.

"We were behind a good part of that game but a fascinating experience happened," Taulbee said. "There was never a doubt in my mind or with the other players that we would win it. The entire game we had the sense that,

Blaine Royer (45) was an honorable mention all-American in his only season as a Redbird starter, leading the Redbirds to a surprising 1969 NCAA Tournament final. Bob Rath gets ready to set a pick for Royer, who was drafted by the San Diego Clippers.

Mike Green breaks through the Redbird poster before an Illinois State home game. Seated on the right is then-Redbird football coach Gerry Hart.

like cats, when we got tired of playing with this little mouse we would gobble it up."

But Taulbee still has trouble digesting the 41–35 loss in the national tournament to Ashland (Ohio) College. Ashland, coached by Bill Musselman, lulled opponents to sleep with a ball possession offense and frustrated them with a trapping zone defense.

Taulbee regrets that the Redbirds didn't take the ball inside more often. "That zone was not as bothersome as the slow-down offense," he said. "Their middle man on defense was so slow you could have driven a caterpillar by him. Their defense was not that difficult but their offense was a killer."

Royer posted the third-highest single-season total in school history with 583 points and a 20.1 average. He shared the league's most valuable player award, joined teammate Taulbee on the all-conference team, and was selected by the San Diego Rockets in a National Basketball Association supplemental draft.

But the team's 19-9 record, conference co-championship and three tournament titles truly resulted from a team effort. Seven players averaged in double figures scoring. "This would have been a great team if we had Cirks all year," Collie said.

◆   ◆   ◆   ◆   ◆   ◆

Illinois State basketball reached the end of many eras with the 1969–70 season. Jim Collie's coaching career, the 62-year-old IIAC, and the historic basketball rivalry with Illinois Wesleyan all came to an end.

The year of change began with Athletics Director Milt Weisbecker's early announcement that Illinois State would adopt a full NCAA scholarship program and move up to major college basketball status in 1970.

As a result, Illinois State would sever ties with the IIAC after the 1969–70 school year and join Northern Illinois, Southern Illinois, Ball State and Indiana State in a new league to be known as the Conference of Midwestern Universities. That left only three teams remaining in the IIAC, so the remnants of the old "Little Nineteen" voted to disband after the year ended.

Dramatic spotlight introductions stirred the crowd and intimidated opponents in the 1960s at Horton Field House where coach Jim Collie's Redbirds ruled the roost.

Illinois State's decision to offer full athletic scholarships prompted Wesleyan to announce an end to football scheduling between the schools after the 1969 game. After Illinois State's athletic board voted to do the same in basketball, negotiations broke down between athletic administrators, and the schools decided to end the series with the January 13, 1970, game at Illinois State.

There were plenty of changes on Jim Collie's basketball roster, too. Virtually all of the players were gone from his three championship seasons. Handy and Crabtree, part-time starters the previous year, were the only returnees with significant experience.

"This will be the most inexperienced team we have had in a long time," Collie admitted.

Greg Guy, a sophomore transfer from Indiana State, and Sherrill Campbell, a senior transfer from Hofstra, provided additional experience. Guy was a 6-foot-3 guard who became the team's leading scorer. Campbell, a

shooter with exceptional range, was valuable when the team needed an outside threat.

Willie Williams led the freshman team in scoring the previous year. Although only 6-foot-4, he opened at center. Two other sophomores, Jim Smith and Myron Litwiller, were 6-5 and worked their way into the lineup.

The Redbirds raised hopes by winning three of their first four games before plunging into a five-game losing streak. After a couple more victories, they lost eight of the next 10 games. Clearly, it was not going to be a successful season.

One of those defeats was administered by Illinois Wesleyan in the last basketball game between the schools. Illinois State held a one-point lead late in the game, but Wesleyan inbounded from center court with four seconds remaining and Tom Gramkow threaded a jumper through the cords with time running out to give the Titans a 69–68 victory.

Still, Collie's overall record against Wesleyan

was 13 victories against 12 defeats—the best mark by any ISU coach against the university's time-honored rivals.

Collie didn't feel well that season. Doctors diagnosed his illness as multiple sclerosis. Early in January, when the Redbirds held a 5-6 record, he decided the timing was right for a career change. Collie announced that he would accept a position in the Office of Admissions and Records after 21 seasons of coaching.

"I long ago recognized that with the exception perhaps of people like Adolph Rupp, Hank Iba and Paul Hinkle, that we all have to quit sometime," he said. "Knowing this, I did want to make this decision at the right time.

"The factors that I considered necessary were: (1) That it be my decision; (2) I did not want to leave after an unsuccessful season; and (3) I did not want to leave when the talent 'well' had run dry. We do have good young material. The fourth point, of course, was the opportunity for a better position."

Collie was right about the talent well not running dry. He had full scholarships to offer that year for the first time. In a typically kind act, he gave all but two of them to seniors "who had played free for three years."

The other two went to freshmen Dan Witt and Doug Collins, a late-blooming guard from Benton, Ill., who turned down a scholarship offer from Illinois. Collins played high school ball for Rich Herrin, who had been Collie's captain at McKendree.

Collie did not have the opportunity to coach Collins and Witt on the varsity level because of the freshman rule, but Collins would become the greatest basketball star in Illinois State history, an NBA All-Star and coach, and a bright basketball commentator for network television.

Thirty years after he retired, Collie, in a wheelchair, attended Illinois State games on a regular basis. He also attended University High and Wesleyan games because his grandsons played for those schools and his son-in-law, Cal Hubbard, coaches at U-High.

Collie maintained his droll sense of humor, which he used to needle his grandson, Nathan Hubbard, a sophomore starter on Illinois Wesleyan's 1997 NCAA Division III champions.

"I told him that I never thought I would see the day when a grandson of mine would attend and play basketball at Illinois Wesleyan."

Gentleman Jim Collie's brilliant career not only elevated Illinois State basketball to levels previously unachieved, it also prepared the program and the university—now with more than 17,500 students—to join the highest level of collegiate athletic competition.

Chapter 18
WILL ROBINSON, TRAILBLAZER (1970)

Jim Collie's announcement in January 1970 that he would leave coaching at the end of the season gave Athletics Director Milt Weisbecker ample time to search for a successor to build a major college basketball program at Illinois State.

Weisbecker had already constructed the foundation by adopting a full NCAA scholarship program with the blessing of President Samuel Braden, following similar decisions by Southern Illinois and Northern Illinois. Two other Illinois schools, Eastern and Western, expressed a desire to stay in the Division II ranks with the reduced level of aid prevalent in the disintegrating IIAC.

The number of schools remaining in Division II was dwindling and Illinois State's enrollment had zoomed from 4,400 to 17,500 students in one decade. The timing was right to make a move. Weisbecker and his counterparts at NIU, SIU, Indiana State and Ball State agreed to form a new major basketball league, the Conference of Midwestern Universities.

"We made the decision, and I took a lot of hell for it, that the one sport we could really make an impact in was basketball," Weisbecker said. "I just felt that we really had an opportunity because of the nature of the school, the size of the school, and the field house, which was new at the time so we had a very nice facility."

Weisbecker contacted some of the best high school coaches in Illinois and college assistant coaches, then broadened his search by talking with such nationally prominent figures as Sam Jones and K.C. Jones, two former Boston Celtics, and Wayne Embry, another former pro basketball star. All three of them are African-American.

No major college basketball program in the nation had a black man as head basketball coach then, but Weisbecker was convinced he should go that direction after seeing the results of state high school tournaments in Illinois, Indiana and one other nearby state.

"I watched all three state championships on TV and when the final six teams took the court there were 29 black players and one white player. So I thought, geez, if we're going to win we're going to need some black players. Maybe if we hired a black coach that would be the thing to do."

Weisbecker theorized that a black coach would not only have a recruiting edge but also would provide strong leadership for his athletes during a time when college campuses were torn by civil rights battles and anti-war protests.

At that point, Weisbecker's mail brought letters recommending Will Robinson, a 58-year-old high school coach from Detroit, Mich., whose list of former players included such well-known athletes as Spencer Haywood, Ralph Simpson, Mel Daniels, Gene "Big Daddy" Lipscomb, Ted Sizemore and Sammy Gee.

After checking with Michigan colleagues who knew the coach, Weisbecker arranged to interview Robinson at the time of Illinois State's basketball game at Mt. Pleasant, Mich., on February 14, 1970. Discussions began in the afternoon and extended late into the night. Weisbecker became convinced he had found the right man.

"If you've got enough courage, I'm your guy," Robinson told Weisbecker.

Weisbecker had the courage.

On March 1, 1970, the *Pantagraph* devoted its entire lead sports page to the announcement that Robinson was coming to Illinois State as the first black head coach at a predominantly white Division I school. K.C. Jones of Brandeis University was the only African-American coach in the NCAA's College Division then, except for the predominantly black colleges.

"Bring on some more typewriter ribbons and copy paper," *Pantagraph* sports editor Jim Barnhart exclaimed. "Will Robinson is the head coach at Illinois State University!"

The frank-talking Robinson had no illusions as he contemplated the task of taking Illinois State into the major ranks of college basketball.

"I've reached a goal, I've broken a barrier," the coach told Charles Chamberlain of the Associated Press. "But I've collected scars along the way and I hope they don't show too much.

"I've wound up in the most illogical area in the world for a black coach. This is a farming community and there aren't many blacks."

Illinois State's enrollment of 17,500 included only 700 to 800 African-American students at that time.

"But don't get me wrong. I've wanted a head coaching job on the university level for most of the 38 years I've been in the business and it took an unprejudiced man like Milt Weisbecker to give me my chance."

◆　　◆　　◆　　◆　　◆　　◆

Robinson was born in Wadesboro, N.C., on June 3, 1911, and grew up in the tough steel mill town of Steubenville, Ohio. Football was the school's big sport but it was unusual to have

Will Robinson's great perspective on college basketball meant he wasn't above a little levity...

...during a game. In this sequence, he shares an anecdote with assistant coach Warren Crews...

black player on the team.

"Back in those days, black people didn't even attend high school," Robinson recalled for a *Detroit News* sportswriter. "We had three black kids on a squad of 80 players."

In Robinson's senior year, he quarterbacked Steubenville to the ultimate perfect season: unbeaten, untied and unscored upon in 10 games.

Robinson, who won 14 letters in five sports, also finished second in the Ohio High School golf championship in 1930 at Scioto Country Club in Columbus. Unlike other players, all of whom were white, he wasn't allowed to practice at the exclusive club nor could he stay with the team in a hotel. Instead, he roomed at a downtown YMCA.

After working as a lifeguard for a couple of years and playing semi-pro football, basketball and baseball, Robinson entered West Virginia State, an all-black school in the segregated 1930s. He won 15 letters in four sports and quarterbacked the football team to the National Negro College Championship in 1936.

Robinson entered coaching in 1938 at the Centre Avenue YMCA in Pittsburgh. His basketball team won four straight state YMCA championships, and the swimming team took five straight titles. His 1939–40 basketball team was runner-up for the National YMCA championship.

He moved to Chicago in 1942 as athletics director for the Wabash Avenue YMCA in Chicago and coach of football and swimming at Du Sable High School.

Robinson left Chicago reluctantly in 1943 when Detroit's school superintendent recruited him to help improve race relations in the wake of the Belle Isle race riots.

His coaching assignment at Miller High School was daunting. The school had no gym, pool or football field but in 13 years Robinson's teams played for 10 city championships in football and basketball.

His basketball team won the first city championship game between public and parochial champs in 1947 before 16,051 spectators, then the largest crowd in the nation ever to witness a high school game.

He adopted a full-court pressing defense for the entire game in 1947, becoming the first coach to use that aggressive style of play. Some people were shocked by the strategy.

"Fact of the matter, when I started that, people told me I was going to kill my kids because they were running all the time by pressing," he said.

One of his top 1947 players, Sammy Gee, became the first prep all-American from the state of Michigan. Gee signed a minor league baseball contract with the Brooklyn Dodgers, but was cut despite a .300 batting average.

Ironically, Robinson's college roommate, sports reporter Wendell Smith, was a key figure in Jackie Robinson's successful entry into major league baseball with the Dodgers.

Will Robinson moved to Detroit's Cass Technical from 1957–60 and then to Pershing High School for the next 10 years. Pershing won state championships in two of his last four seasons. In 38 years of coaching, he won 85 percent of his games.

...as Dennis Murray (51) looks on from the bench.

One of Will Robinson's most gifted players was Robert "Bubbles" Hawkins, a prep all-American from Detroit.

Will Robinson's youthful appearance belies the years he not only spent coaching youngsters, but breaking down barriers.

Beginning in 1957, Robinson also scouted for the Detroit Lions of the NFL and uncovered such talent as Roger Brown from Maryland State College and Lem Barney of Jackson State.

Meanwhile, his high school teams produced such prize basketball pupils as early American Basketball Association stars Haywood, Simpson and Daniels, as well as the late Big Daddy Lipscomb of the NFL, and Sizemore, baseball's National League rookie of the year in 1969. Major colleges came running for his athletes but not for the coach.

❖   ❖   ❖   ❖   ❖   ❖

"I never went after the job here," he said after taking the Illinois State position, "but in years gone by I've asked for coaching jobs at Michigan and Michigan State. Fritz Crisler and Biggie Munn—close friends—always put their arms around me. They said, 'You're a great coach, a fine man, but...'

"It wasn't that I was too old. I was too black."

Robinson's frustration reached its peak in a situation involving Haywood and the University of Detroit. Robinson was both coach and legal guardian for Haywood.

Haywood led the U.S. Olympic basketball team to the gold medal in 1968 after spending a year at Trinidad (Colo.) Junior College, then transferred to the University of Detroit with the understanding that Robinson would become coach after Haywood's sophomore year. But when Bob Calihan retired from coaching at the end of the season, Detroit gave the job to Jim Harding instead.

"They promised me the job," Robinson said. "After I gave them Spencer, they reneged on the issue when it came down to hiring."

Haywood left school and signed with the Denver Rockets of the ABA. Eventually, his legal case paved the way for any underclassman to become eligible for the NBA draft.

Detroit's snub of Robinson in 1969 set the stage for his move to ISU just a year later.

After waiting so many years for the opportunity,

Robinson had to wait another 22 days before beginning duties at Illinois State because his Pershing High School basketball team kept winning games in what was supposed to be a rebuilding season. Led by sophomore superstar Robert "Bubbles" Hawkins, the Doughboys gave Robinson his second state championship as a farewell gift. Eventually, all of Pershing's starters would join him at Illinois State.

Robinson approached his new position with confidence.

"I want a team that when we go down south we win," he told sportswriters. "I want a team that when we play UCLA at UCLA, we win."

Statements like that one grabbed everyone's attention but he also was in a reflective mood when he expressed gratitude for the chance to finally coach college basketball as he approached his 59th birthday.

"I am but one generation removed from slavery and I cannot put into words what it means to me to get an opportunity to succeed at something that I love so dearly," he said. "That's what this country is all about."

Chapter 19

WHERE THERE'S A WILL, THERE'S A WAY (1970–1972)

W ill Robinson had to use the hand he was dealt in his first season at Illinois State because of the freshman rule. While he stockpiled awesome height on his freshman team, the varsity squad he inherited possessed just moderate size.

But it did have Doug Collins, the all-state guard from Benton who was destined to become the most celebrated basketball player in school history.

Collins and point guard Dan Witt, a Little All-State selection at Kaneland, moved up from the previous year's freshman team. They joined holdover regulars Greg Guy, Myron Detwiller and Jim Smith to form the early-season starting lineup.

Guy, the top scorer in the previous season, was not fully recovered from a broken ankle in a summer game at Lincoln. He re-injured the ankle during the season, and Robinson reshuffled the starting lineup to include Dennis Murray, who was Spencer Haywood's understudy on Robinson's 1967 state championship team. Murray, 6-foot-5, transferred from Burlington Junior College in Iowa. He and Smith were the tallest starters on Robinson's first Illinois State squad.

"We definitely do not have an exceptionally big man, and that in itself makes you uneasy in basketball competition," Robinson said as he prepared for the season. "We're being open minded about it, though, and hoping for the best."

The freshman team was another story. Robinson recruited a dozen lofty players topped by 6-foot-8 Clarence Weaver, 6-foot-9 Epney Bacon, 6-foot-10 Steve Nelson, 6-foot-10 James Floyd and 6-foot-11 Ron deVries.

Robinson brought his Pershing High School assistant, John Parker, with him to work with the freshmen and added native Illinoisan Bob Ortegel to the staff for recruiting help. The veteran Warren Crews, an assistant for two previous ISU coaches, was Robinson's varsity assistant.

Fans were so eager to see Robinson's varsity matched against his towering freshmen that 5,000 showed up for a game-type scrimmage. The more mature varsity team barely won, 76–73, but ticket demand and media coverage continued to soar.

Although the university had declared for an NCAA University Division ("major") status, Illinois State still had a College Division schedule and presented Robinson with an 80–67 victory over Bemidji State in his first collegiate game.

The Redbirds had a target on their backs for their next assignment, a tournament with their former IIAC opponents at Macomb. ISU split the two games, but Collins gave a hint of what was to come by totaling 53 points and winning the tourney's MVP award unanimously.

"Doug hasn't even scratched the surface yet," Robinson declared. "He has excellent potential because he has such tremendous desire. He wants to learn and he works at it all the time."

Collins led his team in scoring for 13 of the next 14 games with high marks of 40 against Indiana State, 39 in an overtime victory at Southeast Missouri and 37 at Ball State. He ranked among the nation's top 10 scorers with a 28.3 average.

Deep into February, however, the Redbirds were struggling with an 11-10 record and mired in the second division of the Midwestern Conference. By contrast, the freshman team was sailing along with a 14-2 mark.

At that point, their fortunes changed. The frosh blew a lead in the final minute of a disappointing 75–73 loss to Illinois and dropped their final four games. On the other hand, the varsity closed its campaign with five straight victories for a 16-10 record.

During that span, the Redbirds drew more than 8,000 fans for an 87–76 victory over league champion Southern Illinois, which was on the schedule for the first time since 1962. Collins, who had 34 points, and Smith, who scored 26 when the teams played at Carbondale, both hailed from the southern region of the state.

Three of the late triumphs came on the road. The Redbirds finished with a flourish when Collins scored 44 points and Smith leaped high to swat Southwest Missouri's last shot away in a thrilling 89–88 overtime victory at Springfield, Mo.

Collins shattered Fred Marberry's 15-year-old season scoring record with 743 points, a 28.6 average. He won all-Midwestern Conference honors and became a second-team academic all-American.

Robinson told the *Pantagraph's* Jim Barnhart that Collins could tote a higher scoring average next year when those tall freshmen became eligible.

"It depends on how I set up the club and how they take to him," the coach said. "If they take to him, he'll score more than he does now. With his talent, he'll be great."

Illinois State's first seven-footer, Ron deVries holds or shares every Redbird rebounding record.

Until the 1972–73 season, freshmen weren't eligible for varsity competition. Freshman teams often included players from other sports. Dan Roan, a Redbird golfer from 1971–75, played on the last Redbird freshman team. He became WGN-TV's sports director.

A transition player from the Collie era to the Robinson era, Greg Guy gave the Redbirds some finesse.

◆　◆　◆　◆　◆　◆

Doug Collins did reach for greatness during the 1971–72 season, starting with a 40-point salvo against Oral Roberts and finishing with an invitation to the U.S. Olympic tryouts—an honor that thrust him into the international spotlight after he was selected to play in the

Munich Olympics.

Robinson was successful in securing a University Division schedule, and Collins drew attention as one of the nation's top scorers. Collins broke his own school record with 847 points, a 32.6 average, and finished third behind Dwight Lamar of Southwestern Louisiana (36.3) and Richard Fuqua of Oral Roberts (35.9) for the national scoring championship.

Collins' high game of 55 points against Ball State, which broke Al Meyer's school record by four points, was the second-highest game by a major college player that season.

Collins and Fuqua met head-to-head in the opening game and Collins won the battle, 40–31. But Fuqua's team won the war, 95–93, on Elden Lawyer's last-second shot with evangelist Oral Roberts beaming from his seat in Horton Field House.

Collins scored 30 points or better 15 times that season. In addition to the 55-point peak, he had four games in the 40s. The accelerated schedule didn't slow him down, either. He scored 39 points against Iowa State's "bellybutton defense," prompting Cyclone coach Maury John to declare, "If there is a finer guard around, I'd like to know who he is." John made that comment a week after his team played UCLA.

However, the Redbirds lost the Iowa State game, and they learned more about the perils of the road when they played back-to-back games at Pacific and Long Beach State in February.

Pacific made 41 of 53 free throw attempts en route to winning its 35th straight home game, 107–94, at Stockton Civic Center, which Jim Barnhart described as "an old-time opera house that was built in 1925 and obsolete in 1926."

Illinois State outscored Pacific by five field goals but lost four players on fouls, including Collins, who scored 42 points before departing with 1:32 left to a standing ovation from the partisan crowd.

Three days later, Jerry Tarkanian's nationally ranked Long Beach State team won its 51st straight home game, 88–63. Illinois State trailed only 42–35 at halftime with Collins scoring 22 points, but Tarkanian switched his team to a zone and held Collins to four points in the second half.

Robinson still shakes his head about those games and others like them as he tried to entice established major teams to the ISU schedule. He was at their mercy for dates, location and officials.

"We couldn't get teams to play us, except at their place," he said. "And always the fix was in. You couldn't beat teams there.

"When we played Tarkanian out in Long Beach, I said to him, 'Did you want to win that bad?' after the game. He ignored my comment all together."

Robinson also had to weather an NCAA investigation during the season. In January, the NCAA issued a reprimand because the university used an improper grant-in-aid form and Robinson, in his enthusiasm, had inadvertently conducted a tryout early in his tenure. There were no sanctions against him or the university, though.

The Pacific and Long Beach games, followed by a 99–85 home loss to Northern Illinois, left Illinois State with a 10-10 record. But just as they had the year before, the Redbirds closed with a winning streak for a second straight 16-10 record.

This time the streak was six games (seven including an exhibition with Athletes in Action). Two of the Redbirds' finest performances came against conference rivals Northern Illinois and Southern Illinois.

NIU was riding high with an 18-3 record and a post-season tournament bid seemingly locked up when Illinois State scored an 86–85 upset at DeKalb. The Huskies led by five points with 2:22 to play but Collins stole the ball twice for driving scores and connected from the corner to put the Redbirds ahead. Northern tied the game on a free throw, but Dan Witt, playing near his hometown, won the game with his only free throw of the night with eight seconds left.

Their victory hunger satisfied, the Redbirds went to a nearby restaurant and downed some 60 hamburgers after the game.

Illinois State's victory knocked the Huskies out of tournament consideration despite their fine season record of 21-4 and conference championship mark of 7-1.

The season finale with Southern Illinois became the first Illinois State basketball game to be televised live on a commercial station. Peoria's ABC affiliate, then known as WRAU, beamed the signal throughout central Illinois and sports director Lorn Brown, who became the Chicago White Sox broadcaster, handled the play-by-play.

The game had a special significance for Collins and Smith, who hailed from the southern part of the state, and also for Athletics Director Weisbecker, who played football and baseball at SIU.

A record crowd estimated at 8,500 squeezed into Horton Field House and saw the Redbirds capture a pressure-packed 88–84 triumph. Collins came through with 36 points and 6-11 sophomore center Ron deVries, only 18 years old and still growing, chipped in with 21 points and 22 rebounds.

As it turned out, that was Illinois State's last game in the Midwestern Conference. The league folded after the season when Northern Illinois and Ball State joined the Mid-American Conference to secure a home for their football teams.

The victory over SIU left fans eager for the next season. Tall sophomores deVries, Stepney Bacon and Clarence Weaver gained significant playing time behind senior starters Jim Smith and Myron Litwiller.

Bacon was on the all-tournament team at the Chip Cage Classic in Mt. Pleasant, Mich., where he hauled down 22 rebounds in one game. Weaver moved into the lineup when Dennis Murray left school and was on the all-tourney team at the Dominican Holiday Tournament in Racine, Wis., which the Redbirds won. DeVries averaged better than 11 rebounds a game and was second to Collins in individual scoring.

Help was on the way from the freshman team, too. Rick Whitlow, a magnificent athlete from Michigan City, Ind., actually had beaten Collins to the 55-point plateau in an early-season freshman game and led the yearlings with a 26.7 average. Calvin Harper, the center for Robinson's state champs at Pershing, awed fans with his raw power the night he had 26 points and 27 rebounds and then, when attacked by frustrated opponents, tossed several of his tormentors to the floor like so many Beanie Babies.

Collins was coming back, too, despite being drafted by the Denver Rockets of the American Basketball Association.

"We've got some winning to do around here before I go anywhere else," Collins said.

n 1970–71, Doug Collins burst onto the college basketball scene with style.

Chapter 20

DOUG COLLINS, OLYMPIC HERO (1972–1973)

Basketball season never ended for Doug Collins in 1972.

A steady stream of honors flowed his way, highlighted by the Chicago Press Club's Abe Saperstein Award given annually to the nation's top player. Previous winners were Austin Carr, Spencer Haywood, Elvin Hayes, Kareem Abdul-Jabbar and Cazzie Russell.

Will Robinson took special pride in the award because his college roommate from four decades ago, Wendell Smith, presented the huge trophy to Collins at halftime of a Harlem Globetrotters game at Chicago's International Amphitheater. Smith was president of the Chicago Press Club.

Then came the crowning achievement: an invitation to the U.S. Olympic tryouts and selection to the 12-player team that would represent America in the Munich Games. It was a dream come true.

"It's the greatest thing that ever happened to me," Collins told one reporter.

Collins became an American folk hero with his gutsy performance against the Soviet Union in the most controversial basketball championship in Olympic history.

The young American players, all college students except for one AAU player, trimmed a 10-point Soviet lead to one. It was 49–48 and the Soviets were freezing the ball with time running down.

With six seconds left, Collins made a brilliant steal near mid-court and drove desperately for the American basket. As he leaped for a layup, he was knocked headfirst into the basket support. Stunned, he lay motionless on the floor for several seconds.

Then, his head clearing, he sank two pressure-packed free throws to give the Americans their only lead of the game, 50–49, with three seconds to play.

Broadcaster Jim Durham, Athletics Director Milt Weisbecker and Doug Collins watch Will Robinson at the microphone with Robinson's former college roommate, Wendell Smith, as Collins receives the Abe Saperstein Award during halftime of a Harlem Globetrotters game at Chicago's original International Amphitheater.

The "Backcourt Magician" was the first Illinois State athlete to get his picture on the cover of *Sports Illustrated*.

Those three seconds will live forever in basketball infamy.

The Soviet Union was handed the ball and passed inbounds, but play was stopped as the time hit one second because a Soviet coach was on the floor. Referees returned the ball to the Russians with one second to go, a full-court throw missed the mark, and the Americans pummeled Collins happily in celebration of an apparent victory.

Then, unbelievably, an international basketball executive intervened and ordered the final three seconds to be replayed. This time the Russians threw an 85-foot pass to Aleksander Belov, who knocked down the two players guarding him and made the short layup to win it.

It was the first time in 36 years of Olympic basketball that the United States had lost, a streak which had reached 63 games. U.S. coach Hank Iba protested the game, to no avail. The Americans boycotted the awards ceremony and to this day have not accepted the silver medals for second place.

"We didn't do it as a protest," Collins said. "We just felt inside us that we had won the gold medal."

The Olympics ended in September after classes had started for the fall semester. Collins came home to a hero's welcome with a rally at Hancock Stadium. His hometown of Benton greeted him with a 15-vehicle motorcade including fire trucks with sirens escorting the convertible that carried Collins around the town square and to the high school football stadium, where he spoke to some 600 townspeople.

The 1972–73 basketball season was fast approaching and Collins hardly had time to catch his breath before a series of exhibition games in Joliet, Pekin and at Rend Lake Junior College near Benton.

◆　　◆　　◆　　◆　　◆　　◆

The 1972–73 season was one of the most anticipated basketball campaigns in school history and not just because of Doug Collins' great Olympic performance. Will Robinson had assembled another awesome array of incoming talent, and this year the NCAA began allowing freshmen to play varsity basketball.

The freshman class included Bubbles Hawkins, the prep all-American who led Robinson's last Pershing team to the Michigan state championship; Roger Powell, another prep all-American from Joliet Central; Mike Bonczyk, the playmaking guard for the great Dolton Thornridge High School teams that posted a 64-1 record while winning 1971 and 1972 state championships; and Richard Jones, an all-state forward from Alabama.

Bonczyk also played baseball at ISU and was the centerfielder on the 1976 NCAA regional team. His father, Ed, had been a baseball pitcher at Illinois State and then coached at Thornton Community College. Gene Smithson, who joined Robinson's coaching staff the previous year, used his south suburban coaching contacts to help recruit Bonczyk.

Rick Whitlow, a guard with big-time skills, and Calvin Harper, the 6-foot-7 strong man, were up from the freshman team.

Then there were the three junior giants: Stepney Bacon, Ron deVries and Clarence Weaver formed an imposing trio of players for the front line.

Finally, there were the two seniors, Collins and point guard Dan Witt. Both had started for two seasons. By now, Collins was one of the most celebrated athletes in America.

Robinson's task was to blend those players together for Illinois State's first season as a basketball independent in more than six decades. It proved to be a difficult assignment.

In retrospect, it is obvious that the team's abundant talent was not matched by maturity. More than half of the players had no college basketball varsity experience. They were eager to display their ability but it would be difficult for Robinson to find enough minutes to satisfy all of them.

"They better be used to each other before the first game," Robinson said. "If they take a few games to get going, we're in trouble."

The group never really came together as a unit. The Redbirds were 11-1 at home, 1-0 on a neutral court, and 1-11 on foreign floors. Defeats in five of their last seven games cost them an opportunity to capitalize on Collins' public acclaim with a National Invitation Tournament bid.

"If we had not had the freshman eligibility rule kick in, that team might have been different," Whitlow speculated years later from his vantage point as a television sports director in Jackson, Miss. "We had great super stars but there was a chemistry thing that was doomed from the beginning because there were so many elements and factions. There wasn't enough time or enough of anything to mesh this all together."

Whitlow, a superb shotmaker, was thrust into an unfamiliar role as point guard because he was too talented to leave out of the lineup. "That team just did not have a rudder," said Whitlow. "I could have been that rudder, but I didn't have the point guard mentality."

But they had good times, too, in their eye-catching uniforms with red, white and blue vertical stripes on the pants.

Their lone road victory was a beauty, an 81–67 triumph before a hostile crowd and unfamiliar officiating at Arkansas in the third game on the schedule. It wasn't easy, Robinson said.

"We rebounded the ball and ran a fast break down the floor and the referee blew the whistle and said the basket didn't count. Three-second violation. And we were on the fast break! How the hell is it going to be a three-second violation?"

When the players were on the same page, they put together awesome numbers: 119–67 over Central Missouri; 118–70 over Winona State; 137–72 over MacMurray (a scoring record that still stands). But team harmony suffered when they left home.

When the Redbirds lost games at Pacific and California over the winter holiday, Robinson shoved freshmen Jones and Bonczyk into the starting lineup with Collins, deVries and Harper in a home game with LSU-New Orleans.

"We have to get something going," Robinson said. "I'm unhappy that we haven't played better. Our potential is better than our performance has been."

Collins responded with a school-record 57 points. He made 10 straight points in an overtime period, but fouled out with about two minutes to play. Bubbles Hawkins made a pair of jump shots in the last minute to give Illinois State a 103–98 victory.

Curry Kirkpatrick of *Sports Illustrated*, who was in town to interview Collins, was impressed. Kirkpatrick made Collins the focus of his feature story on the nation's best guards, and Collins' picture was on the magazine's cover instead of a football photo during Super Bowl week.

As coach and player, Will Robinson and Doug Collins elevated Illinois State basketball.

At the end of one of his signature steal-and-layup moves, Doug Collins soars over the north goal at Horton Field House as Rick Whitlow (22) trails the play.

But Kirkpatrick also saw the Redbirds out of sync when he accompanied the team to a game at Ball State. Collins had 20 points at halftime and the Redbirds led by nine, but the team was disorganized. Once when Collins made a steal, Hawkins cut in front of him to take the ball and go in for a layup. Collins missed nearly eight minutes of the second half with an upset stomach and Ball State won the game.

The Redbirds regrouped for their first appearance in the Big Apple a few days later. They played Morehead State at Nassau Coliseum in a doubleheader with Southwestern Louisiana going against Cincinnati. The games showcased SLU's Dwight "Bo" Lamar, the nation's leading scorer the previous year, and Collins, the Olympic hero who finished third.

The two engaged in a shooting exhibition the previous day at halftime of a New York Nets game and Collins won the event handily by making 17 of 25 shots from 25 feet or more away from the basket. Lamar made 12 of his attempts.

Robinson put another freshman, Powell, into the lineup against Morehead State and the long-range bomber pumped in 30 points to lead a 107–91 triumph. Whitlow scored 28, Harper had 14 rebounds, and Collins contributed 21 points and nine assists. It was an impressive showing for the Redbirds' first foray into New York.

The famous "*Sports Illustrated* Jinx"—noted athletes meeting untimely injuries after appearing on *SI's* cover—struck Collins when the January 15 issue came out with his photo on the cover. Soon after the magazine reached the newsstands he cracked his left thumb in a practice session. Fortunately, he was right-handed.

A song called "The Ballad of Doug Collins," based in part on the *Sports Illustrated* article, became a big hit on local radio. The opening lines of the song, composed and performed by Michael LeGary, included a nickname inspired by Collins' toothpick-thin frame: "It's Doug the Jet, ol' 'Pick' Collins, slidin' through the trees. He moves as quick as lightnin' as the defense seems to freeze."

The game the Redbirds enjoyed most was Pacific's visit on January 20. To a man, the

Few athletes provide as much personal and public support for their former schools as Doug Collins, shown here during one of his appearances at an Illinois State fund-raiser.

"Doug the Jet" wasn't a million-seller, but it was a hit record in central Illinois. Michael LeGary, who composed and sang the song, is pictured at left.

players felt they had been victimized by hometown officiating in two previous games in Stockton, Calif. They had something to prove.

Illinois State jumped on the Tigers for an 8–0 lead in the first 90 seconds and thrilled the wildly cheering Horton Field House crowd with a 95–56 conquest. "It was a hell of a ball game for the ISU fans because they didn't believe basketball can be played that well," Robinson said.

DeVries savored the victory. "We wanted to find out how much better we were," he said. "We knew we were better than they were but we weren't sure by how much."

Thirty-nine points better, it turned out. "Sure this means something special," Collins added. "Our people can see now how much better we are. Those losses hurt out there."

Pacific's coach, Stan Morrison, was gracious after the blitz. "Our basic problem was that we got our brains beat out by a great team which was inspired and a team which played well

together," he said.

The Redbirds nourished hopes for a National Invitation Tournament bid after beating Indiana State to go 11-7 with seven games to play. Then Ball State jolted them with their only home-court defeat, signaling a four-game tailspin. They ended up losing five of the last seven games to extinguish post-season hopes.

Even though they lost, the Redbirds were entertaining. Their game at Oral Roberts matched two of the nation's premier guards, Collins and the Titans' Richard Fuqua. Collins scored 41 points, hitting 10 of his first 11 shots and needing only 26 attempts for his 19 baskets. Fuqua scored 49 points but put up an amazing 49 shots, hitting only 19 of them.

The Redbirds saw basketball great Bill Russell the next day when they stopped at the Houston airport on their way to Jacksonville, Fla., and Collins mentioned

Fuqua's shotgun game. "It takes a lot of heart to put the ball up there 49 times," Russell said in amusement.

Hawkins had his best game of the season with 30 points at Jacksonville and Collins produced 21, but it wasn't enough and the Redbirds lost, 95–86.

Collins scored 39 points against Western Illinois in his final home game as a collegian. Collins' uniform number 20 was retired in an emotional post-game ceremony. "If I had it to do all over," Collins told the throng, "I would still enroll at Illinois State."

Collins finished with Illinois State's single-game, season and career scoring records, amassing an amazing 2,240 points in three seasons. He became the school's only consensus all-American with first-team honors on virtually every dream team that was announced.

His subsequent achievements are well known to basketball fans.

As coach of the Chicago Bulls, Doug Collins molded a young team which became one of the best in NBA history.

Collins became the National Basketball Association's No. 1 draft pick and signed a contract for more than $1 million dollars with the Philadelphia 76ers.

Coincidentally, Jim Durham, the bright young broadcaster of Redbird basketball on WJBC radio, also went to the NBA that year as the voice of the Chicago Bulls. Durham would have a long and illustrious basketball television career as well.

The diminutive Durham's successor was the robust, golden-voiced Art Kimball, who would be part of the central Illinois and statewide sports scene for most of the next quarter-century. When Kimball departed WJBC for a brief stint in Peoria television in 1981, his successor was the affable Dick Luedke, who would describe more than 500 consecutive Redbird basketball games before leaving broadcasting after Illinois State's 1998 NCAA Tournament appearance. All played key roles in continuing a tradition of excellence in play-by-play announcers for Redbird basketball.

◆   ◆   ◆   ◆   ◆   ◆

Collins' all-star career with the Sixers was cut short by injuries but he has stayed in the game as coach of the Chicago Bulls, an NBA commentator with TNT, coach of the Detroit Pistons, and today as an NBA commentator for NBC television.

Collins was just as competitive and successful in the classroom as he was on the basketball court. In 1995, when he joined an elite group in the GTE Academic All-American Hall of Fame, he told the audience in Washington, D.C., about his drive to excel as a student.

"When I walked into a classroom I wanted to be the best student," he said. "I hated it when someone saw me walk into a classroom and said, 'Don't look off my paper today.'

"I said, 'Don't even think about that. I'm going to kick your butt on this test.' And I would."

Collins has maintained meaningful ties with Illinois State. He is active in contributing to the Redbird Education and Scholarship Funds and has spearheaded other fund drives. The Chicagoland golf outing that carries his name has emerged as one of the athletics department's key annual events.

His number, displayed on a banner hanging from the rafters of Redbird Arena, is the only one to be retired in the first century of Illinois State men's basketball.

Horton Field House was a warm and friendly home of Redbird basketball from 1963 to 1989.

Chapter 21
WILL POWER
(1973–1975)

The year 1 A.D. (After Doug) was the dawning of a new era. For the first time since Robinson had come to Illinois State, all of the players on the roster were his recruits.

Seven returning lettermen for 1973–74—Stepney Bacon, Ron deVries, Calvin Harper, Bubbles Hawkins, Roger Powell, Clarence Weaver and Rick Whitlow—all had starting experience.

They were challenged by demanding road games at Purdue, Louisville, Idaho State, San Diego State and Oral Roberts.

But one big-time team came to Illinois State that year, and the Redbirds seized the opportunity by beating Washington State of the Pacific Eight, 72–63. Powell made 12 of 18 shots, but it was scoring balance and the rebounding of deVries and Harper that kept the Redbirds in front throughout the game.

Three weeks into the season, Illinois State was the only undefeated team among Illinois' eight major schools with a 5-0 record and was averaging about 20 points and 20 rebounds a game more than its opponents. The Redbirds had a different scoring leader in each game, too, with deVries, Hawkins, Harper, Powell and Whitlow taking turns.

"I am very happy that the scoring has been passed around like that," Robinson said. "This makes for a very wholesome situation."

That brought the Redbirds to the most dangerous phase of their schedule: six road games in the next seven starts beginning with Purdue—Illinois State's first Big Ten opponent in 54 years—at West Lafayette, Ind. Robinson understood the challenge.

"We've come to the mountain top," he told a friend in the locker room while his players were warming up at Mackey Arena.

Thanks to Powell's 7-of-9 shooting and 18 points, the score was tied seven times before Purdue moved to a 51–45 halftime lead. Purdue's defensive pressure turned a tight game into a 114–85 rout in the final seven minutes. Both teams shot 62 percent from the field, but 32 ISU turnovers gave the Boilermakers 21 more attempts.

The grinding road schedule took its toll. After a talent-laden Oral Roberts team handed the Redbirds their sixth straight loss, ORU coach Ken Trickey noted that "Illinois State has had to go all over America to play. You put them in the Missouri Valley and see if they can't play. You put them in the Big Ten and see if they can't play. I'll guarantee you, they have a fine ball club."

Robinson drew little comfort from the praise. "It's not much fun to play well and lose," he said. "I'd rather play bad and win."

His team kept its confidence, though, and won 12 of the last 15 games to finish with a 17-9 record, the best in Robinson's tenure. The exciting windup produced a school-record 58-point outburst by Hawkins and a memorable shootout against nationally ranked Louisville.

But first, Horton Field House was the scene of a bizarre controversy that cost Bill Harrell of Morehead State his coaching job.

Harrell left his top six players at home to prepare for Ohio Valley Conference games and showed up in Normal with a collection of seldom-used underclassmen. Illinois State thrashed the depleted Eagles, 113–74, but Harrell's actions angered Robinson.

"If I'd do what he did," Robinson said, "I'd get run out of coaching."

Athletics Director Milt Weisbecker was steaming, too.

"This was a hoax on our team, a hoax on our students, and a hoax on our fans," Weisbecker said. "A guy like that should not be in college athletics, and I told him that."

Harrell resigned a week later amid a firestorm of national media criticism.

Back on the basketball court, the silken-smooth Hawkins rocked Horton Field House by scoring 58 points—NCAA Division I's best single-game performance of the year—in a 130–93 rout of Northern Illinois on February 20. The total broke Collins' record of 57 set the previous year.

Hawkins' roommate, Mike Bonczyk, set the table by dishing out a school-record 20 assists. What's more, Whitlow chipped in with 32 points in the same game despite sitting out the final 10 minutes. The Hawkins-Whitlow combination accounted for 90 points, still a school record for two players.

Illinois State carried a 17-8 record and glimmering hopes for a post-season bid into the final game at nationally ranked Louisville, the Missouri Valley Conference champion. The Redbirds went down with their guns blazing, 117–107, against a Louisville lineup featuring all-Americans Junior Bridgeman and Allen Murphy. The combined 224 points set a collegiate record for Louisville's Freedom Hall.

Whitlow had his finest game of the season with 38 points and Hawkins delivered 29. DeVries capped his college career with 17 points and 19 rebounds.

"It was a damn good effort," Robinson said.

Philadelphia 76er superstars George McGinnis (30) and Julius Erving (6) got quite a battle from New York Net players Butch Van Breda Kolff (left) and Bubbles Hawkins (right). Hawkins, who left ISU after his junior year, led the Nets in scoring in 1977.

"We could have folded when we were down 13 in the first half and they were shooting so well but we came back and took the lead. I'm really proud of that effort."

DeVries, the team's most valuable player, set season and career rebounding records that still stand and he shares the single-game record of 24. He is the only player at Illinois State to have more than 1,000 rebounds in his career and he totaled more than 1,000 points, too.

DeVries, who also lettered in tennis during

his freshman year at Illinois State, had come a long way in basketball since growing too tall for ice hockey in high school.

"Anyone who saw me play as a freshman and again as a senior would know that Coach Robinson is a great coach," he said. "I was a pitiful freshman."

But he was a great senior. He played well in the Aloha Classic at Honolulu and in other post-season events, leading to his selection by the Los Angeles Lakers in the NBA draft. The Lakers

were grooming him for a roster spot when a back injury ended his playing career.

◆   ◆   ◆   ◆   ◆   ◆

Robinson won his greatest victory just by coming back for the 1974–75 season, his fifth at Illinois State. He had surgery for prostate cancer shortly after his 63rd birthday the previous June.

"I feel fortunate to be alive," Robinson said.

A prep football all-American quarterback, Rick Whitlow proved his skills on the basketball court were top drawer, too. Since his playing career ended, Whitlow has been a successful sportscaster, including a stint as analyst with Art Kimball at WJBC radio.

Other problems seemed minor by comparison with cancer, but they had to be faced when he returned to work. Scheduling was a continuous headache. Fans grumbled because name teams refused to come to Horton Field House.

"Criticism is so unfair," Robinson said. "People just don't know what's involved. We just can't dictate our scheduling.

"I've been calling two schools regularly for three weeks. I haven't been able to get in touch at either one. It isn't because they're not in.

They just don't want to talk to me.

"This does something to you as a person."

Major college coaches friendly with Robinson when he was developing high school talent did not want to play against him at ISU. Al McGuire of Marquette was one of the coaches that Robinson contacted.

"Al was the most honest with me," Robinson said. "Al said, 'Will, I'm not going to play you until I see you play. And should I play you, I'm going to play you at my place and you're not

going to get a return game.' Al said that to me. I didn't like it, but he was honest with me."

Robinson also had to adjust to new leadership in the athletics department. Milt Weisbecker was now directing the university's development and alumni offices. Robinson did not enjoy the same trusting relationship with the new athletics director, Warren Schmakel.

Prospects looked rosier on the court, however. Robinson gathered the most talented basketball squad ever assembled at Illinois

Roger Powell's offensive game packed a deadly combination of long-range marksmanship and slashing moves to the basket.

State for the 1974–75 campaign. The Redbirds had no fewer than five former prep all-Americans: Bubbles Hawkins and Roger Powell from previous seasons and newcomers Billy Lewis, Cyrus Mann and Jeff Wilkins.

For that matter, Rick Whitlow and Calvin Harper were high school all-Americans, too, but in football instead of basketball. In fact, Harper became Illinois State's starting offensive tackle in 1974 and bulked up so much for football that he dropped basketball after a few games.

Wilkins, a powerful 7-foot sophomore, and incoming point guard George Tometich had played at Black Hawk College for John Parker, who had left Robinson's staff in 1973 for a head coaching position. Lewis (6-6) and Mann (6-10) were blue-chip freshmen.

The schedule was a barrier to instant success. Illinois State had only 11 home games on a 26-game schedule.

So it was no wonder that the Redbirds started the season with a 1-3 record. Lewis showed he was ready for college basketball with 25 points in his debut but they lost to St. Louis by two points in overtime at the old Kiel Auditorium. Then they lost by two points in Florida State's stifling Tully Gym and by one point on a last-second shot at Butler's historic Hinkle Field House.

Their next road game was at UNLV, where Jerry Tarkanian waited with another power-house that prevailed by 11. Aside from Hawkins' 32-point game, the best part of the Las Vegas experience came when Robinson took several members of his entourage backstage before a late-night show to meet the Mills Brothers, his friends from long ago in Pittsburgh.

But the Redbirds were too good to stay down. They strung together a four-game winning streak highlighted by Whitlow's 51-point outburst in a 91–84 overtime victory over Southern Illinois and future NBA star Mike Glenn.

"It's funny how things work out sometimes," said Whitlow, who hit 19 of 31 field goals and 13 of 14 free throws against SIU. "I went into that game thinking defense. You have to be defensive oriented when a player like Mike Glenn comes to town."

Two nights later, Whitlow pumped in 38 points to pace a 107–98 victory over Oral Roberts. He was averaging 22.8 points a game with a glossy 54.5 percent field goal accuracy.

But another succession of road losses at Bradley, Pacific and South Alabama threatened team unity. Hawkins, Powell and point guard George Tometich all were sidelined.

Tometich's injury spelled opportunity for

Bonczyk. He picked Northern Illinois apart for the second year, raising his school record from 20 to 23 assists in one game against the Huskies. The chief beneficiaries were Whitlow with 34 points and Hawkins with 22.

The Redbirds had one other significant squad loss late in the season when Robinson suspended Mann, the talented freshman, with five games remaining. Mann's great potential was evident the night he had 22 points and eight rebounds against Southern Illinois center Joe Meriweather at Carbondale, but he had a troubled personal life. He left after that season as the Boston Celtics drafted him in the fourth round.

Once again the Redbirds finished the season with a flourish, winning the last six games for a 16-10 record. As tough as the road had been, Robinson achieved his two most gratifying victories away from home in West Virginia, the state where he had attended a segregated college.

Illinois State handed Marshall its first home-court loss, 80–77, late in January at Huntington, W.Va., with a balanced team effort led by Whitlow's 22 points.

The Redbirds topped that effort with a stunning performance in the final game of the season at West Virginia. The Redbirds broke from a 40-all tie to lead, 57–50, at halftime and held off the Mountaineers, 105–99. Whitlow and Lewis were the leaders with 31 and 28 points.

Beating the two West Virginia schools was the crowning achievement of Robinson's career at Illinois State.

"When I attended college at West Virginia State, which was an all-black school, I couldn't even go to watch them practice," he said. "I couldn't even go to see a game. They wouldn't sell you a ticket. It was that segregated. That was in the Thirties. Then in 1970-something I'm playing those teams and beating them at their place."

Once again, a tournament bid eluded the Redbirds. "We're the best non-rated team in the country," Robinson said.

However, post-season honors did go to Whitlow, the team scoring leader who made 57 percent of his shots and averaged 22.2 points. He played in the annual Pizza Hut Classic at Las Vegas, scored six points for the East and was drafted in the fifth round by the Houston Rockets. One of his Pizza Hut Classic teammates was C.J. Kupec of Michigan, who later became an assistant athletics director at Illinois State.

Hawkins, a junior, entered the NBA draft and was selected in the third round by the Golden State Warriors. He played one season at Golden State and two with the New Jersey Nets. He led the Nets in scoring during the 1976–77 campaign with a 19.3 average, but the Nets released Hawkins after 15 games the following year. Eventually he spiraled into a bleak world of crack cocaine and was shot to death in Detroit at the age of 39 in 1993.

Robinson resigned as Illinois State's basketball coach on August 18, 1975, to become director of scouting for the NBA Detroit Pistons.

He compiled a 78-51 record in five seasons at Illinois State and left a lasting legacy as the first black to be named head coach of a major university basketball program, blazing a trail for many who have followed.

"I have always felt proud of opening that door," Robinson has said.

Coming in late summer, Robinson's move caught Illinois State athletics administrators by surprise.

"I wish I could defer it for another year," he said, "but you have to take the opportunity when it presents itself. It's a wonderful position."

So, at the age of 64, when most people are retired or contemplating it, Robinson moved into the professional sports arena.

In 1998, at age 87, he is still there. He has two championship rings from the Detroit

Pistons' title seasons of 1989 and 1990; teams he helped shape. He also has a championship ring from the Detroit Lions' 1957 title season during his years as a scout for that NFL organization.

Robinson was reunited for a time with Doug Collins, when Collins became head coach of the Pistons in 1995.

Robinson has reaped a harvest of honors over a lifetime of sports achievement. He is a member of at least five halls of fame, including Illinois State University's, and in 1992 he received the John W. Bunn Award given by the Basketball Hall of Fame for outstanding contribution to basketball.

More than 300 of Robinson's former players attended college on full scholarships, and more than 25 earned doctorates. Fourteen of his Detroit high school players played professionally in the National Basketball Association, American Basketball Association or with the Harlem Globetrotters.

NBA or ABA teams drafted nine of his Illinois State players: Doug Collins, Ron deVries, Bubbles Hawkins, Randy Henry, Billy Lewis, Cyrus Mann, Rick Whitlow, Jeff Wilkins and James Floyd. Roger Powell had a tryout with the Chicago Bulls, and Stepney Bacon, who had a productive year in Europe, was about to join an NBA team when he was killed in a car accident between Chicago and Detroit.

The mark of Will Robinson, the man, is that he is just as proud of the 25 Detroit police officers who played for him.

His impact on the Illinois State basketball program is immeasurable. Against all odds, he took the university into the major college basketball ranks within a year of his arrival, took the Redbirds coast to coast to develop a major schedule, and maintained a winning tradition.

"Will Robinson is a one of a kind person, and I mean that in a complimentary way," Doug Collins said. "I can honestly say I've been a success in life because of my association with him. He's given me a tremendous amount of guidance and wisdom."

Chapter 22

MTXE: GENE SMITHSON'S TEAMS WIN WITH STYLE (1975–1978)

O n August 22, 1975, Gene Smithson succeeded Will Robinson as head coach, and Redbird basketball began its climb to national prominence as a team.

Robinson's coaching and the play of Doug Collins and other talented individuals had dominated the early 1970s. Nearly unbeatable at home and more successful than Robinson's teams on the road, Smithson's squads achieved national ranking and played in two National Invitation Tournaments.

And he did it with style. In a fun-loving era of permed hair, leisure suits and disco dancing, the Redbirds' new coach talked the talk and walked the walk.

Smithson, whose colorful appearance included a frizzy Afro hairstyle and mustache, introduced Illinois State and the college basketball world to MTXE: Mental Toughness, Extra Effort.

Not long after Smithson was hired, red and white buttons with MTXE stamped on them began popping up around Horton Field House. Redbird uniforms had the slogan prominently displayed on them; MTXE was stitched on the bottoms of the undergarments of the ISU cheerleaders, and MTXE towels were sold to fans.

"Every place you could put MTXE, I put it," said Smithson, who produced a carnival-like atmosphere at Horton Field House with MTXE girls in the little red MTXE electric car delivering the game ball to the officials at center court prior to the game.

ISU players entered the court via a red MTXE carpet rolled out for their arrival prior to warmups. At one game, Smithson even had the Redbird mascot swoop down from the rafters

Gene Smithson brought the MTXE basketball motto to Illinois State along with his permed hair and leisure suits.

via a rope to present the game ball to officials.

"MTXE was not a gimmick," said Smithson. "It was a way for me to promote my philosophy."

And promote it he has. After three superior

seasons at Illinois State, his eight years at Wichita State included national rankings and NCAA Tournaments, but ended in controversy as he was fired amid an investigation for NCAA

In the mid-1970s, the dunk was back and seven-footer Jeff Wilkins made the most of it.

rules violations. Now, he serves as head coach at Central Florida Community College in Ocala, Fla.

"When I first got into coaching I was always talking about mental toughness and extra effort to my players," he said. "It's always been my philosophy in life that success relies on people having mental toughness and giving extra effort."

Smithson holds the copyright to MTXE and his teams still display it. His son, Randy, a former ISU player and now the head coach at Missouri Valley Conference rival Wichita State, is allowed to use MTXE2 logos on his team's uniforms.

It was that MTXE philosophy that produced 20 or more victories in each of his three seasons. The Redbirds were 20-7 in Smithson's initial year, and it marked the first time since joining the Division I ranks in 1970.

As expected, Smithson's first team did not lack for pizzazz. There was Roger "The Mad Bomber" Powell knocking down shots from long distance; slick Billy "Smooth" Lewis gliding up and down the court with the greatest of ease; seven-footer Jeff "The Big Dipper" Wilkins controlling things in the lane; and the self-assured Mike "The Bonz" Bonczyk running the show from the point guard position.

The Redbirds showcased Smithson's penchant for a fast-breaking, explosive offensive team that played tenacious defense right at the start, blowing out undermanned Lewis, 129–72, and Long Island, 100–78.

ISU would eclipse the century mark in three other games that season and end as one of the nation's top offensive teams, averaging 91.3 points per game. They started the year with six straight victories, including an 88–83 triumph over Bradley in the Braves' tournament. It was in that game that MTXE received its first true test as the Redbirds were forced to hold off a furious Bradley rally by future NBA player Roger Phegley and Company.

Twenty-four points by future NBA All-Star Robert Parish led Centenary, coached by ISU graduate Larry Little, to a 76–72 victory in the next game. It was the first of only three losses ISU would suffer at Horton Field House in 45 games with Smithson at the helm.

That loss was followed by a road win that

made the basketball world sit up and take notice. The 'Birds bucked a sellout crowd in Winston-Salem, N.C., and handed No. 14 Wake Forest an 81–79 setback as Powell and Wilkins scored 19 apiece and Lewis added 18.

A more confident road team, the Redbirds finished 20-7. Euphoric Redbird fans believed the magical 20-win plateau would earn them a bid to the 16-team National Invitation Tournament, but the call never came and the Redbirds bid farewell to talented seniors Powell, Richard Jones, Randy Henry and George Tometich.

"Naturally, we were all disappointed we didn't make the NIT, but you have to remember that was at a time when the NIT was a much stronger, quality tournament," said Smithson. It was true. A total of 98 teams get NCAA or NIT bids today compared to just 32 in the NCAA and 16 in the NIT in 1976.

The Redbirds made sure the NIT would call the next two years, though.

◆   ◆   ◆   ◆   ◆   ◆

Smithson's second team (1976–77) was a relatively young squad that was led by All-American candidates Wilkins and Lewis. The 7-foot Wilkins was the lone senior starter and was joined in the starting lineup by Lewis, a 6-6 junior; heady 6-1 sophomore guard Derrick Mayes; wiry 6-4 freshman Ron Jones and burly 6-7 freshman forward Del Yarbrough. Again ISU started fast, winning 12 of its first 14 games before consecutive losses on the road at San Jose State and Oral Roberts. A rare home loss to St. Louis in double-overtime had Redbird fans worried, with good reason.

Ahead loomed one of the juggernauts of late 1970s basketball: coach Jerry Tarkanian's Nevada-Las Vegas Runnin' Rebels. UNLV came to Normal February 3, 1977, ranked No. 3 by United Press International and No. 4 by the Associated Press.

All-American Reggie Theus was supported by other future NBA draftees Glen Gondrezick, Larry Moffett and Sam Smith. The run-and-gun Rebels averaged 108 points per game—best in the nation.

More than 8,000 people shoehorned into

High-flying Billy Lewis brought some of the excitement of MTXE to his game.

Horton two hours before tipoff, marking the first time an ISU home game had been sold out in advance since the 1972–73 season when Doug Collins was a senior.

"I probably played in as many games in Horton Field House as anybody at that time between my high school career at Bloomington High School and my college career," said Joe Galvin, a freshman reserve when UNLV came calling. "And the place was never more electric than that night. It was an amazing game and a game that really put ISU on the map as a national power."

Smooth Ron Jones was a complete guard for three Redbird NIT teams from 1976–80.

Tarkanian, quite a showman himself, admitted the Redbird crowd was a factor in Illinois State's 88–84 win, which snapped his team's 14-game winning streak.

"This is the noisiest place I've ever been in," he said. "This was a great crowd. It's a tribute to Illinois State. It was a boost for their whole team. It was great for college basketball."

The Redbirds never trailed in the contest as the youthful guard tandem of Mayes and Jones would combine for 40 points (20 points apiece) and 21 of ISU's 53 rebounds. Wilkins added 17 points and

14 rebounds while Lewis threw in a game-high 21 points as the Redbirds recorded one of their more memorable victories.

Smithson remembered that game as a turning point for Illinois State basketball. He also believed the game proved something to the Horton faithful as well.

"The Vegas game indicated to our own fans that we had a program that could compete against anyone in the country," he said. "Even in my days at Wichita State where we had some big wins, I don't know that I ever saw a victory party at the conclusion of a game like the one I saw after we beat Vegas. It was incredible. That game was definitely one of the highlights of my coaching career."

The victory over the Runnin' Rebels started ISU on an 8-1 roll to finish the regular season 21-6 and under consideration for a post-season trip to the National Invitation Tournament.

"Sooner or later, people have got to recognize that new basketball powers are emerging on the scene," said Smithson prior to "Selection Sunday" in 1977. "It's my only hope that the committees will consider our team's outstanding record over the past two years."

Smithson's hope and ISU fans' dreams came true less than 48 hours later when then Athletics Director Warren Schmakel received a call from the NIT selection committee telling him the Redbirds were in the 16-team field and would play at Creighton.

In those days, only opening-round NIT games were played on campuses, with the final eight teams going to New York.

Led by Wilkins' 21 points and 12 rebounds, ISU beat Creighton in Omaha 65–58 and earned a date against powerful Houston—starring guard Otis Birdsong and coached by the legendary Guy V. Lewis—at famed Madison Square Garden.

Birdsong and the Cougars had the Redbirds down 14 at halftime, but that never-say-die MTXE spirit nearly prevailed. ISU had been behind since leading 3–2 before freshman guard Ron Jones earned his nickname—"The Ice Man"—and tied the score with a pair of free throws with one second left in regulation time to send the game to overtime.

Was the freshman guard nervous? "At the time I wasn't thinking about it," answered Jones. "I was just trying to keep us in the game."

Incredibly, ISU completed that comeback after big guns Wilkins and Lewis fouled out. The Redbirds appeared headed for the semifinals against Alabama when Galvin tipped in a missed shot with 15 seconds left in overtime to give ISU a 90–89 advantage.

However, Birdsong dashed ISU's hopes by canning an 18-foot jumper with five seconds to go.

Wilkins, who would go on to a solid career in the NBA and a pro playing stint in Europe, was the only senior on the 22-7 team. The seven-footer left a giant impression on Redbird basketball in just three seasons. He ranks 13th in points, seventh in rebounds and third in blocked shots on ISU's career lists. His senior season he averaged 21.8 points, 11.1 rebounds and blocked 103 shots.

◆　◆　◆　◆　◆　◆

Because the Redbirds returned everyone but Wilkins from the NIT-tested team, excitement for ISU basketball reached a fever pitch for 1977–78.

The team didn't disappoint either, winning its first 12 games and reaching No. 16 in national polls—the first time an ISU team had been ranked since moving to Division I.

The Redbirds were 13-1 heading into a rematch with another nationally ranked Nevada-Las Vegas team.

With 11 minutes, two seconds remaining in the game at the Las Vegas Convention Center, the Redbirds trailed by 16 points to a team that had won 72 of 73 home games. But ISU refused to fold and scratched back to within three points at 93–90 on a Ron Jones jumper with less than a minute to play.

Reggie Theus made two free throws with 43 seconds remaining, but the second was disallowed as a Las Vegas player was guilty of a lane violation. Sophomore guard Randy Smithson, a Normal Community graduate and the coach's son, pulled the Redbirds to within two points at 94–92 on a jump shot.

A turnover and a missed free throw gave Smithson two shots to tie the game in the final

11 seconds, but neither fell in and UNLV held on.

Jones scored a career-high 34 points and grabbed 10 rebounds, while Galvin added 19 points and nine rebounds.

Eight days later the Redbirds found themselves going against Indiana State, ranked No. 4 nationally in both wire service polls. Junior forward Larry Bird, who would lead Indiana State to a second-place finish in the NCAA Tournament the next year, was the Sycamore star.

"Nobody knew what Bird looked like, so we spent all of our time during warmups trying to figure out which one he was," said Galvin. "You didn't have the television coverage and media exposure then that you have now. The scouting reports were what you read in the press releases or in the newspaper. Once the game started, it didn't take long to figure out which one he was."

Much like the Nevada-Las Vegas game the previous year, the ISU faithful were ready for the Sycamores. A sellout crowd in excess of 8,000 people saw the Redbirds rally from an eight-point deficit in the final 14 minutes for an 81–76 victory.

Del Yarbrough's husky body and soft hands were an excellent low-post combination. No. 21 is Illinois State guard Derrick Mayes.

The crowd was so loud that Bird was called for a technical foul for dunking the ball after the whistle had blown—illegal at the time. Bird had stolen the ball from Smithson, but was guilty of a foul on the play. He never heard the whistle blow, though, as the roar of the crowd was much greater, and he continued downcourt for the dunk.

"There weren't many crowds in college basketball like the ones at Horton Field House," reflected Gene Smithson, whose 1977–78 team never lost at home. "The excitement and energy generated by Redbird fans were worth some points to us in a lot of games. The ISU crowds back then were second to none."

It took four consecutive pressure-packed free throws by Jones and Smithson to hold off Indiana State in a game that was marred by a scuffle with 10 seconds remaining. Ron Jones and Indiana State's Harry Morgan were ejected after Randy Smithson became sandwiched between Morgan and Bird. Morgan was charged with a foul, then tempers flared.

Smithson's two free throws sealed the win and handed the Sycamores only their second defeat in 15 games. It also boosted Illinois State's record to 16-2. Billy Lewis' 25-point, 12-rebound effort led the Redbirds as a counter-punch to Bird's 37 points and 17 rebounds.

Unfortunately for the Redbirds, it wouldn't be the last time they would see Bird and Company that season. Despite a 24-3 record and a No. 13 national ranking, ISU couldn't overcome a 96–84 loss at DePaul in a regular-season finale between the top two independents in the Midwest—and maybe the country. The nationally ranked Blue Demons, coached by the legendary Ray Meyer, had Dave Corzine, Gary Garland, Joe Ponsetto and Clyde Bradshaw and earned a berth in the NCAA Tournament ahead of ISU with a 25-2 record.

Illinois State had to be content with accepting its second straight bid to the National Invitation Tournament, with the opening game at Indiana State in Terre Haute.

"You have to go somewhere," said Gene Smithson upon hearing the Redbirds were rejected by the NCAA. "We're happy to be going to a tournament at this time of the year. If you're not in one, you can't win one."

The Redbirds weren't in the tournament very long, though, as Bird scored 27 points to help

play professionally in Turkey.

The Chicago Farragut High School all-stater who played prep ball for ex-ISU standout Wardell Vaughn, was the first Division I player at ISU to start every game during his four-year

The 1970s began with seven-footer Ron deVries in the post for the Redbirds and finished with Bloomington's Joe Galvin (32), who still holds Illinois State's single-game blocked shot record.

Indiana State avenge its earlier season loss, 73–71. It brought an end to the winningest season (24-4) the Redbirds had enjoyed since 1967–68 and marked the end of the stellar four-year career of Lewis, who would go on to

career (110). Lewis still ranks second behind Doug Collins in career points scored (1,962) second in field goals made (841) and fifth in rebounding (869).

Lewis was among eight players coached by

Smithson who were drafted by NBA teams. The others were Wilkins, Randy Henry, Derrick Mayes, Del Yarbrough, Galvin, Jones and Randy Smithson.

◆　　◆　　◆　　◆　　◆　　◆

While everything seemed encouraging on the ISU front for the next season with all the players returning but Lewis, one person was discouraged. Gene Smithson wasn't satisfied with just going to the NIT. He wanted to coach a team in the NCAA Tournament.

Smithson was among the hot young coaches in America because of his teams' 66-18 record in three seasons, and it didn't take long for other schools to begin courting his services. Smithson turned down an offer from West Virginia.

But just 10 days later, he accepted the head coaching position at Wichita State at a substantial raise from what he made at ISU.

It wasn't easy.

"It was a tough decision," said Smithson, "but it was discouraging to me that we were able to compete with the best teams in the country at ISU and we still couldn't get in the NCAA."

To this day, Smithson claims the three years he served as the Redbirds' head coach "were three of the greatest years of my life. They were some of the most fun years I've had in life."

Smithson said it has always been his design to get his program to a level of prominence on the national scene and he believes he accomplished that at Illinois State.

"I had an excellent staff [Ron Ferguson, Bill Flanagan and Warren Crews]. We were outrecruiting everybody in the state of Illinois," said Smithson. "And we were able to beat teams that were nationally ranked. We scheduled those teams to give us a presence on the national level and try to impress the NCAA selection committee. I truly believe our victories over

Nevada-Las Vegas, Florida State, Wake Forest, Bradley and Indiana State made people stand up and take notice."

But lack of a conference affiliation, according to Smithson, was a major factor in his decision to leave. Ironically, three years later the Redbirds would be facing his Wichita State teams after ISU joined the Missouri Valley Conference.

"Those [quality] victories also made ISU attractive to conferences and set the stage for ISU ultimately getting into the Missouri Valley. Had ISU been moving toward joining a conference while I was coaching there, I probably would have stayed."

Instead, Smithson packed his MTXE belongings—not to mention his talented son, Randy—and took his show to Wichita State.

In just three years, Gene Smithson and the magic of MTXE took Illinois State to higher levels of team success. Smithson and MTXE were style, but they produced substance.

The exterior of Horton Field House.

Chapter 23

NEW STYLE, SAME RESULTS: DONEWALD ERA BEGINS (1978–1980)

As Gene Smithson moved west to Wichita State, Redbird Athletics Director Warren Schmakel looked east and chose Indiana University assistant coach Bob Donewald to lead the team into its next phase of basketball growth.

From the hottest program in college basketball, Donewald brought the experience of 121 wins and an undefeated 1976 NCAA Championship in five seasons assisting Bob Knight.

He more than kept the wins coming at Illinois State. In 11 seasons, Donewald led the Redbirds to 208 wins, a school-record three straight NCAA Tournament appearances, three National Invitation Tournament berths and five seasons with 20 wins or more. He was instrumental in Illinois State joining the Missouri Valley Conference and stumping for votes during the student referendum campaign to build Redbird Arena.

The Bradley-Illinois State rivalry became one of the nation's hottest when Bradley coach Dick Versace (second from left) and Illinois State coach Bob Donewald (second from right) were leading their respective teams to national prominence.

Hank Cornley muscled through an Illinois opponent as Dwayne Tyus eyed a possible rebound.

Smithson era ended—at Terre Haute, Ind., facing Indiana State and Larry Bird. And like the previous season, the Redbirds would come up short again in a 78–76 loss.

In defense of Donewald and crew, nobody else beat the Sycamores in their first 33 games of the 1978–79 season. Indiana State's only loss was to Michigan State and Earvin (Magic) Johnson in the championship game of the NCAA Tournament.

The Redbirds posted the school's fourth of five straight 20-win seasons. ISU jumped to a 14-4 record before splitting its final 12 games to finish at 20-10. Still hampered by an independent's scheduling woes, eight of the final nine games were on the road. Already lacking depth, the Redbirds were further weakened when Yarbrough broke his hand with eight games remaining.

That season featured a matchup of rookie head coaches which foreshadowed exciting times in the 1980s. Bradley's first-year mentor was the brash, silver-haired, self-proclaimed Shakespearean scholar, Dick Versace.

Illinois State beat a young Bradley squad, 74–61, January 3 at Horton Field House behind Mayes' 26 points. The end of the game was marred by a pushing-and-shoving match which centered around Versace and Redbird guard Ron Jones. Versace admitted he didn't realize how intense the rivalry was between ISU and Bradley.

"I've seen the Big Ten and I've seen the Chicago Public League and no place have I seen anything like this," said Versace. And, with the benefit of hindsight, it's safe to say he hadn't seen anything yet.

◆　◆　◆　◆　◆　◆

Donewald's helping man-to-man defensive strategy really punched in during the 1979–80 season as Illinois State limited opponents to 62.4 points per game, 10 fewer than the previous season.

Behind senior starters Jones, Yarbrough and the seven-footer Galvin, the Redbirds were a young team. Dale White, Anthony Jones and McKay Smith were joined by a freshman class made up of burly all-state center Rick Lamb;

It all began with a style change. The high-flying, 80-points-per-game style taught by Smithson was replaced by the control-tempo, defensive-oriented regimen popularized at Indiana.

Meticulous preparation featured detailed game plans prepared from long hours of film study by the Donewald staff. It was a style opponents respected with good reason—it worked. In fact, opposing coaches frequently expressed how tough it was to face Donewald's

teams when they had three days or more to prepare.

◆　◆　◆　◆　◆　◆

At the start, Donewald inherited some fine players with successful post-season experience. Juniors Joe Galvin, Ron Jones and Del Yarbrough, plus seniors Derrick Mayes and Rick Ferina, were the backbone of Donewald's inaugural season, which opened where the shooting guard Dwayne Tyus, who played for ISU alumnus Wardell Vaughn at Chicago Farragut; and jack-of-all-trades forward Raynard Malaine.

The Redbirds' fifth straight 20-win season (20-9) earned a return to the National Invitation Tournament after a one-year hiatus.

After a 3-3 start, Illinois State found itself in the championship game of the Illini Classic at Champaign—the first basketball meeting between Illinois and Illinois State in 58 years.

Although playing without Galvin, who had a sprained foot, the Redbirds were within striking distance of the Illini late in the game, but a controversial technical foul for "non-action" (this was well before the shot clock) helped the Illini pull away to win, 47–40. Despite Illinois' championship, Ron Jones was the tournament's most valuable player.

Later, during a seven-game Redbird win streak, Jones earned MVP honors of the Illinois State Holiday Classic after leading the Redbirds to a 94–62 victory over Billy Tubbs' Lamar team. Tubbs later moved to Oklahoma and coached the Sooners against Illinois State twice in the 1980s.

That win streak propelled the Redbirds to a 14-5 mark and had fans talking about a possible NCAA bid. That hope was dashed by another broken hand—this one on Galvin, whose career ended at least eight games too soon. ISU's 5-3 regular-season finish included a 97–81 loss to No. 1-ranked DePaul at Alumni Hall.

The loss to DePaul left ISU with a 19-8 mark and a spot in the NIT field, which was expanded from 16 to 32 teams for the first time in history.

West Texas State, now West Texas A&M, turned out to be a worthwhile draw. The Buffaloes found out they were going to Normal as they deplaned in Amarillo, Texas, after returning home from losing the Missouri Valley Conference Tournament championship game to Bradley in Peoria.

A lively crowd saw Ron Jones score 22 points, Anthony Jones earn career highs with 17 points and 12 rebounds, and the spidery Smith shut down 5-foot-9 WTSU star Terry Adolph during an 80–63 Redbird victory.

The victory gave ISU its fifth straight 20-win

With assistant coaches Terry Smith and Pat Cunningham plus rugged Rick Lamb (53) looking on, Bob Donewald took command in the Redbird huddle.

season and set up another showdown with Illinois in Champaign. And, like the first time the two teams met, ISU was without Galvin.

The 75–65 Illini victory was the last straw in an unhappy experience for the 'Birds.

First, Illinois shorted Illinois State's promised ticket allotment and delayed release of those tickets. Then, the Redbirds' game-day shooting practice at Assembly Hall was in shivering cold and the building's personnel struggled to find a way to get the over-the-court

lights on. That night, Redbird pep band members were allowed access—with tickets—but their instruments were not. First-year Redbird Athletics Director Don Kelley was not permitted access to the locker room area until after the game began because of Illini security policies.

The loss also ended the fine careers of Galvin, Ron Jones (who was described as "a loose bag of spare parts running down the floor" by Tyus) and Yarbrough. All were

1,000-point scorers and starters for much of their four years at ISU.

Jones still ranks first in career steals with 232, fourth in career scoring with 1,839 points and second in career assists with 597. Yarbrough has the fourth-best career field goal percentage (53.3), is ninth in career free throw percentage (77.8) and eighth in career rebounds with 750. Galvin still holds the school record for blocked shots in one game with nine and ranks second in career blocked shots with 132.

But one of the biggest events in Redbird basketball history came to pass that summer. After two years of planning, politicking and overall athletics program upgrades, Illinois State became the newest member of the Missouri Valley Conference, to begin basketball competition in 1981–82.

Raynard Malaine's 225-pound frame combined with his perimeter skills to give the Redbirds a player who made a difference at both ends of the court.

Chapter 24

A VALLEY FULL OF FUN: REDBIRDS JOIN NCAA ELITE (1980–1985)

With 17 wins each in 1980–81 and 1981–82, Donewald's Redbirds didn't get calls from the NCAA or NIT, but developed important players to add to the nucleus of Rick Lamb, Dwayne Tyus and Ray Malaine.

They were joined by powerful 6-foot-7 Hank Cornley and scholarly 6-foot-8 Mark Zwart in 1980–81. A superb quartet from Indiana—clever point guard Michael McKenny (Gary), exciting Rickie Johnson (Indianapolis), sharp-shooting Brad Duncan (Anderson) and versatile big man Lou Stefanovic (Merrill-ville)—arrived a year later.

The 17-10 record in 1980–81 marked the Redbirds' finale as a Division I independent. The next year, it was on to the Valley—famous for its fast-paced teams, top-quality athletes and colorful-but-successful coaches, including Gene Smithson at Wichita State, Dick Versace at Bradley and Nolan Richardson at Tulsa.

The deliberate Redbirds were entering the Valley when it was the nation's highest-scoring conference.

But, win or lose, the Valley was a necessary elevation for the Redbirds. President Lloyd Watkins, Athletics Director Don Kelley, Donewald and a host of others had spent some two years meeting what Drake Athletics Director Bob Karnes would call "the toughest standards ever set for admission to the Valley."

Pantagraph sports editor Jim Barnhart, now retired, reflected on the Valley's value to Illinois State.

"The entrance into the Missouri Valley Conference provided Illinois State with a preaching pulpit and a solid schedule—unlike the Robinson years when the Redbirds would

be forced to make two trips yearly to the West Coast in order to play enough games to meet NCAA requirements," related Barnhart. "The conference clout also enabled Illinois State to beef up its non-conference schedule."

◆   ◆   ◆   ◆   ◆   ◆

The Valley coaches aroused Horton Field House fans. Versace would rankle the fans before his team would even play at Horton by coming out personally to scout a preceding ISU home game, helping himself to a courtside press row seat and waving to fans who chanted "Go home, Dick!" When the Braves came to Horton, student fans donned frizzy white wigs to mimic Versace's hairstyle.

Some fans cheered the stylish Smithson as a favored son returning home. Others hooted at Smithson, whose Shockers featured future NBA stars like Antoine Carr, Cliff Levingston and Xavier McDaniel, but struggled under the shadow of NCAA sanctions.

Richardson, muscular arms folded across his polka-dotted shirt topped by a piercing scowl, riled Redbird faithful from the moment his teams took the court.

Often, pre-game sound bites among coaches fueled the flames.

"The Valley was a publicity man's dream in the 1980s," claimed Barnhart. "Versace, sporting his English-barrister hairdo…and who can forget Richardson, who came out of the barrios of El Paso, Texas, to coach a national championship junior college team, a National Invitation Tournament champi-onship team at Tulsa and later an NCAA champion at Arkansas?"

Barnhart recalls enjoying the by-play among the coaches.

"Richardson would challenge Versace to a fight in a game at Peoria and refer to the Braves head coach as a 'Sissy.' But there was a soft side to Richardson, a side not many people saw."

◆   ◆   ◆   ◆   ◆   ◆

For trivia buffs, the Redbirds lost their first Valley game (72–68 at Southern Illinois) but rebounded in their next league matchup to defeat Drake at home, 59–49.

To the surprise of many, ISU finished fifth in the Valley's regular-season standings in 1982, but the biggest surprise was yet to come.

In the semifinals of the MVC Tournament, the Redbirds upended top-seeded regular-season champion Bradley, 55–50, in overtime in Peoria to advance to the league's post-season tournament championship game at Tulsa. A 90–77 loss to the Golden Hurricane left ISU with a 17-12 record and without a post-season tournament berth. Angered by an NCAA snub, Bradley overpowered four opponents to win the NIT. That Illinois State victory turned out to be Bradley's last loss in ancient Robertson Fieldhouse before moving to Carver Arena.

◆   ◆   ◆   ◆   ◆   ◆

The golden years of the mid-1980s began as the Redbirds roared off the starting line in 1982–83 with 16 wins in their first 17 games, taking up residence in the nation's Top 20 with their lone loss coming to Illinois in the champi-onship game of the Illini Classic in December.

The 11-game victory string which followed

Chevrolet Most Valuable Player Rickie Johnson snipped a share of the net after the Redbirds won their first Missouri Valley Conference title by beating Tulsa in the 1983 MVC Tournament at Horton Field House.

four-year starter at point guard, Michael McKenny's cool under fire helped the Redbirds to NCAA Tournament bids in 1983, 1984 and 1985.

Mark Zwart (45) beat Ohio University's Victor Alexander for this rebound, but the Bobcats nipped the Redbirds in Illinois State's first NCAA Division I Tournament game. No. 52 is Hank Cornley.

The CBS-TV crew featured Verne Lundquist on play-by-play and Irv Brown's analysis. The pair stood on the court at Horton Field House doing the still-common "pre-game stand-up" to set the stage for the game.

The stand-up became a videotaped tribute to Redbird fans. Brown's one-minute summary of Tulsa's speed against ISU's power was performed while the frenzied Horton faithful were welcoming the Redbirds back to the court before tip-off. It was so loud, Lundquist could not hear the shrilling Brown even through his earplug. So he had to lean ever closer to his partner as the speech continued. Brown nudged Lundquist to indicate he had finished, and the veteran of NFL, college basketball and Olympic events admitted, "Irv, I have no idea what you just said, but you can sure hear the excitement here at Illinois State...we'll be back with the tip-off after this."

◆　　◆　　◆　　◆　　◆　　◆

And after the tip-off, the Redbirds blew past Tulsa, 84–64. Although neither started the game, senior Raynard Malaine and sophomore Rickie Johnson led the victory party.

Johnson, who carried the nickname of "Slick," was named the Chevrolet Most Valuable Player by the CBS television crew for scoring a career-high 22 points. The bull-like Malaine added 18 as ISU shot a sizzling 59 percent from the field.

"That was probably the biggest game of my career because it seemed to jump-start my career," recalls Johnson, now a career specialist in the Student and Alumni Placement Services at ISU and junior high girls basketball coach at Metcalf Laboratory School. "Plus, a lot of historical things were riding on that game— the school's first NCAA Tournament berth and the first time ISU was on national TV. It was also the first time my mom got to see me play in person at Horton Field House. Needless to say, I was juiced."

It began during that pre-game entrance.

"I remember walking out of the locker room with Ray [Malaine]. He said, 'Slick, let's just go out and not worry about anything. Let's just play and not worry about making mistakes and

included wins over Valley kingpins Bradley, Tulsa and Wichita State. A three-game losing streak and an injury to sharpshooting guard Dwayne Tyus began a mid-winter slump for the Redbirds, who fell out of the Top 20. They would finish second to Smithson's Shockers, whose only league loss was to the Redbirds. ISU finished second to the Shockers at 13-5, but WSU was on NCAA probation and ineligible for the MVC Tournament.

"Smithson's return trips to Horton Field House instigated split loyalties among the

Redbird followers," recalled Barnhart. "Some wanted Radar Gene back, and others just wanted him dead."

In the early 1980s, the No. 1 seed meant home-court advantage for the tournament. The top-seeded Redbirds disposed of Southern Illinois and Bradley at home in the first two rounds and found themselves hosting the championship game against Tulsa in the first nationally televised game from Horton Field House, with an automatic NCAA Tournament berth on the line.

etting taken out of the game.' "

The 6-foot-5 Johnson was one of the all-time great crowd-pleasers at Illinois State because of his quick leaping ability and natural enthusiasm. Against Tulsa, Johnson jump-started the Redbirds with what would become his patented play: jumping the passing lane, making the steal, streaking to the basket for a dunk, and then, without breaking stride, circling back to the defensive end while shooting his left fist into the air. It made Horton Field House vibrate.

"I happened to be on the weak side and read the pass," said the left-handed Johnson, who was pumping his fist higher into the air with each ISU basket late in the game. "I just stepped in and took the pass and went all the way. We didn't just try to break their press, we tried to attack it."

In the last 56-team NCAA Tournament, ISU had a No. 8 seed and drew Ohio University of the Mid-American Conference in its first-round NCAA game on March 17, 1983, at the Sun Dome on the campus of the University of South Florida in Tampa—where 1920s Redbird star Harris Dean was acting president. The winner faced No. 1 Kentucky, who had a first-round bye.

Facing a green-clad team on St. Patrick's Day, coached by ex-Notre Dame assistant Danny Nee (of Irish descent), the Redbirds still looked like a winner with a 43–37 lead with 6:39 left. But missed free throws, a ballhandling gaffe and a defensive strategy which enabled Ohio freshman guard Robert Tatum to swish a falling-down 20-footer at the buzzer did them in.

After Ohio took a 49–47 lead, ISU knotted the score as Malaine drained a baseline jumper with three seconds remaining. After an Ohio timeout, Donewald substituted Zwart for McKenny to get his tallest lineup on the floor.

Ohio's Jeff Thomas threw the ball the length of the court. Zwart and Cornley went airborne for the ball in the OU free throw lane, and Zwart batted it toward the ISU basket. However, the tap went right to Tatum, who ducked a flying Malaine to get off his game-winning shot.

"We all went after it," said Zwart after the game. "Instead of grabbing it, I just swiped at

Before the three-point line, Brad Duncan had the range.

it. I should have grabbed it, but I didn't want to get a foul."

The loss still rankles Johnson.

"You talk about a roller coaster ride of emotions within a week," said Johnson. "We didn't want to foul the guy, so we just stood there. We didn't go for the ball and the guy slings it up and it goes in."

The Redbirds finished 24-7, the most victories that an ISU Division I team would have until the 1996–97 team would match the 24 victories and the 1997–98 squad would reach the 25-win mark.

With the loss of leaders Lamb, Tyus and Malaine—and the Valley improved—some saw a dip in the Redbirds' fortunes for 1983–84. Not Hank Cornley.

At 6-foot-7 and weighing 250 or more, a smiling Cornley was a charming, teddy bear of a man. But a scowling "Big Henry" often could look scary. A master at using his ample rear end to pin opponents helplessly behind him under the basket, a fire-eyed Cornley would clap his hands together and bark at teammates "give me the rock [ball]." Failure to do so would earn the offending teammate an icy glare as the Redbirds fell back on defense.

Before the 1983–84 season, the "give me the rock" Cornley made a locker room speech. Moving from player to player, he reminded each that this was *his* senior season and *nobody* was going to mess it up. And there would be *no excuses*.

Fellow senior Zwart, juniors Johnson, Duncan, Stefanovic and McKenny, along with 7-foot freshman center Bill Braksick and slender 6-6 freshman forward Derrick Sanders all took Cornley's message to heart and made it into the nation's Top 20 at No. 17 by mid-January with a 13-3 record.

After a February slump, the Redbirds found themselves trailing Tulsa by one game with two to go: home dates against archrival Bradley and Tulsa. ISU dispatched Bradley, 55–46, setting the stage for the showdown with Nolan Richardson's No. 9-ranked Tulsa team.

A standing-room-only crowd of 7,801 people was on hand at Horton Field House to celebrate as an ISU team, plagued by flu problems earlier in the week, registered a 91–81 triumph and tied Tulsa for the Valley's regular-season championship. The loss was only the third for Tulsa, and ISU had been responsible for two of them.

Cornley and Zwart went out with a flourish in their final regular-season home game. Cornley scored 25 points and grabbed 10 rebounds, while Zwart, who carried a 3.8 grade-point-average, added 16 points.

Winning a share of the league championship—and winning the season series from Tulsa—also gave the Redbirds the home-court advantage throughout the Valley post-season tournament. ISU thrashed Drake, 91–62, before Creighton, coached by NBA Hall of Famer Willis Reed and led by future NBA player Benoit Benjamin, stunned the Redbirds, 64–59, at Horton in the semifinals. The loss left ISU with a 22-7 record—still good enough to earn an at-large bid to the newly expanded, 64-team NCAA Tournament.

Again, the Redbirds received the No. 8 seed, but this time they were placed in the Midwest Regional at Lincoln, Neb., against No. 9 seed

Alabama. Again, the first-round game would be a cliffhanger.

However, the ending would be much sweeter against the Crimson Tide as Lou Stefanovic's 16-foot jump shot with eight seconds remaining lifted the Redbirds to a 49–48 victory, the school's first triumph in NCAA Tournament play at the Division I level. Ironically, he was in the game only because McKenny suffered an eye cut late in the contest.

Alabama led, 48–47, with 24 seconds to go when ISU called time out to set its final strategy. Donewald's late-game strategy was typically

hit many clutch shots in his career, Stefanovic confidently drained his open jumper for the ISU win.

Disappointed was the way ISU felt after its 75–61 second-round loss to nationally ranked DePaul. The Redbirds, who finished the season with a 23-8 record, were hoping to avenge a 69–66 loss to the Blue Demons earlier in the season.

"DePaul is good," said Zwart after the game "but we've played with a lot of other good teams longer than that. We didn't play as hard as we should have and that makes it disappointing."

With NCAA bids came media attention like this 1984 NCAA Tournament press conference in Lincoln, Neb. Bob Donewald is flanked by two of the Redbirds' bruising best: Lou Stefanovic (left) and Hank Cornley.

open-ended and this was no exception.

"I told them not to worry about the time left, but if they had a good shot to take it even if only two seconds had been run off," said Donewald. "I told them that if it got really late, everyone was to go to the boards."

Stefanovic said no one was designated to take the final shot.

"I was the open man because we had good ball movement," said Stefanovic. "It could have been Rickie [Johnson]; it could have been Brad [Duncan]; it could have been me. I did not shoot the ball well in the first and second half, but I had a feeling I had to hit this one."

A physically and mentally tough player who

Legendary DePaul coach Ray Meyer, who retired after a subsequent loss to Wake Forest in the regional semifinals, was confident his team would win.

"I have the greatest respect for Bob Donewald and Illinois State," said Meyer. "But they just don't have our talent. We did a better job on the boards than the last time we played them."

◆   ◆   ◆   ◆   ◆   ◆

Cornley and Zwart would pass the torch of success onto one of the more talented senior classes ever assembled in Stefanovic, Johnson, Duncan and McKenny the following year.

Stefanovic was known for his hard-nosed defense, rebounding and baseline shooting. Johnson was still providing ISU fans with plenty of excitement with his jumping ability and slam dunks. ISU has probably never had a deadlier outside shooter than Duncan, who would have flourished with today's three-point field goal.

ISU has had some talented point guards—Richard Thomas, David Cason and Jamar Smiley—since McKenny's departure in 1985. But, against the best opponents, McKenny would take a back seat to none and he always had control of the Redbirds' pulse.

The bigger the game, the bigger McKenny seemed to play—some of his best efforts came in the face of Tulsa's relentless full-court press when both the 'Birds and Hurricane were nationally ranked.

Until Dan Muller came along 13 years later, McKenny held the school record for minutes played in a career at 3,845. Like Muller, McKenny was a disciplined defender, too.

Lacking experienced depth behind the front-liners, the 1984–85 Redbirds won with a unique confidence which showed up at critical moments.

One such moment came in the championship game of the University of Pacific Tournament in Stockton, Calif., against a superbly talented Texas A&M team. ISU struggled for 30 minutes and trailed by nine when Donewald called a timeout near the 10-minute mark of the second half. After the timeout, the team went back on the floor, but re-huddled with Stefanovic doing the talking.

A tougher Redbird team emerged, erased the Aggie lead and had a chance to win in regulation time when freshman Tony Holifield was fouled in the final seconds. Holifield finished his career as the Redbirds' field goal percentage leader, but free throws were another story. These would be the first of his career, and he missed both, sending the game to overtime.

Before he left the floor, Stefanovic had his arm around the unhappy freshman, telling him, "It's all right; you did a good job…I promise we'll beat them in overtime." And they did, with ease.

Stefanovic's leadership was shared by the always-upbeat Johnson, the steady McKenny and the fun-loving Duncan. They were a class to remember.

That talented senior class, supported by junior William Anderson, sophomores Sanders and Braksick along with freshmen recruits Holifield, Matt Taphorn, Jeff Harris and Cliff Peterson, cruised through the 1984–85 regular season with a 21-6 record, including a stretch where they won three of four straight overtime contests. ISU finished with an 11-5 mark in the Valley and a second-place tie with Wichita State, one game behind Tulsa.

But Indiana State's only road victory of the season was a 66–61 win at Horton in the first round of the MVC Tournament. Donewald and Company waited nervously for a third straight NCAA bid and a second straight at-large invitation.

It came. The Redbirds were given the No. 9 seed in the Midwest Regional at Oral Roberts University in Tulsa. The No. 8 seed was Pacific 10 champion Southern California.

And for the second straight year, the Redbirds advanced past the first round as they rallied from a seven-point deficit to register a 58–55 victory over the Trojans. ISU did it with defense as it held Southern California's leading scorer Wayne Carlander scoreless in the second half. Sanders and Stefanovic limited Carlander to just two shots in the final 20 minutes.

The Redbirds' sagging defense, which left the area under the basket resembling a fire drill, limited Southern California to a 37 percent shooting average and 25 points in the final 20 minutes.

Braksick, playing 40 minutes for the first time in his collegiate career, made the pivotal play with 11:39 remaining. He went high into the air, pulled down a long rebound, and then moved back forcefully inside to score. He was fouled on the play and made the free throw to give the Redbirds a 41–40 lead.

The victory would send ISU into a second-round matchup with Oklahoma—coached by Billy Tubbs—the No. 1 seed in the Midwest Regional and the No. 4 nationally ranked team. The Redbirds played with courage and determination.

But the Sooners had Wayman Tisdale and used the three-time all-American's 29 points and eight rebounds to hold off underdog ISU, 75–69, and finish the Redbirds' season at 24-8. A crowd in excess of 400 people met the team at the Bloomington Airport on its return trip home from the tournament.

Chapter 25
THE LAST YEARS AT HORTON (1985–1989)

With the departure of the talented senior class the previous year, Illinois State fell to 15-14 in the 1985–86 campaign, but Derrick Sanders, then a junior, along with the sophomore quartet of Tony Holifield, Matt Taphorn, Jeff Harris and Cliff Peterson emerged during the season along with point guard Todd Starks.

With the dawn of the three-point field goal and shot clock, they led the Redbirds back to post-season play in the 1986–87 campaign. The Redbirds made the NIT with a 17-12 regular-season mark even though center Bill Braksick transferred to Illinois Wesleyan over the summer for his senior season.

ISU drew Akron, coached by Bob Huggins (who gained later fame as head coach at Cincinnati), at Horton Field House in the opening round of the NIT and zapped the Zips, 79–72, as Starks dished off 11 assists and Holifield scored 23 points. Then, it was off to Cleveland State to face Kenny (The Mouse) McFadden, thought by many to be the nation's best player under six feet.

Sanders, the team's lone senior, made his first eight shots of the second half to match a career high with 27 points as ISU posted a 79–77 upset victory to move into the quarterfinals against LaSalle and future NBA players Tim Legler and Lionel Simmons.

Sanders, who would go on to have a successful professional career overseas, finished his brilliant four-year stint at ISU by scoring 26 points against LaSalle at The Palestra in Philadelphia in a 70–50 loss. The Redbirds were 19-13 at the end.

Stylish Derrick Sanders led the Redbirds in scoring and rebounding in 1985–86 and 1986–87.

Seniors Jeff Harris, Matt Taphorn, Cliff Peterson and Tony Holifield would get the Redbirds their second straight NIT appearance during the 1987–88 campaign. It was a season that was marked by a number of oddities.

For starters, it would be the final full season that the Redbirds would play at Horton Field House. The $17.4 million Redbird Arena would open in the middle of the next season. It also was a season that the Redbirds would score one of the bigger regular-season victories in school history with an 89–88 victory over Iowa of the Big Ten Conference in the All-College Tournament in Oklahoma City.

Taphorn scored the game-winning shot with three seconds remaining to give Illinois State its first triumph over a Big Ten team. Sparked by Harris, who was having trouble breathing because of bronchitis, and Taphorn, whose playing time was limited because of a stress fracture in his right leg, the Redbirds rallied from a 16-point deficit in the second half.

Sophomore Rickey Jackson began that rally with back-to-back open-court steals which could have resulted in dunks, except that the always-creative Jackson disdained the drive and pulled up to hit three-pointers both times.

Harris, who was so weak that he had difficulty practicing earlier in the week, scored a career-high 30 points, making five of eight from three-point range. His roommate Taphorn, who injured his back in the first half to go along with his stress fracture, scored a career-high 25 points and made seven of 11 shots from three-point range.

"I have to credit Taphorn," said Donewald after the game. "He missed the one shot with 21 seconds left and it would have given us the lead. Then, he came back to make the game-winner."

The Redbirds, who shot 64 percent from three-point range, trailed 75–59 with 8:36 remaining before outscoring the Hawkeyes, 19–2, and grabbed the lead at 78–77. But Iowa moved to an 83–78 advantage with 2:16 left before Taphorn drilled two straight three-pointers.

Future NBA star B.J. Armstrong knocked

Long-shooting Jeff Harris also was a GTE Academic All-American for the Redbirds.

down a three-pointer with less than a minute to play to give the Hawkeyes an 88–86 lead. Taphorn then missed a shot with 21 seconds to go, but then forced Iowa's Michael Reaves to

travel with 18 seconds remaining to give ISU the ball and Taphorn the opportunity to hit the three-point winner.

"When Iowa attempted to inbounds the ball, I stepped in front of the intended receiver to force a traveling violation," recalled Taphorn, who later became a color commentator on the Redbird television broadcasts. "When we regained possession, we ran the clock down until five seconds were left when I received the ball. I made a shot fake to lose my defender and stepped up to make the three. It was definitely the biggest shot of my career."

The Redbirds would finish third in the conference standings, but found success in the post-season tournament by posting victories over Drake and Wichita State. Bradley, which was serving as the host for the tournament, would be ISU's opponent in the championship game at Carver Arena.

The beginning proved to be the end for the Redbirds, though, as the Braves reeled off nine straight points to start the game before securing an 83–59 victory. All-American and future NBA standout Hersey Hawkins scored 29 points to lead Bradley.

The loss offset a 13-point, 13-rebound effort from the normally low-scoring Cliff Peterson, who would lose his life in 1994 when a Molotov cocktail was tossed into the front room of his family's home in Detroit. Like Dan Muller a decade later, the slender, 6-foot-8 Peterson could guard any opponent from point guard to post player.

Despite the defeat to Bradley, Donewald was confident the Redbirds would receive a second straight NIT bid and he was right. Oddly, Illinois State was sent to Cleveland State in a rematch of the previous year's tournament game. This time, though, Mouse McFadden and Cleveland State gained a measure of revenge with an 89–83 overtime victory, ending ISU's season at 18-13.

The 1988–89 season was one of anticipated excitement. Despite losing key senior contributors from the previous season, the Redbirds appeared in good shape with the return of arrod Coleman, Randy Blair, Jackson, Jon Pemberton, Sonny Roberts and Sam Skarich.

This also was the season the Redbirds would move into Redbird Arena in early January. The arena was a direct result of three straight NCAA Tournament appearances in the mid-1980s.

"The success of the men's program was the primary reason Redbird Arena was built, although then-school president Dr. Lloyd Watkins was instrumental in holding the project together when it appeared that building costs might keep the new facility from becoming a reality," said retired *Pantagraph* sports editor Jim Barnhart. "Watkins went out on the proverbial limb and provided the tenacity necessary to get things done."

While Redbird Arena would be classy, Horton was a classic.

"An empty Horton Field House might not have appealed to high school recruits," said Barnhart, "but anyone who observed one of the crazy sold-out contests had to come away impressed with the fact that the boisterous fans might have had a great deal to do with the increased revenue in the hearing aid business."

◆   ◆   ◆   ◆   ◆   ◆

Illinois State opened the season at Indiana in the pre-season National Invitation Tournament and the Hoosiers blistered ISU, 83–48. Few Redbird fans knew at the time that game set the tone for a losing campaign.

ISU won its next two games before suffering a heartbreaking 78–77 loss to DePaul in the final game at Horton Field House after 25 years. It was a game that the Redbirds felt they actually won.

DePaul's Terence Greene drained a shot in the final second before a sellout crowd of 7,725 people. How many points the shot was worth inspired debate. The referees signaled a three-pointer. Television replays showed that Greene's feet were inside the three-point arc, meaning the basket should have only counted for two points.

Further, replays showed that DePaul should not have even had the ball for that final shot. Andy Laux's baseline shot for the Demons a few seconds earlier hit the rim and bounded

out of bounds untouched.

"I really credit Terence Greene for knocking the ball in the basket, but we just flat out got cheated," said Donewald moments after viewing the tape of the final seconds.

Even DePaul coach Joey Meyer admitted he thought the game was headed for overtime.

"But Coach Mo [future Bradley coach Jim Molinari, then an assistant at DePaul] grabbed

Tony Holifield ranks No. 1 in career field goal percentage at Illinois State at .618.

me and said it was a three," said Meyer. "I looked up at the scoreboard and said, 'Let's get the hell out of here while we're still ahead.'"

The Redbirds were 3-9 heading into the Redbird Arena inaugural January 11, 1989. A crowd of 9,724 saw Illinois State beat Chicago State, 71–70.

Blair made the first basket in Illinois State's new home; Skarich hit the first three-pointer; Scott Fowler had the first dunk; and Coleman

blocked the first shot. Coleman paced ISU with 17 points and 13 rebounds while Fowler, a freshman forward, added a career-high 16 points and Jackson had 14.

Then-President Lloyd Watkins, who still lives in Bloomington-Normal, has a special appreciation for Redbird Arena.

"Nothing was easy," said Watkins. "Every time I drive by it, I think of all the blood, sweat and tears that went into that building. We had a lot of hurdles to overcome. We got the support of the students, but it was a tough sell to the Board of Regents."

After the successful opening of Redbird Arena, things got a little better for the Redbirds, who split their final 16 games, including a 66–60 upset victory over No. 2 seed and host school Wichita State in the opening round of the Valley tournament. ISU seeded seventh, then lost to sixth-seeded Southern Illinois, 69–61, in the semifinals to bring an end to a 13-17 season. It was the first losing season since ISU joined Division I in 1970.

Little did ISU fans know that it would be the final game in which Donewald would be the head coach. With the backing of new President Thomas Wallace, Athletics Director Ron Wellman would remove Donewald eight days

created conflict for Donewald, who opposed rule changes like the shot clock and three-point line. Despite that, he used the changes to his advantage both defensively and in unleashing long-range shooters like Harris and Taphorn.

"That's Donewald for you," said former Drake coach Gary Garner. "Opposes the hell out of the new rules, then uses them to beat you."

played a key role in the impetus for Redbird Arena, greater fan support and expanded media attention.

In the end, Donewald's supporters and detractors would probably agree that he showed himself true to his background as a rugged disciplinarian, a tireless worker, a tenacious teacher and a proven winner.

Not long after his departure from Normal, Donewald became the head coach at Western Michigan.

Cliff Peterson usually drew the other team's toughest offensive player no matter what position. The 6-foot-8 Peterson had the quick feet to guard perimeter players.

Matt Taphorn is No. 1 in single-season and career three-point field goal percentage at Illinois State and, in the 1990s, served as analyst for Redbird basketball on TV.

later, bringing an end to his 11-year Illinois State career.

In the 1980s, many of the top college basketball coaches were flamboyant personalities who, in the spirit of the decade, pushed the envelope and fed on the burgeoning media growth. Donewald's conservative style was a study in contrasts.

Even the evolution of the college game

Several who had routine dealings with the complex Donewald found him to be difficult and contentious, traits that probably contributed to his dismissal. But Donewald, who diligently guarded his privacy, could also flash a charming side, perhaps too infrequently.

Still, it must be noted that Donewald's teams, through their string of victories, championships and post-season tournament bids,

Chapter 26
BENDER HEALS, WINS (1989 – 1993)

After firing Bob Donewald, Athletics Director Ron Wellman wanted the next Illinois State coach to be an energetic individual with a strong basketball background who had the charm and charisma to reach out to the community.

"I knew there would be a group of folks who thought the decision to fire Bob Donewald was wrong, and therefore was not going to be a part of the program anymore," said Wellman. "And, I knew they would be very vocal about it."

Wellman interviewed four candidates he felt might fit that scenario for four to five hours in Chicago. He readily admits it became very

obvious to him who he wanted as the next coach an hour into his conversation with one of the applicants.

Thirty-one-year-old Bob Bender fit the bill perfectly. He had the traits Wellman was looking for: strong people skills and six years of experience as an assistant coach under Mike Krzyzewski at Duke, one of the premier programs in college basketball.

Bender had been a winning player as well, having been a freshman on the 1976 NCAA Championship team at Indiana before transferring to Duke in time to play in the 1978 NCAA Championship game against Kentucky.

He also was a native son, of sorts, having graduated from Bloomington High School in 1975 with all-state and all-America basketball honors. His roots were all Illinois. He grew up in Quincy before moving to Bloomington for his sophomore year when his father, Bob Sr., became the head coach at BHS.

Bender stayed four years at Illinois State, posting a 60-57 record while guiding the Redbirds to a Missouri Valley Conference post-season tournament championship and a berth in the NCAA Tournament in his first season at the helm. His teams also won back-to-back Valley regular-season championships in his

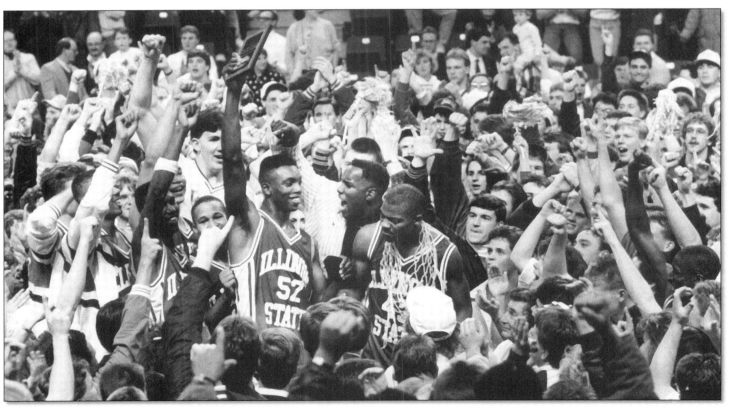

Jarrod Coleman (left) and 1990 MVC Tournament MVP Rickey Jackson got mobbed after Illinois State's 81–78 championship game win over Southern Illinois March 6, 1990.

A versatile scorer for the early 1990s, Rickey Jackson could drive to the bucket as well as shoot the three.

"While these kids might have struggled the year before, they knew how to win," said Bender. "They had been well-coached and they understood the way that I believed in playing too. I knew they would be well-versed defensively with man. I knew motion offense was something they had already been running. The main thing I wanted them to understand was that I wanted to allow them more freedom."

Typically, it took time for the veteran players and new coaches to come together. The Redbirds were a struggling 6-9 in mid-January.

Things began to jell in a 63–62 home victory against Drake, and Illinois State won eight of its next nine games before heading on a two-game road swing to Wichita State and Southern Illinois. The Redbirds dropped a 66–52 decision at Wichita and trailed league-leading Southern Illinois by a game when they arrived in Carbondale—just one win from a share of the MVC title. That title was denied by virtue of an 85–79 loss.

The Redbirds finished the regular season with an 83–77 victory at home over Creighton as Jackson netted a then-Redbird Arena record 32 points. What made Jackson's feat even more remarkable was the fact that his mother lay critically ill in a hospital in Mount Morris, Mich.

"I was thinking about winning the game for her. I wanted to play exceptionally well for her," said Jackson. "I dedicated this game, this season and the rest of my life to her."

The win also sent the Redbirds into the Valley's post-season tournament as the No. 2 seed behind Southern Illinois. For the final time, the MVC Tournament was awarded to a campus site based on competitive bids. Illinois State's Redbird Arena, just 14 months old, was the 1990 site.

Fowler's 16 points led to a 77–62 first-round triumph over Drake. Next came a 69–64 semifinal win over Creighton, the tournament's No. 3 seed, despite 32 points from Creighton's Bob Harstad.

Bender was openly crying following the victory. They weren't tears of joy, though.

They were tears of sorrow for Jackson, whose mother had passed away earlier in the day. Jackson carried the burden by himself into

final two seasons.

The Redbirds returned all 12 lettermen from the previous year. The nucleus was built around the talents of seniors Rickey Jackson,

Jarrod Coleman, Randy Blair, Jon Pemberton and Sonny Roberts. Rugged sophomore forward Scott Fowler and heady freshman point guard Richard Thomas added to the mix.

the game, telling Bender not to say anything to his teammates.

Jackson proceeded to hit his first three shots from the field, including two from three-point territory, and four straight free throws to help the Redbirds build a 17–9 advantage. Jackson finished with a team-high 19 points.

"I just wanted to come out and give us a lift at the start," said Jackson, who indicated after the game that he would play in the championship game against Rich Herrin's No. 1-seeded Salukis, who already had 26 wins.

With ESPN's "Championship Week" cameras rolling, the title game lived up to all the pre-game hype and excitement it had generated. A lively sellout crowd of 10,625 people (the largest crowd to watch a game at Redbird Arena) arrived early and stayed well into the night celebrating Illinois State's 81–78 victory, which earned the Redbirds their first NCAA Tournament berth since 1985.

Jackson, who scored 16 points in the second half, and Coleman combined for 43 points to lead the winning charge. Coleman finished with 23 against a talented SIU front-line while Jackson added 20 to earn the tournament's most valuable player award.

"I had hoped this, but I never dreamed it would happen," said Bender after the game. "My goal was for this team to compete like we did in the regular season and make a good showing in the tournament because it was here."

It was far from easy as Illinois State saw a 13-point lead of 50–37 with 16:58 remaining evaporate as Southern Illinois went on a 12–1 run to cut the margin to 51–49.

The Salukis forged ties at 59 and 61. However, the Redbirds never fell behind. Thomas hit an 18-foot jumper with 7:46 remaining to give the Redbirds the lead for good at 63–61. The advantage stretched to 75–69 with 3:23 to go behind 10 of Jackson's points.

SIU made a final run and cut the gap to 79–78 with 39 seconds to go. Jackson bagged two free throws with 34 seconds left for the final margin, although Southern got off two potential game-tying shots from three-point range in the final eight seconds.

One of the Missouri Valley's best defenders, Randy Blair contributed scoring and leadership to the Redbirds.

The defense, keyed by Blair, the MVC Defensive Player of the Year, went a long way in securing the victory.

Nearly 1,500 people joined the Illinois State team at Redbird Arena to watch the NCAA pairings show on TV, enjoying concessions and the MVC title game on tape. The Redbirds had to wait until the last regional field (the West

Talented and athletic, Jarrod Coleman was capable of beating a whole team full of defenders.

Regional at Long Beach, Calif.) was announced to know their fate. They received the No. 14 seed and a date against defending national champion and No. 3 seed Michigan, coached by former Redbird guard Steve Fisher.

Fisher had guided the Wolverines to the NCAA title as interim coach the previous year. Had Michigan not advanced that far, Fisher could have been coaching the Redbirds instead of Bender. Fisher reportedly had conversations with Wellman concerning the ISU position.

Seldom have No. 14 seeds beaten No. 3 seeds in the NCAA Tournament, but the Redbirds nearly went against the form. They played Michigan even for nearly 39 minutes. A Jackson steal and dunk tied the score at 70 apiece with 1:44 remaining.

Michigan took a timeout after Jackson's dunk to set a play to get the ball to all-American guard Rumeal Robinson. However, Illinois State switched from a man-to-man defense to a zone, and it forced the Wolverines to swing the ball to Sean Higgins, who hit an open three-pointer with 1:13 left to put Michigan in control.

"I was scared," Fisher said afterwards. "Illinois State played hard. I'm pleased they played the way they did, but I'm more happy that we won."

The Redbirds, who made 12 of their first 21 shots, led by five points twice in the first half, then saw their shooting touch fall cold in the second half as Michigan came on strong.

"Had we hit a couple of shots we would have knocked off the national champions," lamented Roberts, one of five seniors to finish their careers at Illinois State. "We all knew we could have beaten them. Believe me, that was difficult to deal with. We didn't want to accept it, but we had to look at our season and be happy. We wanted to get to the NCAA Tournament and we made it."

The Redbirds finished their first year under Bender, 18-13. Coleman, who played in 123 games, and Jackson, who played in 122, ended their stellar four-year careers 18th and 22nd, respectively, on the school's all-time scoring list. After the 6-9 start, the Redbirds won 13 of 17 games in a fairy-tale run to their fourth NCAA Tournament bid.

In the Redbird tradition of no-nonsense big men, Sonny Roberts parlayed hard work into Illinois State victories.

◆　◆　◆　◆　◆　◆

Thirty minutes before the Redbirds were to board a bus to Dayton for their 1990–91 season opener, junior forward Fowler tore the anterior cruciate ligament in his left knee. His season was over, and the 1990–91 nightmare was just beginning.

Skarich, whose career never fully blossomed because of knee injuries, was the lone senior,

Scott Fowler was a key cog in the Redbirds' run to the MVC title in 1990. His knee injury was the first of many setbacks the following year.

and the only returning starters were Fowler, who joined the opening lineup during the 1989–90 second-half sprint, and the sophomore Thomas.

Still, the upbeat Bender was optimistic about his team's chances because of a strong recruiting class that included Reggie Wilson from nearby Lincoln Junior College, and freshmen Todd Wemhoener, Mike VandeGarde, Scott Taylor and Charles Barnes.

On the heels of Fowler's injury, Dayton slammed the Redbirds, 109–69, in an ESPN nationally televised game. The first of a record 12 straight losses led to a 5-23 record, the fewest number of victories in the program's 63 years.

It wasn't until January 14 that the Redbirds tasted victory when little-known sophomore guard Todd Kagel, a graduate of Normal Community High School who made the team under Bob Donewald as a walk-on, hit a 22-foot three-pointer with three seconds remaining to lift Illinois State past Indiana State, 56–55, at Redbird Arena.

Kagel's heroics started the Redbirds on a three-game winning streak, with all the victories coming in the waning seconds. For the first time of many, 6-foot-7 Mike VandeGarde was the hero in a 57–55 win over Drake at Des Moines. That time, he hit a shot from deep in the right corner at the buzzer. It was the first of four times in his career that VandeGarde scored the late points to beat the Bulldogs.

Wemhoener was the man of the hour for the Redbirds in the next game against Creighton as he made two free throws with 23 seconds to preserve ISU's third straight victory—a 71–68 decision over the 1991 MVC champions before another ESPN national television audience.

The Redbirds returned home for a rare February non-conference game against Chicago State, which had won only three games. The game was physical from the outset and with one second remaining in the first half a fight broke out between Illinois State's Taylor and Chicago State's Derrick Van with Illinois State holding a 39–23 lead.

After Van shot a three-pointer, he and Taylor became entangled trying for the rebound with Van falling on top of Taylor. Van then grabbed Taylor around the neck and the melee broke out.

Eleven of the 13 Chicago State players and Redbird guard Antoine Hicks were ejected from the game for fighting and/or leaving the bench during a fight. Because it didn't have enough players to compete, Chicago State was forced to forfeit the game and Illinois State was awarded a 2–0 victory.

Bender, trying to act as peacemaker, suffered a broken nose in the Redbirds' final win of the season. At the time, though, Bender believed his team was developing despite the adversity.

"We were just not a very good basketball team," said Bender. "There are no excuses to be made. But in the adversity of that season, the freshman players probably grew up a lot quicker. So, then coming back, I knew without any question that third year we'd be right back to where we wanted to be and that was challenging for a championship."

Wilson led the team in scoring (15.2) and rebounding (7.0) and was voted the league's top newcomer.

◆　　◆　　◆　　◆　　◆　　◆

A healthy Fowler led a group of 11 lettermen—all with starting experience—to open the 1991–92 season. But, like all four of Bender's Illinois State teams, the Redbirds struggled out of the gates. They were a disappointing 4-5 through December before heading to Omaha to meet Tony Barone's talented Creighton Bluejays with a chance to go 2-0 in Valley play.

Bender had said before the season that if the Redbirds were going to contend for the championship, defense would have to be the team's trademark. His team showed it with a 56–49 triumph at Creighton. However, the victory was bittersweet because Wilson suffered a career-ending broken right leg and torn knee ligaments 12 seconds into the game.

Sadly, three years later, the likable and always polite Wilson was shot to death in his hometown of Chicago, the victim of a random carjacking.

The Redbirds followed the Creighton victory with three more wins to lead the Valley, heading for an always-tough two-game road swing to

Bob Bender addressed the crowd and media after Illinois State secured the 1993 Missouri Valley Conference regular-season title at Redbird Arena.

Wichita State and Tulsa. Illinois State figured to win at Wichita State, but knew the odds would be long at Tulsa.

However, Wichita State stunned the Redbirds, 66–50, and a livid Bender made a point after his team arrived in Tulsa the next day. Road practices between games ordinarily involve shooting and stretching, but Bender made this an exception and put his club through a long and tough workout. The team responded the next night for a 73–72 win.

Kagel, nicknamed "Money" by his teammates because of his ability to make clutch free throws, calmly deposited three charities with 0.05 seconds left in the game. He was fouled by Gary Collier as he attempted to get off a three-point shot deep in the left corner.

"I didn't know he [Collier] was there," said Kagel. "I just knew there wasn't much time left and I just wanted to get my feet set square to the basket. I wasn't thinking about getting fouled. I just turned and the guy was there in my face."

Now 6-1 in the Valley, the Redbirds were looking ahead to a showdown with Southern Illinois at Redbird Arena. Southern would win that game, as well as the game against ISU at Carbondale, but the teams tied for the league regular-season championship with 14-4 records.

Seven straight victories at the end of the regular season helped secure Illinois State's first regular-season title since 1983–84. It also marked only the fourth time in the 85-year

history of the Valley that a team had vaulted from last to first in one season. The successful year earned Bender the league's coach of the year honors.

The Redbirds were the No. 2 seed in the conference tournament, but never got a third meeting with top-seeded Southern Illinois. Southwest Missouri State saw to that with a 61–58 overtime win in the semifinals. With an 18-11 record, the Redbirds were hopeful of their first NIT bid since the 1987–88 season, but that call never came.

The regular season had included perhaps the most bizarre game in Redbird Arena history, a 54–51 win over Drake that was interrupted twice for non-player medical emergencies.

Bender, an emotional sideline coach, apparently passed out in front of the Redbird bench in the first half. He remained on the bench and returned for the start of the second half. However, he began feeling weak midway through that frame and left the bench. He was driven to the hospital by Wellman (with the radio off supposedly) where he was checked and

Steady point guard Richard Thomas controlled the Redbird offense during the entire Bender era.

To raise funds for a European tour for the Redbirds, Bob Bender subjected himself to a roast in the summer of 1992. Among those who came to Bloomington-Normal for the event were, from left, Duke head coach Mike Krzyzewski, former Duke and NBA standout Mike Gminski and noted national sportswriter and author John Feinstein.

released with a clean bill of health.

In a separate incident, Drake forward Kevin Sams and veteran referee Ron Berkholtz collided under the basket, resulting in a broken left elbow and a head injury for Berkholtz. The game was delayed 23 minutes and Berkholtz was eventually transported to BroMenn Regional Hospital where he was treated for the injuries.

Berkholtz returned to action the next year. In his first return engagement at Redbird Arena, the fans gave him a standing ovation.

◆ ◆ ◆ ◆ ◆ ◆

With only Fowler and Wilson graduated from the previous year, the Redbirds returned nine lettermen and four starters for Bender's final season in Normal.

Led by four-year regular Thomas at point guard, steady Kagel and a cast of juniors including VandeGarde, Taylor, Wemhoener and Barnes, the Redbirds were pre-season favorites

to win a second straight Valley title.

Illinois State opened with wins over Lewis and Butler before promptly losing six of its next eight, including three of four league games.

VandeGarde, who had scored 25 points in a 63–60 loss at lowly Indiana State, followed that performance with a 26-point effort at Redbird Arena to give Illinois State an 88–74 victory over Southern Illinois that turned the Redbirds' season around.

They won nine of their next 10 games to jump back into the conference race at 9-4. In fact, the Redbirds would lose only one more conference game during the season to finish with a 13-5 record and their first outright regular-season title since Jim Collie's 1967–68 team.

The Redbirds wrapped up sole possession of the league championship with a 71–59 win in their regular-season finale with Northern Iowa at Redbird Arena.

It also marked the final home game for

seniors Kagel, Steve Fitch and Thomas, whose sterling four-year career left him 24th in all time scoring with 1,170 points and sixth in assists with 424.

While the seniors were honored, the night belonged to VandeGarde, who made 15 of 20 shots from the field on the way to a career-high 32 points as the Redbirds became the first team since Tulsa in 1984–85 to win back-to-back regular-season championships.

The Redbirds entered the conference tournament as the No. 1 seed and had to rally from a 14-point deficit to avoid an upset in the semifinals against Drake. And, again, it was VandeGarde who turned back the Bulldogs by making a pair of free throws with 11 seconds remaining to earn the victory.

"I'm sure he [Drake coach Rudy Washington] cringes every time he sees me at the line," said VandeGarde, a fan favorite at Illinois State with a knack for making big plays.

The Redbirds ran into Southern Illinois in

Reggie Wilson was the MVC Newcomer of the Year in 1991. A broken leg ended his senior season prematurely, then he met a tragic death shortly after finishing his Illinois State career.

A former walk-on player, Todd Kagel will long be remembered for making three free throws with 0:00.5 seconds left to beat Tulsa and lift Illinois State to the 1992 MVC Championship.

Mike VandeGarde's nifty low-post moves often fooled defenders.

the championship tilt and could never really get untracked. The Salukis used a pair of offensive spurts to topple the Redbirds, 70–59, to earn the league's automatic NCAA berth and leave the 'Birds with a 19-10 record and forced to play the waiting game for a possible NIT berth.

While the 19 victories was the most by a Bender-coached team, it wasn't enough to get the Redbirds a bid to the NIT. Southwest Missouri was taken from the Missouri Valley ahead of Illinois State.

Days later, Bender resigned as head coach to take the same position at the University of Washington.

"Leaving Illinois State was not an easy decision because I was very happy there. But it was an opportunity in my career I couldn't pass

up," said Bender. "During my third year as coach, Ron [Wellman] asked me to put together a list of schools that I would be interested in if they ever showed an interest in me. That list included Texas, Georgetown, Michigan, Florida and Washington."

Wellman had left the previous fall to become athletics director at Wake Forest and was succeeded by Rick Greenspan. Bender still believes the Illinois State job is a good one.

"It's a job that has a tremendous history and tradition of being successful," said Bender. "And very rarely do you find a community that supports a program the way Illinois State fans do. Redbird Arena is a testament to the support the community gives. If it weren't for that support, there wouldn't be a Redbird Arena."

Chapter 27

WITH BACKGROUND A-PLENTY, STALLINGS COMES TO TOWN (1993–1995)

Rick Greenspan hadn't been on the job as athletics director for two months when he was faced with the task of finding a replacement for Bender. But because Bender's name had surfaced for other coaching vacancies other than Washington late in the season, Greenspan had already begun formulating a list of potential candidates in his mind should the need arise.

Just as when Bender was hired, ISU was able to lure another former Illinois all-state high school player and top-flight assistant coach from one of the best college basketball programs in the nation to its job.

Introduced by Greenspan as "our first and only choice as head basketball coach," 32-year-old Collinsville native Kevin Stallings became the 15th men's coach in school history.

"He had a thorough understanding of the conference, the university, the understanding of the community, how he wanted to recruit and who he wanted to recruit," Greenspan said. "What I saw in Kevin was somebody who would not leave a stone unturned for our path to success. While we had an open search to fill the job because I wanted to see what type of candidates we could attract, Kevin was the guy I was comparing people against."

Stallings, who also excelled as a collegiate player at Purdue, spent six seasons as an assistant coach under Gene Keady on the Boilermakers' staff following his playing days. And before coming to ISU, Stallings served as an assistant under Roy Williams at Kansas where the highly successful Jayhawks posted a 132-43 record and earned two Final Four berths during Stallings' time there.

"There will be many things I will try to take

from Roy Williams, many things I will try to take from Gene Keady and many things I will try to take from my high school coach [the legendary Vergil Fletcher]. This is certainly a dream come true," said Stallings when introduced as head coach. "My teams will be very competitive. They will scratch and fight and play hard."

Stallings wasn't just blowing smoke when he made those comments April 29, 1993. His first five years resulted in one of the most successful eras in school history. Aside from his first season at ISU, when he was forced to install his sophisticated system in a relatively short period of time, the Redbirds have been one of the most successful programs in the country.

That success is a tribute to his eye for talent and his sharp mind.

The Redbirds landed National Invitation Tournament berths during Stallings' second and third seasons, then qualified for consecutive NCAA Tournament berths in years four and five.

The Redbirds are a sparkling 107-48 during Stallings' tenure, giving him a .690 winning percentage which ranks second in school history behind Smithson's .786.

Stallings' fifth team (1997–98) also became the first in Missouri Valley history to win back-to-back regular-season and post-season tournament conference championships.

◆   ◆   ◆   ◆   ◆   ◆

In Stallings' first season, he inherited 10 lettermen and four returning starters from a team that finished 19-10 and won the league's regular-season championship in the

previous year.

Because of the number of returning players learning a new system under a new coaching staff that employed a change in philosophy, the Redbirds understandably struggled in the early going. They dropped their season opener at Northwestern and went on to lose two of their next three games before winning three straight to boost their record to 4-3.

ISU had a 9-9 record when Tulsa, which went on to win the regular-season championship, came to Redbird Arena in early February. The Redbirds disposed of the Golden Hurricane, 61–56, and started a seven-game winning streak (the longest such streak for a Stallings-coached team).

Included in the streak was a 92–88 overtime victory at Creighton where Mike VandeGarde, who had the uncanny knack for drawing charging fouls and scoring baskets with up-and-under moves around the basket, turned in a gutsy performance.

The gangly 6-foot-8 forward scored 27 points, including eight of ISU's 13 points in overtime, and handled six rebounds while playing 37 of 45 minutes with a stretched posterior cruciate ligament in his right knee.

"I honestly did not expect him to play," said Stallings after the game. "I figured we would put him in the first time and we would find out that his knee was not going to be well enough for him to continue to play the rest of the day."

VandeGarde's status was so much in doubt that his father phoned Stallings in Omaha the night before the game to get an update on his son's injury.

"We had 19 or 20 friends and relatives [from Iowa and his home state of Minnesota]

With a pedigree which included a playing career in the Big Ten Conference and assistant coaching stints with Purdue's Gene Keady and Kansas' Roy Williams, Kevin Stallings brought a winning background and a sense of confidence to Illinois State.

coming to the game to watch Mike play," said VandeGarde's father. "I wanted to let them know that they might get to see Mike play for only a couple of minutes or not at all."

"I couldn't let them come all that way just to watch me sit on the bench," said VandeGarde, who finished No. 20 on the school's all-time scoring list with 1,225 points, No. 1 in blocked shots with 134 and No. 8 in free throws made with 296. He also finished No. 9 in minutes played (2,603) and became the school's first academic all-American in six seasons during his senior year in 1994.

The seven-game winning streak pushed the record to 16-9, but then the Redbirds suffered back-to-back losses to Southern Illinois in the regular-season finale and to Northern Iowa in the opening round of the conference tournament.

Illinois State made good on Stallings' promise to be more offensive-minded as it set school records for three-point baskets made with 145 and attempted with 434. The Redbirds also notched their best scoring average (73.8) since the 1979 season.

The loss to Northern Iowa not only signaled the end of the season but the conclusion of the careers of VandeGarde, Scott Taylor, Todd Wemhoener and Charles Barnes, who were largely responsible for the back-to-back regular-season titles during their sophomore and junior campaigns.

In some ways, though, it also marked the beginning of the *real* Stallings era.

◆   ◆   ◆   ◆   ◆   ◆

Stallings and his staff of assistant coaches (King Rice, Jeff Wulbrun and Tom Richardson) were forced to replace eight lettermen and four starters from their first team, which finished with a 16-11 record.

The staff did that by signing eight newcomers, six of whom would become instrumental in raising the standard of excellence for Redbird basketball. It also marked the first of two straight recruiting classes that were ranked among the top 40 nationally for playing ability.

Included in the recruiting class were junior college transfers Maurice Trotter, who became

the first ISU player since Derrick Sanders in 1987 to earn first-team all-conference honors, and power forward Kenny Wright.

The class also consisted of sophomore Marcus Franklin, a throwback to the players of the 1970s with his Afro hairstyle and his knee-high socks; redshirt freshman Rob Gibbons; and true freshmen Dan Muller, Jamar Smiley and Kenneth Pierson.

Franklin lasted just one season with the

Chad Altadonna was a Bob Bender recruit whose career crossed over into the Stallings era. He then returned to Stallings' staff as an assistant coach in 1997.

Redbirds, but Muller, Smiley and Gibbons went on to make a significant mark in Illinois State basketball history.

The Redbirds returned just one starter, senior point guard David Cason, the first ISU player to ever lead the Missouri Valley in assists, and three other lettermen for Stallings' second year.

The other lettermen included seniors Chad Altadonna and Brian Kern and junior Antonio Cooper. That trio along with Cason and the aforementioned newcomers blended together to produce a 20-13 record.

The group, which consisted of seven first-year players on an 11-man roster, also would give ISU its first National Invitation Tournament berth since the 1987–88 season and a second-place finish in the regular-season conference standings.

That season may have been the best coaching job by Stallings at Illinois State as he turned what was supposed to be a rebuilding campaign into the first of four straight 20-win campaigns.

The Redbirds were barely keeping their head above the .500 mark at 12-10 when they

A relentless defender, Todd Wemhoener ranks No. 3 in career steals at Illinois State.

won three straight before losing at Drake. Then came a home game against Southern Illinois, one of the games that stands out in Stallings' mind.

His team twice rallied from eight-point deficits in the second half and a four-point deficit with a little over one minute to play to post a 104–98 double-overtime Valley win over Southern Illinois before 9,170 people at Redbird Arena.

Cason, who set an arena record with 16 assists, made the play that saved the day for the Redbirds as he stripped the ball away from Chris Carr (who scored an arena-record 38 points in the game) under the Illinois State basket and scored on a layup to cut the deficit to 78–74 with 59 seconds to play in regulation.

Trotter then hit a 12-foot jump shot in the lane with two seconds remaining in regulation to force the first overtime. The Redbirds trailed by four points with 31 seconds remaining in the first extra period, but battled back to force a second overtime when Franklin tipped in a missed Trotter shot with seven seconds to go.

The hot-shooting Trotter secured the lead for good at 95–93 in the second OT with a jump shot at the 3:03 mark. The victory was the first of five straight, including a 75–72 win over Southwest Missouri State in the opening round of the Valley Tournament.

Illinois State lost in the semifinals of the tournament to Southern Illinois, 72–68, before a tournament-record 13,271 people at the Kiel Center in St. Louis to finish with a 19-12 record and cast doubt on an NIT bid.

A week later, though, the smile on Kern's face told the story.

"We had the world's tallest leak," said fellow senior teammate Altadonna, who had joined the rest of his teammates in the Redbird Arena locker room for a meeting when Kern walked in. "With that huge smile on his face I knew we were in. Someone in the media had told him and Coach Stallings came in a few minutes later and confirmed it."

What Stallings confirmed was that the Redbirds had been selected to play in the 32-team NIT and would face Utah State in Logan, Utah, in the opening round.

Like Redbird players from many eras, Brian Kern played his best basketball as a senior, helping Illinois State advance to the NIT quarterfinals in 1995.

Redbird Arena fans cried "Cooooooop" whenever 5-foot-9 Antonio Cooper launched his patented three-point shot. A popular specialist, his 93 three-pointers provided some electrifying moments.

"I'm happy as a bird. It's a great feeling. I definitely had my doubts because of what happened a few years ago," said Kern referring to his sophomore year when the Redbirds were passed over by the NIT selection committee. "Chad and I felt our chances were 60-70 that we would make it. I told Coach Stallings I felt like I had been handed another

life. Now I want to do everything I can to make the most of it."

The 6-foot-9 Kern, who blossomed during his senior season, did indeed make the most of his opportunity. He scored 16 points and grabbed a team-high six rebounds, but more importantly, he blanketed Big West Player of the Year Eric Franson (5-of-15 from the field)

Kevin Stallings' high-energy offense was ignited by his first signee, David Cason.

Maurice Trotter was the leading scorer on the 1995 and 1996 NIT teams.

to help the Redbirds earn a 93–87 overtime victory over the Aggies.

The Redbirds also received a career-high 29 points from Trotter, who scored seven of ISU's 13 points in overtime.

Illinois State appeared to have won the game at the end of regulation, but the officials ruled that Smiley's rebound basket came after the horn had sounded with the score knotted at 80. The lead changed hands five times in the overtime period and the score was tied four times.

The victory marked the first 20-win season since the 1984–85 campaign and the first triumph in post-season play since 1987.

The second-round matchup was with Washington State at Redbird Arena and the game turned out to be one of the classics of Stallings' tenure. The Redbirds suffered an 83–80 loss, but it was one of the rare times Stallings, while disappointed, wasn't upset with a defeat.

"That was a great college basketball game," he said after watching his team finish 20-13. "It

was one of the few times when I felt we played as well as we could play and just didn't win."

Rarely over the subsequent three season would Stallings have to spend much tim bemoaning a loss.

Kenny Wright's high-flying style of play could change the momentum of a game.

Chapter 28

THE GANG'S ALL HERE (1995–1997)

For the first time in his head coaching career, Stallings didn't feel like a rookie coach when he greeted his third team at the beginning of the 1995–96 season.

"We're actually beginning a season where we have a slight bit of carryover from a prior year," Stallings said at the team's annual media day. "I have felt like we have essentially been through two year No. 1's.

"Our first year we inherited a senior-laden group and we probably neutralized their experience factor by coming in new. Then, last year we had so many newcomers to try and involve in the process again that it felt like we started over from square one."

The returning starters were seniors Maurice Trotter and Kenny Wright along with 6-foot-6 sophomore forward Dan Muller, who became the first Illinois State player to earn the Valley's Freshman of the Year honor by playing sound defense and averaging 10.2 points and 4.8 rebounds per game.

Not bad for a guy who the Redbirds would not have recruited had sophomore Markku Larkio decided to return for his junior year. Instead, Larkio opted to return to his native country of Finland.

The coaching staff was aware of Muller, but chose not to recruit him because he would play the same position as Larkio.

"We knew Dan would have to play the No. 3 spot [small forward] and we already had Markku there," explained Stallings. "We didn't want to recruit another player for that spot, but when we heard Markku might not return, we decided to pursue Dan."

Muller became the Cal Ripken of ISU basketball during his career. He started every game, a school-record 128, and also set school marks for career minutes played (4,169) and average minutes per game (32.6).

"I never thought I would start every game," said Muller, one of the more popular and unassuming players to ever don a Redbird uniform. "I came from a small high school [Central Catholic in Lafayette, Ind.], so I didn't know what to expect when I got here.

"I didn't have any expectations or goals when I got here. We had nine new players on the team my freshman year, so everybody was in the same position. I just wanted to come in, work and play hard, and get my degree."

Only once during his career did Muller sit out an entire practice session, and that was because of a sprained ankle. A management major, he also was named a Bone Scholar, the highest academic honor at ISU, and was a second-team GTE Academic All-American as a junior and senior.

Aside from the three returning starters, the Redbirds also returned three-point specialist Antonio Cooper, big man Rob Gibbons and Smiley, who became the school's all-time career leader in assists (No. 2 in the Valley) with 740.

Illinois State gained the services of burly 6-foot-7 center LeRoy Watkins, who was forced to sit out his freshman year under NCAA rules, and lanky 6-foot-8 leaper Kenneth Pierson, who redshirted his freshman year.

While that was enough to generate excitement among the fans, little did they know how one of the more celebrated recruiting classes (6-foot-6 forward Rico Hill and 6-foot-3 guard Kyle Cartmill) would fit into the mix.

"As excited as we were about that season, the fact was that we still lost four of our top six scorers and four of our top seven rebounders from the previous year," said Stallings. "We had four first-year players who we really needed to make some significant contributions."

The Redbirds opened the season innocently enough by posting a 7-5 record before catching fire. ISU won five straight and seven of its next eight games before a trip to nationally ranked Cincinnati for a midnight start on ESPN. The Redbirds suffered a 91–57 blowout.

The Redbirds rebounded to win five of their next six games, including a 74–52 decision at Drake when they made a school- and conference-record 17 shots from three-point range. Trotter led the Redbirds with 25 points while Cooper added a career-record 21 points. Smiley handed out a career-high 14 assists.

"Jamar was the key," said Stallings, whose team made its 17 treys on 31 attempts for an amazing 55 percent. "He was able to penetrate inside their defense and kick the ball back out. Our shooters were receiving the ball squared to the basket."

The Redbirds, who were picked to finish third according to the pre-season poll, found themselves with a chance to win the league title when they traveled to Peoria to meet Bradley in the next-to-last regular-season game.

"It was like two heavyweight boxers just slugging it out," was the way Bradley coach Jim Molinari described his team's 65–64 victory. "We were just fortunate to have the last punch."

While the loss was devastating at the time, it turned out to be the beginning of an unlikely two-game losing streak as the 'Birds dropped their

Conference award-winner, academic all-American and team leader Dan Muller led his teams to national post-season tournaments four straight years. His layup in overtime closed Illinois State's 82–81 first-round win over Tennessee in the 1998 NCAA Tournament.

final regular-season game at Indiana State, a team firmly established near the bottom of the league.

Illinois State notched its 20th victory for the second straight year with a win over Northern Iowa in the opening round of the Valley tournament in St. Louis before falling to Tulsa in the semifinals, 69–52.

After finishing second in the conference standings, an NIT berth came in the form of a first-round home game against Mount St. Mary's. An easy 73–49 triumph in that game set up a date at Wisconsin with the Badgers.

Fans were primed for the matchup against a Big Ten Conference school as six buses and nearly 600 Redbird followers made the trip.

"It felt funny coming out of the locker room because we were expecting boos," said Hill. "But when we stepped on the court, there were Redbird fans everywhere. They were loud and it felt great."

The 6-foot-6 Hill and Muller recorded their second straight double-doubles in leading the Redbirds to an impressive 77–62 thrashing of the Badgers. The outcome ranks as one of the more memorable victories in recent times and also advanced the Redbirds a step deeper than they had ever been in the NIT under its expanded format.

"Everyone thought last year was going to be a rebuilding year," said Stallings following the victory. "We were able to overcome that and get into post-season play and get to the second round [of the NIT]. This year we've gone one step farther. It shows we are making progress."

Watkins also turned in one of his better performances. Playing with torn ligaments in his thumb, Watkins scored 14 points and grabbed seven rebounds.

There was little time to savor the victory, though, as the Redbirds found themselves in New Orleans two days later, facing Tulane in the quarterfinals.

Outmatched in athletic talent and size, ISU scrapped and clawed, but came up short, 83–72.

The setback ended the most successful season in 10 years with a 22-12 record.

Piloting the Redbird running game with precision made Jamar Smiley the all-time Illinois State assist leader and helped players like Rico Hill (trailing) compile impressive point totals.

Nothing but good vibes surrounded the Redbirds as they prepared for the 1996–97 season. They returned eight lettermen, including four starters, from the previous year's team and added the services of long-range shooter Skipp Schaefbauer, who had transferred from East Carolina the previous season.

"We're excited because we think we have a chance to have something special," Stallings told the media before the team's first practice. "We're confident in the players' work ethic and character. The whole group is really cut into what we're trying to do."

What the Redbirds were trying to do that season was win the school's first Valley regular-season championship since 1993 and earn their first NCAA Tournament berth since 1990.

"Anything less than a league championship and NCAA Tournament bid would be disappointing," said junior co-captain Gibbons. "But we all know that we have a lot of hard work ahead of us to accomplish those goals."

Illinois State rolled to a 14-4 record to win the regular-season championship by two games over Southwest Missouri State and Bradley.

ISU opened its fourth season under Stallings with an impressive victory on the road at Pittsburgh. Interestingly, for as much success as Stallings had as the Redbirds' coach, none of his previous teams had opened the season with a win.

Schaefbauer made an immediate impact by leading the Redbirds with 16 points. Five of his six baskets came from beyond the three-point arc, a sight that became very familiar over the next two seasons.

The Redbirds won their next three games, including a satisfying 75–50 thumping of DePaul at the Kiel Center in St. Louis. It marked the first time the Redbirds had beaten DePaul since the 1982–83 campaign, and it also marked the first time ISU had opened the season with three straight victories since the 1984–85 campaign.

The only negative to come out of the DePaul game was that junior guard Steve Hansell, who earned the league's sixth man award at the end of the season, suffered a broken fifth metatarsal

The power in the paint for Illinois State's 1997 and 1998 NCAA Tournament teams was supplied by left-hander LeRoy Watkins.

bone in his right foot, which forced him to miss eight games.

Hill also gave Illinois State fans a glimpse of what would turn out to be an outstanding season by scoring a then-career-high 23 points.

Following a fourth straight victory at the expense of Ohio, the Redbirds laid an egg on another trip to Pittsburgh when Duquesne dropped them, 91–64. It was a sobering loss for the team, but one that got its attention.

The Redbirds, who did not lose two games in a row all season, responded with a 19-point victory at Northwestern, a 10-point win over Wisconsin-Green Bay and a 20-point thumping of Illinois-Chicago to conclude the non-conference portion of their schedule with a 7-1 record.

The Valley schedule began with wins over Creighton and Evansville, before Northern Iowa posted an improbable 77–71 overtime victory in Normal.

The resilient Redbirds won their next three games to move to 12-2 overall and 5-1 in the conference before heading to Cedar Falls, Iowa, and a rematch with UNI. Jason Daisy, who scored 24 points the first time the Panthers defeated ISU, was at it again.

Daisy, who would go on to earn the Valley's Player of the Year honors over ISU's Hill, scored 37 points as Northern Iowa handed the Redbirds another overtime loss, this time a 93–86 verdict.

The loss also knocked Illinois State out of first place and moved Wichita State into the top spot. Ironically, the Shockers were up next on the ISU schedule followed by home games against Southwest Missouri State and Bradley.

"That was a critical three-game homestand for us after having lost to Northern Iowa," said Stallings. "We didn't play great, but we played well enough to win all three of those games."

The highlight of the homestand, which put the Redbirds back atop the league standings, was watching Hill blitz Southwest Missouri State with a career-high 37 points and 13 rebounds. It is the most points scored by an ISU player in Redbird Arena and was one point shy of the arena-record 38 points posted by Southern Illinois' Chris Carr in a double-overtime game.

ISU concluded the regular season by winning nine of 11 games to make good on its pre-season No. 1 ranking in the conference with a 14-4 record. Included in the stretch was a 62–53 victory at Wichita State.

With Hill suffering from the flu bug, the Redbirds fell behind the Shockers by 17 points at halftime before rallying for the win. Watkins, despite playing only 20 minutes because of foul problems, scored 17 points to lead the victory march.

The 21-5 regular-season record included the school's first conference championship since the 1992–93 campaign.

Some of the motivation to tack on the post-season crown came the day before the tourney started at the league's annual awards luncheon.

It was there that Jason Daisy was presented the player of the year award, which he earned over Hill in very tight balloting, and Northern Iowa's Eldon Miller received the coach of the year award over Stallings. Interestingly, both of the league's highest post-season honors went to representatives of the fourth-place finisher.

Illinois State blew past Indiana State in the opening round to set up a semifinal date against none other than Northern Iowa. And again, the Panthers gave ISU all it could handle before the Redbirds rallied for a 69–65 victory. Hill scored 29 points and grabbed seven rebounds.

While Redbird fans were celebrating the victory in St. Louis, much of the talk not only centered around the upcoming championship game against Southwest Missouri State, but the Stallings stare."

With his team trailing UNI, 30–21, with three minutes, 46 seconds remaining in the first half and his team huddled around assistant coaches Jeff Wulbrun, King Rice and Tom Richardson, Stallings stood defiantly on the sidelines, his arms folded and his eyes fixed on the officials.

Upset over a couple of earlier calls, he simply stared at the officials for one minute, 55 seconds.

"I wanted to talk to the officials, but they wouldn't talk to me," said Stallings in his post-game news conference.

The officials were positioned near the

British-born Steve Hansell characterized the depth and versatility of the 1998 senior class by playing three different positions and making huge contributions off the bench.

baseline at ISU's end of the court. They talked with one another, but did not return Stallings' glare. Missouri Valley Conference supervisor of officials Jim Bain later said that Stallings "got his message across."

The Redbirds responded with a 12–2 run to take a 33–32 lead into the locker room at halftime.

"He [Stallings] just said to start coaching them, so we all tried to start coaching them,"

said Richardson. "We were just trying to get them to settle down and remain poised."

Stallings said the timeout "was probably the happiest moment of their [the players'] day because I wasn't around."

For Miller, it was a first. When asked if he'd seen such a stare-down in 35 years as a coach, Miller replied simply, "No."

The win over Northern Iowa set up the championship game against Southwest

153

Missouri and a chance for the Redbirds' first trip to the NCAA Tournament since the 1989–90 season. ISU rolled to a 16-point advantage early in the second half before 9,751 people at the Kiel Center.

But Southwest Missouri State, with former Olympic gold medal winner Steve Alford as its coach, came charging back. The Bears used 63 percent shooting from the field in the second half and a 27–11 run to tie the game at 66-all with 4:36 to go. However, ISU never let the Bears have the lead.

Watkins made a short jumper in the lane, Muller made one of two free throws and Hill banked in a 10-foot jumper from the left of the lane to give the Redbirds a 71–66 advantage with 2:59 to go.

"I was going to the left with the ball and got knocked off balance," said Hill, who was named the most valuable player of the tournament after scoring 31 points in the championship game. "I had to lean because I was off balance, so I had to let it go. I watched it kiss off the glass and started back down the floor because I knew it was going in."

The Redbirds secured their ticket to the NCAA Tournament when Muller made two free throws with 4.2 seconds remaining to give ISU a 75–72 win. It also gave ISU a 24-5 record, which equaled the school record for wins in a Division I season.

"I really believe character wins games and there aren't any teams with better character than our team," said an emotional Stallings after the game. "I knew this time would come. I just didn't know when. I didn't know if we could win it without a senior [on the roster]. I knew the players were good enough to do it, but I didn't know if I could coach them well enough. This is just a great experience."

Illinois State was awarded the No. 11 seed in the Midwest Regional at The Palace of Auburn Hills, Mich., and was pitted against No. 6 seed Iowa State of the first-year Big 12 Conference.

Unfortunately, the game was a case of too much Kelvin Cato. The 6-foot-11 center, who is now playing in the NBA, scored a career-high 29 points, grabbed 12 rebounds and blocked a Midwest Regional-record eight shots in leading the Cyclones past the Redbirds, 69–57, before 21,020 people, the largest gathering to ever watch an Illinois State basketball game.

"I'm proud, but bitterly disappointed because we didn't come here for a moral victory. We came here to win," said Stallings. "We had a chance to do that and we didn't get the job done."

Illinois State tied the nip-and-tuck game at 53 on a three-point field goal by Schaefbauer with 4:03 remaining. But that was as close as the Redbirds would get the rest of the way, thus ending one of the most successful seasons in school history.

Redbird Arena has been Illinois State's basketball home since 1989.

Chapter 29
SEASON NO. 100 IS ONE FOR THE AGES (1997–1998)

◆　　◆　　◆　　◆　　◆　　◆

S ome have referred to the 100th season as the best season of all, a mouthful when considering the basketball history at Illinois State.

The 1997–98 squad set a school record for wins at the NCAA Division I level with 25. It also became the first team in Missouri Valley Conference history to win back-to-back regular-season and post-season tournament championships. It also advanced to the second round of the NCAA Tournament (Division I) for only the third time.

Unfortunately, anything less might have been viewed as disappointing by even the most supportive Redbird fans.

"It was a difficult year in terms of injuries, off-the-court problems and high expectations," Stallings said. "During the first four years we had certainly raised the bar for what was expected. But it was certainly a worthwhile year that was obviously capped off by the victory over Tennessee and our ability to advance in the NCAA Tournament."

The reason for the high expectations was simple. The Redbirds returned all 14 players from a 24-6 season that produced an NCAA Tournament berth the previous year. They were ranked No. 16 in *Sports Illustrated's* pre-season issue, No. 26 in the first Associated Press rankings, and they were the pre-season pick to win the Missouri Valley Conference for a second consecutive year.

Because Stallings had propelled the Redbird program so prominently onto the national scene, he became a target for other schools searching for a successful coach. There were some tense moments before the '98 season began.

A week before practice started for teams across the country, Michigan fired Illinois State graduate Steve Fisher as its head coach. Stallings' name was immediately linked to the job.

Michigan eventually promoted assistant coach Brian Ellerbe to the position, much to the delight of many Redbird fans. Those fans had experienced similar anxieties the previous spring when, shortly after the 24-6 campaign concluded, Tennessee and Ohio State courted Illinois State's head man.

Once pre-season practice began, the Redbirds were hit with a rash of injuries. Rico Hill, LeRoy Watkins, Kenneth Pierson and Jamar Smiley all were slowed by various ailments.

Hill, the team's top returning scorer and rebounder, had a stress fracture in his left foot; Watkins had a dislocated shoulder; Pierson was slowed by a swollen knee; and Smiley had tendinitis in his right knee.

Despite the injuries, Stallings was confident that the team still had the components capable of attaining the lofty goals.

Largely responsible for that feeling was a core of seven veteran players: Dan Muller, Skipp Schaefbauer, Rob Gibbons, Steve Hansell, Smiley, Watkins and Hill, who was the league's pre-season player of the year.

The Redbirds, who had the same starting lineup for all 30 games the previous season, were without three starters when they opened the season at home against Oakland, Mich.

Hill and Watkins were sidelined with injuries, while Smiley, who had encountered legal problems over the summer, was serving a coach-imposed suspension.

Illinois State won anyway over a seriously outmanned Oakland team, 101–66.

The triumph helped thrust the Redbirds into the weekly Associated Press rankings at No. 24, marking the first such ranking for them in 15 years.

The ranking proved to be short-lived, though, as the still-gimpy 'Birds suffered an 80–66 loss at Wisconsin.

Lopsided wins over Pittsburgh and Northeast Louisiana righted things momentarily, but the roller coaster dipped again in the championship game of the United Airlines Tournament at Honolulu. Playing without Watkins, who was still nursing shoulder pain, ISU bowed to homestanding Hawaii, 84–63.

"We're just not a very good basketball team right now," lamented Stallings after the game. "We have some injuries, but we're not using that as an excuse. We're just not clicking as a team and until we get things figured out we're going to be in trouble."

That trouble appeared to be subsiding thanks to wins over lowly Drake and an improved Creighton squad. The second of those two games, played at Omaha, signaled the first time since the third day of practice that all the Redbirds were available for game action.

A sluggish performance and loss at Illinois-Chicago raised the question marks again, before the game on which Illinois State's season turned.

Threatened with the possibility of a short or non-existent Christmas break, the Redbirds came to life in the final eight minutes to register a 72–70 win at Wisconsin-Green Bay.

They did what was once thought impossible—rallied from a 14-point deficit in the second half to outscore the deliberate and defensive-minded Phoenix, 34–19, over the final 8:34.

Schaefbauer, who injured his back when he took a nasty fall during the game, hit three straight three-pointers to help his team back. His third trey at the 2:57 mark narrowed the deficit to 64–62.

Muller, who Stallings later said "willed the win," then stole a Green Bay pass and scored on a layup to tie the game.

After a Phoenix miss, Cartmill hit a three-pointer to give Illinois State the lead for good at 69–67 with 1:59 left.

"We finally showed some stuff at the end that we haven't showed this season," said Muller, who finished with 23 points and five rebounds.

The victory afforded the Redbirds a much-needed five-day break.

"It gave everybody, including myself, a chance to get away from basketball. It seems to have recharged everybody and allowed me time to analyze some things we needed to be and needed to become," said Stallings.

"I did not do a good job of keeping us focused through the injuries. I probably didn't do a good job of staying focused myself. I allowed us to get away from some of the things that had made us pretty successful in the past.

"Because we had everybody back and because we had the summer foreign exhibition tour, it was almost like we never stopped playing from last year. I fell into the trap of thinking we wouldn't lose our identity. But we did lose our identity on offense, on defense and from a leadership standpoint."

The Redbirds did indeed restore their identity by reeling off five straight victories, including a 64–63 win at home over highly regarded Pacific (and future No. 1 NBA draft pick Michael Olowakandi) and a 105–70 thrashing of Southern Illinois, also at Redbird Arena. The 105 points established an arena scoring record.

After a loss at Southwest Missouri State (a setback that happened despite 31 points and 10 rebounds from Hill), it was time for the I-74 rivalry game with Bradley at the only MVC

Rico Hill was Illinois State's first Missouri Valley Conference Player of the Year in 1998.

venue that had not yet yielded a win for Stallings or the vaunted senior class: the Peoria Civic Center.

"You always want to finish your career with

at least one win everywhere [within the league]," Muller said on the eve of the game.

That win did come, 57–54, and it started seven-game win string that eventually hoiste

An exceptional student and a deadly three-point shooter, Skipp Schaefbauer's playing career ended with a broken leg in the first round of the 1998 MVC Tournament, but he was back on crutches just two days later to lead the team out for the championship game.

the record to 18-4.

Southwest Missouri State again burst the bubble, this time at Redbird Arena, but Illinois State came back with an overtime triumph at Evansville. Victories over Creighton and Northern Iowa closed out the regular season and earned the Redbirds their second straight regular-season title with a 21-5 overall record and a 14-2 league mark.

They entered the Valley tournament with the No. 1 seed, the coach of the year in Stallings, the player of the year in Hill and the opportunity to become the first team in league history to repeat as both the regular-season and tournament champion.

Hill, the first ISU player to earn player of the year honors, averaged a league-leading 18.9 points and 8.0 rebounds and a conference-leading 50.6 percent marksmanship from three-point range.

It was his one-handed slam dunk off a fast break that got the Redbirds started in the tournament against Southern Illinois. Hill's steal came 41 seconds into a game the Redbirds won easily, 83–73, while shooting a tournament-record 66 percent from the field.

The victory was bittersweet because it came at the expense of Schaefbauer. He suffered a career-ending fractured right femur with 6:10 remaining in the first half.

"He was guarding me at the time, but I don't know what really happened," said SIU's Rashad Tucker. "We both went up for the rebound and when we came down I heard a popping sound."

Schaefbauer, a hard-nosed competitor, lay in agonizing pain for what seemed like an eternity on the Kiel Center court. He still can't recall what happened.

"I heard it pop, but I don't know if it was while I was in the air or when I came down," he said. "I knew my leg was broken and my career was over."

With their thoughts on Schaefbauer, who had undergone surgery the day before, the Redbirds made quick work of Wichita State in the semifinals, 75–54.

"This tournament is going to be won for Skipp Schaefbauer," declared Smiley, who along with the rest of the team visited their fallen comrade following the game.

Schaefbauer was scheduled to be in the hospital for three to five days, but he vowed to himself that he would be courtside with his teammates when they met Southwest Missouri State in the championship game, just 48 hours after surgery.

The Kiel Center was buzzing with excitement as the two teams prepared to battle for the NCAA Tournament berth. Little did anyone, including the Illinois State players, know what was in store.

At approximately 8:28 p.m., nearly nine minutes before the ball was tossed into the air to start the game, a mighty roar went up through the decidedly ISU-partisan crowd.

The ovation was for Schaefbauer, who slowly hobbled out on crutches, leading his teammates onto the court.

"I swear to God when we walked out on the court, I was in tears walking behind him," said Gibbons.

Unbeknownst to his teammates, Schaefbauer had checked out of the hospital earlier in the day. He watched the game from a room inside the Kiel Center and reappeared after ISU had posted the 84–74 triumph to accept the tournament championship trophy from his wheelchair.

"Skipp was definitely in our hearts and on our minds," said Muller, the tournament's most valuable player, who kissed his roommate on the forehead as he was wheeled off with the trophy. "We really wanted to do this for him."

Five players scored in double figures for the Redbirds, who avenged two earlier losses to the Bears. Watkins was the leader with 18, while Muller added 17, Hansell 14, Gibbons 13 and Smiley 11.

"That one was sweeter than the first one because we capped a great career," said Gibbons, who would later experience perhaps even greater euphoria in the NCAA Tournament. "The year before it was a great ending to a great season, but we knew we would be back. This year, we had all the expectations, picked to be No. 1...everything on our shoulders. We had injuries early in the season, but we pulled together and got it done."

At the height of irony, the Redbirds drew

Hard work, hustle and an engaging personality made Rob Gibbons a fan favorite in Redbird Arena.

Kevin Stallings, shown here at an NCAA Tournament media conference, knows the post-season routine well.

took a pass from Cartmill and banked in the game-winning shot from point-blank range. The game-winning shot, which was designed as a safety net in case Tennessee scored on its previous possession, resulted from a play in which Hansell, Hill and Cartmill all handled the ball.

"I was supposed to set a screen for Steve Hansell and roll to the basket," said Hill, who led the Redbirds with 22 points. "They double teamed Steve as he was dribbling around. I popped open, got the ball and started driving. I came off a LeRoy Watkins screen and Kyle flashed open."

Cartmill said when Hill got him the ball he saw an open rim.

"My first idea was to attack the basket," said Cartmill. "Then I saw Dan wide open. His man wasn't guarding him because he was trying to help off on Rico. My first instinct was to get the ball to Dan."

Muller said that when Hill got the ball he headed for the basket.

"When Rico gets the ball you just run to the basket because he's usually going to shoot," added Muller. "It was a great play on Kyle's part. He drove the baseline and at that point in the game, the defense just runs to the ball. That's what happened. I just stood under the basket and Kyle threw me a great pass and I was wide open and laid it in."

Even in the hysteria following the basket, Tennessee managed to get off a reasonable

Tennessee, the same Tennessee that had sought Stallings' services the previous spring, in the opening round of the West Regional at Sacramento, Calif. ISU was seeded No. 9, while the Volunteers were seeded No. 8.

"One of our goals at the beginning of the season was to win at least one game in the NCAA Tournament," said Muller.

The senior forward laid in one of the biggest baskets in Illinois State history with 1.8 seconds remaining in overtime to give the Redbirds an 82–81 win over the Vols.

"That was a big thrill," Muller admitted. "It's something you dream about. You never want it to be too hard a shot, though."

Muller, standing alone under the basket,

good three-point attempt inside the half-court line. It was Muller, putting the celebration on temporary hold, who dashed back downcourt to get a contesting hand in the face of the Volunteer shooter. Typical Muller.

The Redbirds won the game despite playing without their starting backcourt of Schaefbauer and Smiley, who injured his back in practice the day before the game, and foul trouble.

"It was fitting, especially for the senior class, that we pulled the game out," said Stallings. "I can't begin to tell you how resilient they are."

The victory also lifted a huge load off the team. For the first time all year, it could relax because it had met every expectation.

No. 1 seed and defending national champion Arizona waited in round two.

Illinois State controlled the tempo for a little over half the game, and when Muller made a three-pointer 56 seconds into the second frame, the game was knotted at 32.

Unfortunately, that basket seemed to awaken the Wildcats. Employing a stifling press, a strategy that worked well against a team short on guard depth, UA went on a 15–0 run to erase the upset hopes. The final was 82–49.

The game brought to an end the most successful season in ISU history with a 25-6 record, and it capped the careers of the six senior players.

"The seniors were a terrific group," said Stallings. "We told them when we recruited them that they were going to be the core class that we were going to build this program around."

Winning was the rule for the seniors, who solidified Illinois State as one of the top 40 programs in major college basketball. During their careers, the Redbirds won 20 or more games each season to compile a 91-37 record, or a winning percentage of .710.

Muller, Smiley and Gibbons were the first Illinois State players who qualified for post-season play in all four years of their careers.

"I felt like the potential for our team was to be a final 16 team," said Stallings. "I thought we were good enough and experienced enough to do that. When our starting guards were hurt that became very unrealistic. But under the circumstances our team reached its potential.

"The Tennessee win has to be the highlight now because it signifies accomplishing the most. It represented what our program had become in five years. There were a lot of symbolic values to that win as well as the gratification of victory."

The game also was symbolic simply because it was a victory. In his first five years, Stallings posted a remarkable record of 107-48, a mark that is somewhat dwarfed by a staggering 46-16 mark in Missouri Valley Conference games. Through five seasons, he ranked No. 3 in MVC history for winning percentage among coaches with at least 50 league games under their belt. The two men ahead of him? Legends Phog Allen (Kansas) and Henry Iba (Oklahoma State), respectively.

◆　　◆　　◆　　◆　　◆　　◆

Stallings' Redbirds got all those wins with flair, and without being too slanted in their approach. For instance, his teams set records for three-point shooting and defensive field goal percentage in the same season. Almost from the beginning, Stallings' playing style, which also incorporated the use of eight to 10 players per game, was a hit with all who watched.

The 100th season was under sound guidance with Stallings. The team accomplished at least as much if not more than any of its predecessors.

"Fortunately, we were able to have that type of season in our 100th season," said Stallings. "We were able to put an exclamation point on the first 100 years."

The Redbirds also set the standard, in a sense, for what many hope Illinois State basketball will be for the next 100 years.

"That's our task now as we enter the second 100 years: to sustain and build upon what has been established," Stallings concluded.

About The Authors

100 Years of Illinois State Redbird Basketball was written by two men who have witnessed much of the program's successful history—Bloomington *Pantagraph* sports editor Bryan Bloodworth and former Illinois State sports information director Roger Cushman.

Cushman penned this book from the inception of basketball at Illinois State through the Will Robinson era, while Bloodworth's effort begins with Gene Smithson's hiring as head coach and continues through the 100th season.

Cushman retired as Illinois State University's News Services Director in 1995 after more than four decades of communications work as a journalist, publicist and educator.

He began his career as a sports reporter at the *Pantagraph* in 1952 while attending Illinois State and also was sports editor of the Columbia *Missourian* while attending graduate school at the University of Missouri.

Cushman taught journalism at Lincoln College in Illinois, the University of Missouri, Eastern Illinois and Illinois State.

He was sports information director at Eastern Illinois from 1964–66, sports information director at Illinois State from 1966–79 and coordinator of public information and director of News Services at Illinois State from 1980–95. He continues to write an occasional sports column for the *Pantagraph*.

Cushman achieved his greatest distinction in the field of sports information. His 1978 men's basketball brochure was judged the best in the nation by the College Sports Information Directors of America, and he received five other best in the nation awards for posters, schedule cards and other publications.

He was inducted into the Illinois Basketball Coaches Association Hall of Fame in 1980 and the ISU Athletic Hall of Fame in 1992. He also is a recipient of the Campbell "Stretch" Miller

Former Illinois State sports information director Roger Cushman, and Bloomington *Pantagraph* sports editor Bryan Bloodworth.

Award for meritorious service to ISU Athletics and was listed in the 1992–93 edition of *Who's Who in the Midwest*.

Cushman and his wife, the former Elaine Hakey, met as students at Illinois State. They have two children: Lori Ducharme, a registered nurse in Boulder, Colo., and Steven, deputy chief of New York City's contracts and real estate law division. There are three grandchildren.

Bloodworth arrived on the Illinois State campus from Marshall, Ill., in 1974 as a starry-eyed freshman.

His first taste of Redbird basketball came as a sports reporter for the *Vidette*, the campus newspaper, where his journalistic career began in 1975. In 1976, while a junior at ISU, Bloodworth accepted a full-time sportswriting position with the *Pantagraph* and covered ISU basketball on an occasional basis until 1988.

He was named sports editor at the *Pantagraph* in 1987, a position he holds today,

and began covering ISU basketball on a regular basis in 1988. He also has covered numerous other ISU sporting events during his 22-year tenure at the *Pantagraph*.

The author of "Lefty's Corner," a weekly sports column that appears each Sunday in the *Pantagraph*, he has earned writing awards for his coverage of fastpitch softball, auto racing and high school sports.

Bloodworth has had articles published in *The Sporting News'* pre-season basketball magazine, *Basketball Weekly, Athlon's* preseason basketball and football magazines, the Missouri Valley Conference Tournament program and the Illinois High School Association Tournament program.

He was inducted into the Illinois Basketball Coaches Association Hall of Fame in 1996 and is a member of the College Football Writers and Basketball Writers Associations.

Bloodworth and his wife, Lisa, have three children: Cori, Blake and Annie.